For Ellen Ervin and Cork Smith

But the one sport that took precedence over all others was drinking. And drinking in the twenties was really a sporting proposition.

It involved passwords and travel and smuggling and the constant danger of blindness or worse. For some of us it became a career in itself.

— Donald Friede
The Mechanical Angel, 1948

The new taboo is alcohol. Many of the subjects in this volume had lives dominated or ruined by drink, but it is exceptional for this to be even hinted. There are many others whose careers were transformed or foreshortened by alcoholic poisoning, whose difficulties are not detailed. ... For long-term DNB trend-spotters, it will be fascinating to see how long it tries to sustain the illusion that alcohol is a largely innocuous, mass-recreational drug, while other illicit or innovative drugs are viewed as especially evil or marginal aberrations.

— Richard Davenport-Hines
From a 1986 *Times Literary Supplement* review of
The Dictionary of National Biography

Acknowledgments

I obtained a great deal of the specifics about alcoholism by attending more than a hundred Alcoholics Anonymous meetings in New York and California. No other single source offers a more accurate portrait of how alcoholics cope with their disease on a day-to-day basis. My debt to the AA Fellowship is a heavy one.

I wish to extend my thanks to the staffs of the following institutions: the Alderman Library of the University of Virginia (Joan Crane), the Hemingway Collection at the John F. Kennedy Library in Boston (Joan O'Connor), the Berg Collection of the New York Public Library (Lola Szladits), and the Humanities Research Center, University of Texas at Austin (Kathy Henderson). The Research Foundation of the City University of New York awarded me several PSC-CUNY grants during the completion of the book.

I am also grateful to the following individuals, who have made significant contributions to the book but who are in no way responsible for its contents: A. I. Bezzerides, Joseph Blotner, Jerry Brenner, Jackson Bryer, Tony Buttitta, Carvel Collins, Doe Coover, Malcolm Cowley, Edward Davenport, Roderick Davis, Ellen Ervin, Saul Gilson, M.D., Edith Haggard, Evelyn Harter, Benjamin Hellinger, Patricia Lambert, Robert J. Lifton, Thomas L. McHaney, Donald Newlove, Anthony Powell, Michael S. Reynolds, Harrison Smith, Jr., Barbara Probst Solomon, Leroy Sugarman, M.D., Meta Carpenter Wilde, Joan Williams and Donald Wolf.

Contents

Gravy

No other word will do. For that's what it was. Gravy.
Gravy these past ten years.
Alive, sober, working, loving and
being loved by a good woman. Eleven years
ago he was told he had six months to live
at the rate he was going. And he was going
nowhere but down. So he changed his ways
somehow. He quit drinking! And the rest?
After that it was *all* gravy, every minute
of it, up to and including when he was told about,
well, some things that were breaking down and
building up inside his head. "Don't weep for me,"
he said to his friends. "I'm a lucky man.
I've had ten years longer than I or anyone
expected. Pure gravy. And don't forget it."

RAYMOND CARVER
(1938–1988)

Introduction

1

OF THE SEVEN native-born Americans awarded the Nobel Prize in literature, five were alcoholic. The list of other twentieth-century American writers similarly afflicted is very long; only a few of the major creative talents have been spared. In addition to the five Nobel laureates — Sinclair Lewis, Eugene O'Neill, William Faulkner, Ernest Hemingway and John Steinbeck — the roster includes Edward Arlington Robinson, Jack London, Edna St. Vincent Millay, F. Scott Fitzgerald, Hart Crane, Conrad Aiken, Thomas Wolfe, Dashiell Hammett, Dorothy Parker, Ring Lardner, Djuna Barnes, John O'Hara, James Gould Cozzens, Tennessee Williams, John Berryman, Carson McCullers, James Jones, John Cheever, Jean Stafford, Truman Capote, Raymond Carver, Robert Lowell and James Agee. The presence of the disease in so many of our notable writers surely makes it appear that alcoholism is the American writer's disease.

What about the other arts? If we made up a list of modern American painters, for example, would it contain a similar preponderance of alcoholics? The answer is clearly yes, including as it would such names as Mark Rothko, Jackson Pollock and Franz Klein. Since the painters, and other artists as well, have had their own share of the problem, it seems reasonable to ask if some link exists between alcoholism and creativity. Over the years, many of our best artists have accepted such a connection. In fact, several have claimed they had little choice *but* to drink, and heavily at that, if they were to perform at their creative peak.

In this view, creativity flowers at its fullest when the constrictions inhibiting everyday life are swept aside by alcohol. Thus drinking is believed to open the windows of the soul; true vision is achieved only when the mind has been liberated by liquor, an idea expressed in Hart Crane's poem "The Wine Menagerie":

> New thresholds, new anatomies! Wine talons
> Build freedom up about me and distill
> This competence —

Sincerely believing that steady drinking must surely be the right approach to the muse, the writers I consider in this book embarked on writing and drinking careers together, with deadly effect on their creative powers.

The notion that drinking fosters creativity is not a new one. Horace asserted that the poet had a tradition to uphold:

> ... no lyric poems live long
> or please many people ...
> Which are written by drinkers of water. Ever since Bacchus
> Recruited unhinged poets in the ranks of his satyrs
> And fauns, the delightful muses have regularly reeked
> of wine in the morning. By lavishing praises on wine,
> Homer shows that he was a drinker. ...
> "To the sober I assign
> A career in business or public affairs; from the grim
> I withhold the right to write poems."

In the twentieth century the idea of the writer as drinker seems to be a particularly American one: no such line of thinking prevailed among European or English writers, suggesting that on the subject of alcohol we are a nation apart. From the earliest days of the Republic, Americans have displayed so avid a thirst for alcoholic beverages that it astonished such visitors as Tocqueville and Dickens. In the nineteenth century, America was often jokingly referred to as the "Alcoholic Republic," and its best writers, from Poe onward, have acquired a well-deserved reputation for the amount of liquor they consume. This thirst has never been as acute among modern English writers, as Anthony Powell informed me: "Good British writers are apt to be by no means total abstainers, but I should have thought you were right in supposing the matter to be less disastrous, in bulk, than in the US." Most American writers, however, assumed that drinking was good for them, accepting it as part of the rules of the game; drinking writers were, in effect, good writers.

Many of them became alcoholic, a malady that had much, if not all, to do with the erosion of their talents at ages that were characteristically far younger than those of their European counterparts. Nevertheless, many American writers were convinced that they had benefited richly from their early pact with alcohol and remained assured that it had been a necessary ingredient in the brief yet golden period of their youth. This, despite the fact that the muse of alcohol became increasingly deaf to the pleas of these writers as they aged. Fitzgerald's best work was concluded when he published *Tender Is the Night* at age thirty-eight. Hemingway's last notable book to appear in his lifetime was *For Whom the Bell Tolls,* published when he was forty-one, although his decline was evident at least four years earlier in *To Have and Have Not.* Faulkner's immense talent kept him functioning longer than most; he was forty-four when he completed his last important book, *Go Down, Moses.*

A closer look at the long list of alcoholic writers reveals that four were suicides (Jack London, Hart Crane, Hemingway and John Berryman), while nearly all the rest burned themselves out at surprisingly early stages of their careers. A few preserved legendary silences that persisted for decades (Djuna Barnes and Dashiell Hammett), but virtually all the rest continued to write, producing increasingly feeble works, a situation suggesting the relevance here of Fitzgerald's much-quoted remark "There are no second acts in American lives." We've had many brilliant beginnings in American writers but far fewer sustained careers. Unlike many of the chief European writers of the last one hundred years — extreme examples are Tolstoy and Thomas Mann, writing *Hadji Murad* and *Confessions of Felix Krull,* respectively, in their late seventies — the Americans have exhausted their talents very quickly. It is clear that alcoholism has played an immense part in this sad and premature loss of creativity.

Of course, another list can be compiled of prominent American writers of this century who were not alcoholic. It would include T. S. Eliot, Ezra Pound, Edith Wharton, Willa Cather, Thornton Wilder, Robert Frost, Gertrude Stein, Ellen Glasgow, Wallace Stevens, William Carlos Williams, Katherine Anne Porter, Zora Neale Hurston, Saul Bellow, Ralph Ellison, Eudora Welty and Flannery O'Connor. (Although they were heavy drinkers, neither Theodore Dreiser nor Sherwood Anderson appears to have been alcoholic.) This second list is notable for the number of poets it contains as well as for the preponderance of women. With few exceptions, American women writers have not been alcoholic. The commonly held medical view concerning the low incidence of the disease in women is that they have been drinking (and smoking) only within recent memory and that the ratio of male to female alcoholics may narrow in the near future. It is, however, a fact that a majority of the main figures in American writing in this century have been alcoholics. This book is about four of them.

2

THERE HAS BEEN a curious unwillingness on the part of the critical community to deal openly with alcoholic writers. An example of the stonewall approach is that of Christopher Sykes, who, in his biography of his friend Evelyn Waugh, flatly denies that his subject could have been alcoholic despite all the evidence he presents to the contrary. Sykes's position proceeds from his belief that alcoholics are quite incapable of producing anything noteworthy. Since Waugh wrote all those superb books, it follows that he just couldn't have been an alcoholic. A different tack is taken by those who write about Faulkner. Yes, he was undeniably an alcoholic, they acknowledge, but they insist that he exercised a degree of control over his drinking unknown to most alcoholics. Critics also insist that his frenzied drinking had nothing to do with his later creative decline; some of them prefer not to detect any decline and find talk about Faulkner's alcoholism irksomely distracting. In pursuing the subject with people who were close to him, I found a reluctance to discuss the matter, as if the information that would come to light about it would somehow diminish his reputation.

That Faulkner drank heavily all his life is no secret, but the effect of it on both the man and the books he wrote after 1942 is not well known. His continual hospitalizations, his blackouts and the electroshock therapy he received did little to curb his thirst. The immense body of work he created between the late 1920s and the beginning of the 1940s is amazing considering the intense physical handicap he labored under because of his drinking. One may well ask, When and how did he find the time to write the books?

Faulkner's principal biographer, Joseph Blotner, ascribes his subject's heavy drinking to his need for temporary oblivion from the world around him. Blotner views the prolonged binges as experiences that Faulkner chose of his own accord, something *willed*. Yet it is clear that Faulkner did *not* will his binges — they were far too painful and damaging for that. He was always surprised to find himself back in the hospital. The bouts of drinking were, in effect, the inevitable results of a disease over which he had little or no control. Faulkner drank alcoholically for nearly fifty years and remained confident to the end that his extraordinary powers derived, at least in part, from alcohol. When Faulkner remarked that "civilization begins with distillation," he was not joking but stating what he believed to be self-evident: a writer requires the liberating infusion of whiskey in order to reveal the nature of the world around him. Sadly, nearly all the best American writers of this century have agreed with him.

In his early days Faulkner made no bones about his drinking, once telling an interviewer that he always kept his whiskey within reach as he wrote. He seemed invulnerable to alcohol in the great early period of *The Sound and the Fury* and *As I Lay Dying,* but by the mid-1930s his body began to revolt against the huge amounts of liquor he consumed daily. When only thirty-eight, he discovered the other, unfriendly side of alcohol, the destructive side that produced convulsive seizures, a score of hospitalizations and, in time, an erosion of his talent.

We know far more about Fitzgerald than about any of his American contemporaries — perhaps too much. The appetite for information about his life and times has proved to be unending in its search for new revelations about a writer whose reputation reblossomed wondrously in the early 1950s. By 1988 six full-length biographies had appeared. Supplementing these are two books dealing primarily with his wife, Zelda, but which of necessity concern themselves as much with him. In addition, there have been three books of reminiscences from Sheilah Graham, while scores of academics have published hundreds of articles chronicling the minutiae of Fitzgerald's life and works. Dozens of the terrible short stories he wrote for quick cash — the ones he rigorously excluded from his book collections — have been exhumed and published. No letter, no matter how dull or obscure, has failed to make its way into print. The sheer weight of all this material threatens to overwhelm the real quality of a writer who produced a relatively modest body of enduring work.

Although all the Fitzgerald biographies depict their subject's alcoholism, none of them indicates the extent to which alcohol dominated his life after about 1925 or that the decay of his talent can surely be attributed to it. A number of the biographers have simply exercised their moral indignation about something that clearly disturbs them. This approach is clear in the preliminary remarks made by James R. Mellow in the pages of his 1984 dual biography of Scott and Zelda, *Invented Lives,* in which he observes that he has "become less and less sympathetic toward people with major or minor talents in any field who waste their gifts on drugs and drink." Mellow here echoes Cyril Connolly, who had similar views about Fitzgerald's drinking:

> I never want to read about another alcoholic; alcoholism is the enemy of art and the curse of Western civilization. It is neither poetic nor amusing. I am not referring to people getting drunk but to the gradual blotting out of the sensibilities and the destruction of personal relationships involved in the long-drawn social suicide.

Regarding the alcoholism of the Fitzgeralds, Mellow takes on the prim dignity of a high-court judge, stating that in writing his book he decided "the best approach would be not to let the glamorous Fitzgeralds get away with anything." What they might be getting away with so many years after their deaths is perplexing, but Mellow's stance is quite clear: in 1929, for example, Fitzgerald was a man often "not on the wagon [and] there are other bits of damaging evidence." Mellow believes that Fitzgerald's excessive drinking was a clear sign of immorality rather than an indication of his alcoholism. It is fair to say that Mellow and the other Fitzgerald biographers have failed to grasp the implications of a disease that destroys talent as surely as it does health.

It has never been easy to separate the enduring Hemingway from the "Papa" legend that he encouraged to spring up around him over the years. That legend has done much to obscure the fact of his great artistry; to many he is merely a neurotic brawler, a sexually confused buffoon who enjoyed killing living things. Behind the myth is a man who thought writing well brought him the greatest happiness. In the twenties and thirties he was incomparable in his command of a seemingly simple style with which he conveyed the feel of the physical world as did no other writer of his generation.

A vigorous denial that one has a problem with alcohol, even in the face of much evidence to the contrary, is frequently an indication of the presence of the disease. Although Hemingway prided himself on his ability to drink "competently," as he might have put it, he surely became an alcoholic. He knew he could easily outdrink all his contemporaries and, in time, believed he was invulnerable to alcohol. His oft-quoted boast "I'm no rummy" proved to be false. Only when he'd lost his ability to write in those frenzied months at the end did he perhaps suspect that alcohol had played a large part in his creative decline. At the Mayo Clinic Hemingway, like Faulkner, received a dozen electroshock treatments. While still a patient there, he read a volume published by Alcoholics Anonymous entitled *Sedatives and the Alcoholic*.

O'Neill differs from Faulkner, Fitzgerald and Hemingway in the accelerated frenzy with which he embarked on his drinking career. Like the other three, O'Neill was a teen-age drinker. He would drink literally anything if he thought it would make him drunk; none of the others appeared so desirous of achieving oblivion in sordid, life-threatening situations. Influenced by Baudelaire and Swinburne, O'Neill devised a rationale for his drinking similar to Faulkner's. At the age of thirty-eight, however, he realized that if he continued, he would probably commit suicide (he had attempted it when he was twenty-four) or become insane, the fate that befell his brother. But while alcohol might, in time, cost him his life, O'Neill also understood that it would quickly erode his writing talent, the one thing he valued over everything else. Consequently, he alone among these writers managed to stop drinking. His decade and more of sobriety enabled him to produce the two great American works about addiction, *The Iceman Cometh* and *Long Day's Journey into Night*.

These four writers drank heavily not only because of their disease but also for what they thought alcohol could do for them. Their stories explain in part how and why so many American writers have become alcoholics and why so many of them have exhausted their talents tragically early.

*

Alcoholism is a disease with a twofold etiology: the genetic and the environmental. Recent medical findings stress heavily the significance of the genetic aspect of the disease. But this factor alone is insufficient to produce alcoholism; an environmental "trigger" is also required. Before a person can become an alcoholic, no matter what his genetic make-up, he must take the first drink. One such trigger was the introduction of Prohibition in America at the beginning of 1920, just when these writers were beginning their careers. Once alcohol became forbidden, many independent minds believed it was their moral duty to violate the law on every possible occasion. It was a matter of principle to drink; people who had never cared much for alcohol now felt that drinking was the socially correct thing to do. The 1920s became a period when having your own bootlegger was a sign of status.

If alcoholism does have a genetic factor, why haven't European writers been victimized to the same degree as the Americans? It is clear that the American cultural environment has led our artists into drinking patterns that most Europeans found to be dangerous and unacceptable. Glenway Wescott, who knew Hemingway and Fitzgerald in their Paris days, commented on this major difference in attitudes toward alcohol:

> In France no one expects much of anyone who drinks, but in America the drinker is supposed to drink *and* to produce. Some American writers have done it, but the management of drinking and what is expected of the drinker are very different in France.

3

First the man takes a drink,
Then the drink takes a drink,
Then the drink takes the man.
— Japanese saying

THE CONCEPT of alcoholism as a disease rather than as a moral failing has had a long and difficult battle for acceptance. In *The Neutral Spirit,* published in 1960, Berton Roueché quotes the Edinburgh physician Thomas Trotter, who in 1804 produced the first medical definition of alcoholism:

> In medical language, I consider drunkenness, strictly speaking, to be a disease, produced by a remote cause, and giving birth to actions and movements in the living body that disorder the functions of health. . . . The habit of drunkenness is a disease of the mind.

Trotter's insights were neither embraced by the medical profession of his day nor accepted by the then all-powerful clergy. His opinions were far too revolutionary for the time: the doctors, for example, hadn't the slightest notion of how to cope with their drunken patients. The clergy were equally disturbed by Trotter's definition, for they felt it usurped their ordained task of dealing with the immorality of drunkenness. If drunkards were now to be regarded as sick people, what about spiritual redemption? The powerful combination of the medical profession and the clergy prevented alcoholism from being considered a disease for more than another century. The world today has grown accustomed to the fact that alcoholism is a serious disease. But what sort of disease can it be if its victims embrace it so fervently?

Despite its prescience, Trotter's definition contained some

troubling material that assisted in the confusion about the nature of alcoholism. When he stated that it was a "disease of the mind," he clearly pointed the way to the still popularly held view that if alcoholism *is* a disease, it must surely be a self-inflicted one brought about by the demands of some deep-seated personality disorder — the proper concern of the psychotherapist. Roueché's book patently subscribes to this idea. When Roueché quotes Dr. George W. Thompson, it is clear that he is in sympathy with the view that alcoholism is not a separate disease: "Alcoholism . . . is a symptom of disease. The alcoholic individual is emotionally sick." What Thompson failed to note was that the emotional disorder he speaks of may well have arisen *after* the onset of the disease and not before. The fact is that sound emotional health is no guarantee that one won't become alcoholic.

Medical research during the past quarter of a century demonstrates clearly the error in Thompson's line of reasoning that alcoholism is *merely* symptomatic. It is now apparent that the emotional illness of the alcoholic is most frequently the result of drinking and not necessarily the cause of it. Most alcoholics do not drink because they're emotionally ill to begin with. *They drink because they're alcoholics;* the psychological disorders follow.

But isn't it true that alcoholics are usually in bad shape emotionally? Don't they tend to use alcohol as a tool to cope with a world they find both hostile and fear-ridden? The answer is yes to both questions, but their condition arises largely after they have become alcoholic. A frequently cited study by W. and C. McCord in 1960 demonstrates that very few individuals manifested any prior emotional problems before their addiction. On the contrary, they "were outwardly more self-confident, less disturbed by normal fears, more aggressive, hyperactive, and more heterosexual." Such findings completely reverse the still widely held belief that prealcoholics are emotionally sick people who use alcohol to alleviate the pains and torments of life. The truth is that there is no evidence that neurosis produces alcoholism; it is, however, very much the case that alcoholism will often produce neurosis.

Considerable progress has been made in dismantling this "cart before the horse" idea that alcoholism is merely symptomatic. But for decades the picture was not so clear: if alcoholism was indeed only a sign of emotional illness, then surely psychotherapy must be the healing instrument with which alcoholics might hope to recover their mental health and stop their excessive drinking. But psychotherapy was not the answer. After years of disappointing struggles to "cure" their alcoholic patients, most reputable therapists have abandoned such attempts as futile, and the better psychiatric institutions have followed suit. The cure rate for alcoholism treated by psychotherapy is virtually nil. There is, in fact, no cure for this disease except abstinence.

The neurosis explanation of alcoholism did not die easily; it still has its advocates. It was E. M. Jellinek who, in 1960, formulated the currently prevailing view that alcoholism *is* a discrete disease, although ironically enough, even he continued to voice the traditional notion that the disease was of psychological origin: "In spite of great diversity in personality structure among alcoholics, there appears in a large proportion of them a low tolerance for tension coupled with an inability to cope with psychological stresses." Much contemporary research has shown such claims to be false, and some studies maintain that alcoholism is a primary depression disorder.

The best overall study of alcoholism to date is Dr. George Vaillant's *Natural History of Alcoholism,* a volume that summarizes a great deal of the research discoveries in the field since Jellinek's major contributions at the beginning of the 1960s. As Vaillant views it, alcoholism can best be conceptualized as a single disease with a multiple etiology, containing both genetic and environmental factors. Vaillant characterizes the alcoholic in the words of the National Council on Alcoholism: "The person with alcoholism cannot consistently predict on any drinking occasion the duration of the episode or the quantity that will be consumed." Vaillant states his basic definition when he asserts that "alcoholism becomes a disease when loss of voluntary control over alcohol consumption becomes a necessary and sufficient cause for much of an individual's social, psychological, and physical morbidity." He also says that "alcoholism is a unitary syndrome best defined by the redundancy and variety of individual symptoms," which also means, as he puts it, that alcoholism has a life of its own.

Scott Fitzgerald wrote, "Let me tell you about the very rich. They are different from you and me." Had he been speaking of alcoholics, he would certainly have been correct, for the alcoholic is indeed different: the cells of his body have undergone changes. There is a parallel here in the notion that alcoholics are simply people "who drink too much." The fact is that they drink very differently than do nonalcoholics. In the early stages of their drinking, most alcoholics develop the physical ability to ingest large amounts of alcohol; such an ability constitutes cellular, or tissue, tolerance. This tolerance is a metabolic one, produced by physiological changes that take place in the cellular structure of the liver and the central nervous system. The commonly held belief is that an increase in drinking will make the drinker tolerant of alcohol, but the reverse is true: it is the alcoholic's developing tolerance that is responsible for his ever-increasing need for more alcohol.

Some researchers have divided alcoholism into three basic phases: the early, middle and final. In the early stages of the disease, liquor is the good friend, the wonderful substance that makes everything right. By the time the alcoholic has reached the middle phase, everything is no longer fine — he or she feels bad without alcohol and begins to increase the dosage. By this time the cells of the drinker have been altered significantly; this person can no longer function comfortably without alcohol. When alcoholics reach the most advanced stage of the disease, everything in their lives is governed by it. As alcoholics lose control of their drinking, their old tolerance decreases as their withdrawal symptoms steadily increase. When alcoholics go on what is generally termed a "binge," it is usually due to their having entered a cycle of drinking and withdrawal that they are powerless to stop. Their withdrawal from alcohol is so terribly painful that they must drink ever larger amounts to feel better; this ensures their drinking more than their already large tolerance can accommodate. They will then awake to an even worse withdrawal, and the cycle will continue until it is broken by their collapse, an event usually requiring detoxification in a hospital. This was precisely William Faulkner's fate in January of 1936, when he was first admitted to Wright's Sanitorium in Byhalia, Mississippi.

4

"Why are you drinking?" demanded the little prince.

"So that I may forget," replied the tippler.

"Forget what?" inquired the little prince, who already was sorry for him.

"Forget that I am ashamed," the tippler confessed, hanging his head.

"Ashamed of what?" insisted the little prince, who wanted to help him.

"Ashamed of drinking!" The tippler brought his speech to an end, and shut himself up in an impregnable silence.

— Antoine de Saint-Exupéry, *The Little Prince*

Diseases are known by their manifestations as well as their causes, and why alcoholics drink is irrelevant to the diagnosis of alcoholism.

— Donald H. Goodwin,
professor of psychiatry, University of Kansas

ALTHOUGH the ultimate cause of alcoholism is unknown, we do know that it runs along family lines, and this is, as Dr. Donald H. Goodwin has observed, a starting point. To date, we cannot isolate specific genes that determine alcoholism in the same way that we can predict the offspring of a woman who possesses genes that determine color blindness: 50 percent of her sons will be born so. In the color blindness analogy, environmental effects are totally unrelated; the number of color-blind children is genetically invariable. But in the case of alcoholism, it is necessary to provide an environmental trigger in order for the disease to develop and run its course. There are few alcoholics in Saudi Arabia. As indicated earlier, the trigger for the writers in this book was the myth that "good writers are drinking writers." The spirit of the Prohibition era did much to enhance this notion.

But can alcoholism be genetically transmitted? This is a question that fills many people, especially alcoholic parents, with considerable anxiety and that has engaged the growing attention of medical researchers during the past decade. Thinking of alcoholism as an inheritable trait is not at all new and goes back at least as far as the ancients. Aristotle believed that drunken women "bring forth children like themselves," while Plutarch was in complete agreement: "One drunkard begets another." The early American physician Benjamin Rush was convinced that women who drank during pregnancy would surely give birth to drunkards. During the gin fever that swept England during the eighteenth century, many people were certain that the offspring of the tipplers would inherit the trait. In the first two decades of this century, several statistical studies, conducted independently in a number of countries, found a much higher rate of alcoholism among the relatives of alcoholics than in the general population. The studies were in complete agreement that alcoholic parents were many more times as likely to produce children who became alcoholic.

It was the sharp rise in influence of the psychological theorists, starting with Freud and his followers, as well as the additional contributions of the newly developed field of sociology that caused the investigation of genetic factors in studies of alcoholics to be replaced by research of strictly environmental ones. This abandonment of the biological aspects was to last from the early 1920s to the end of the 1960s. Even Jellinek considered alcoholics to be the product of "bad" parents who drank to excess and brought up their children in an anxiety-ridden atmosphere. It was therefore natural for these children to drink heavily in their later years in order to alleviate their anxiety. He thought of the children as being "taught" to drink by the example of hard-drinking parents.

In the seventies and eighties researchers have once again turned their attention to the biological aspects of the disease. The principal difficulty in all such endeavors has been how to keep the genetic factors separate from the environmental. At present, there are three principal methods of investigation in widespread use: studies of twins, studies of adopted children and genetic marker research. While all three methods are successful in varying degrees, the adoption studies have proved to be the most rewarding.

It has been over a decade since Dr. Goodwin revealed the outcome of a series of studies indicating that alcoholism can indeed be genetically transmitted. He relied chiefly on adoption studies because they are the least likely to be challenged by those who find it hard to cut off completely the "nurturing" side of things.

Goodwin's investigation was supported by the National Association of Alcohol Abuse and Alcoholism. All of the field work was performed in Denmark, primarily because the Danish government has maintained astonishingly precise files concerning over five thousand cases of adoption in the period 1924 to 1947. The entire study was a "blind" one from beginning to end. The investigators (all psychiatrists) had no idea whom they were interviewing, and hence no charge of bias could be leveled against them.

Goodwin had two main goals in the initial phases of his research. The first was to determine whether men raised apart from their biological parents were more likely to have drinking problems if one of their biological parents was alcoholic than if neither was alcoholic. Second, Goodwin wanted to find out whether sons raised by their alcoholic parents were more likely to develop alcoholism than were their brothers who had been adopted in early infancy and raised by foster parents who were not alcoholic. (The diagnosis of "alcoholic" was assigned to the various subjects only if there had been at least one hospitalization for the disease, followed by treatment.)

In the first phase of the investigation, Goodwin's data were drawn from a study of 133 adopted males (average age: thirty-three). Fifty-five of the subjects were the offspring of at least one alcoholic parent, and the remaining 78 participants, used as nonalcoholic controls, had no known history of alcoholism in their families. The men with an alcoholic parent had been placed in adopted homes within a few weeks of their birth, and they had no further contact with their parents.

The results were startling. Of the 55 who had at least one alcoholic parent, 10 were found to be alcoholic, while 4 of the controls were similarly diagnosed, although they had never received any treatment for their drinking. The conclusion here is that the offspring of alcoholics had a much higher rate of alcoholism than did the offspring of parents with no known history of the disease. *These sons of alcoholics, who had been raised by nonalcoholic adoptive parents and who had had no contacts with their biological parents since adoption, had a fourfold greater incidence of alcoholism than did the control group*. Characteristically, these men had become alcoholic early in life, most of them in their late twenties. Goodwin also discovered that having a biological parent who was alcoholic increased the likelihood of the son's becoming an alcoholic but did not increase the chance of his being classified as a nonalcoholic but heavy drinker.

In the second situation, in which sons were raised by their alcoholic biological parents, the offspring

> were no more likely to become alcoholic than if they were separated from these parents soon after birth and then reared by non-relations. The alcoholism rate of these non-adopted sons was no greater than the rate observed in their brothers who had been raised by non-alcoholic parents.

The first two phases of these ongoing investigations indicate that alcoholism appears to be transmitted along family lines and that an increased susceptibility to the disease occurred about equally in men raised by their alcoholic biological parents and men raised by nonalcoholic adoptive parents. If there is indeed a genetic predisposition to alcoholism, exposure to the alcoholic parent did nothing to increase the chances of acquiring the disease. In addition, *the 10 alcoholic sons in Goodwin's study were no more likely to receive a diagnosis of depression, sociopathy, drug abuse, or any other diagnosable psychiatric condition than were the 78 controls.* In light of Goodwin's findings, the argument for the genetic transmission of alcoholism has become very powerful.

Faulkner and O'Neill demonstrate the clearest examples of having had a familial susceptibility to the disease. The recent occurrence of alcoholism in Hemingway's granddaughter Margaux suggests that she too inherited the illness. The evidence in Fitzgerald's case is far less clear, since we have little on which to base a judgment. But it is plain that all four embraced the myth of the drinking writer, the myth that has been hard to kill. One writer who became aware that drinking could destroy writing talent was Raymond Carver. He overcame alcoholism and, before his death in 1988, created a series of superb short stories that are often set in the mysterious half-light of obscure drying-out establishments or in the bedrooms of shaky men and women who are desperately attempting to remain sober for another day.

All four of the writers discussed here suffered tremendous physical and spiritual pain through their heavy drinking. Three of them found their creativity irreparably damaged by their alcoholism; only one escaped from the grip of the disease to discover that its very nature would become his greatest subject.

Faulkner

❦

"CIVILIZATION BEGINS WITH DISTILLATION"

1

I usually write at night. I always keep my whiskey within reach.

Isn't anythin' Ah got whiskey won't cure.

— Faulkner

BY THE BEGINNING of 1935 William Faulkner could write with some authority about the devastating effect on the central nervous system of a night of heavy drinking. He begins "The Golden Land," the only story he wrote based on his Hollywood years, by describing the main character's attempt to begin his working day:

> If he had been thirty, he would not have needed the two aspirin tablets and the half glass of raw gin before he could bear the shower's needling on his body and steady his hands to shave. . . . Now it was his trembling and jerking hands that he watched as he shook the two tablets onto the glass shelf and set the tumbler into the rack and unstoppered the gin bottle and braced his knuckles against the wall in order to pour into the tumbler.

At the age of thirty-seven, Faulkner had become knowledgeable about the terrible need for the morning, or "restorative," drink, the drink that makes it possible to start the new day, to start thinking about living again.

Faulkner, November 1950

It was only within a year or so after writing this story, however, that Faulkner's early-morning remedies began to fail him. By January of 1936 his wife, Estelle, and his stepson, Malcolm, discovered that Faulkner could no longer depend on his familiar home treatment, for suddenly it became impossible for him to stop drinking after one or two "eye-openers," those precious few drinks that had always brought him around in the past. His system now demanded an increased dosage of alcohol in order to feel "normal." Upon awakening, he would drink what he'd become accustomed to in the recent past, two or at most three drinks, but these made him drunk again almost immediately; he would then continue to drink until he passed out, only to wake up again several hours later, feeling worse than ever. His plight was now far worse than that of his fictional character in "The Golden Land."

These attempts to adjust his drinking level at the beginning of 1936 were frightening. What he did not know was that his metabolism had changed, so only an increased intake of morning alcohol could make him feel at all comfortable. But these "recovery" drinks were just keeping him drunk; there seemed no way to break out of the cycle. In a few days Faulkner's drinking had assumed around-the-clock proportions. The situation seemed hopeless. Hospitalization, which could supply immediate sedation, seemed the best recourse, and his family had him admitted to Wright's Sanitorium, a small medical facility fifty miles from Oxford, at Byhalia, Mississippi. Wright's was a drying-out place that Faulkner would use more than once; it was the scene of his death twenty-six years later.

Just a few weeks after his release from Wright's, Faulkner returned to Hollywood to resume his scriptwriting job at Twentieth Century–Fox, but three months later, in September 1936, he again entered a local hospital for the same reason. It is unlikely that Faulkner had the slightest notion that he was going to face another forced drying-out period this soon, for he was now in the position of an alcoholic who cannot safely predict either the severity or the duration of a particular drinking episode; he had lost his former ability to drink with impunity. This time his absence from work was noted by his employers, a fact that deeply concerned him. In addition to being a direct threat to his job at Fox, this hospitalization marked a new and dangerous stage in the progression of his alcoholism: it was the first recorded time that he experienced delirium tremens, or D.T.'s.

D.T.'s often occur in alcoholic patients after the sudden withdrawal of alcohol from the system. They can create a wide variety of medical problems, including cardiac arrest, but their most frightening aspect is vivid hallucinations, powerful enough to plunge the victim into a state of acute, frenzied terror. Meta Carpenter, Faulkner's lover during most of his years in Hollywood, recalls an episode in 1936 when he was crouched on their bed, shrieking with fear about the German air force:

> He was a man I no longer knew, and when I tried to touch him, he recoiled from me convulsively.
> "Who?" I asked him. "Who's trying to hurt you?"
> "They're diving down at me. Swooping. Oh, Lordy!"
> "Faulkner, what are you talking about? Who's after you?"
> He turned a face as white as library paste toward me. "The Jerries! Can't you see them?" Suddenly he was doubled over, trying to crawl into himself. "Here they come again! They're after me! They're trying to shoot me out of the sky. The goddamn Jerries, they're out to kill me. Oh, merciful Jesus!"

Meta had had no experience in dealing with D.T.'s, but a quick call to a musician friend informed her about the nature of Faulkner's illness and within an hour or so he was in the hospital to undergo detoxification. This hallucination stemmed from the combat experiences in 1918 that Faulkner frequently boasted of and that were entirely a product of his imagination. Faulkner saw no aerial combat in the First World War, but his fantasies about the Canadian Flying Corps were rich enough to produce a genuinely nightmarish fear while enduring the rigors of delirium tremens.

Only six months later, in April 1937, Faulkner was again hospitalized, but this time his condition had worsened, necessitating a stay of nearly two weeks. An absence of this length placed his job at Fox in considerable jeopardy, for his employers were quite aware of its cause. Heretofore, it had been possible for his friends and co-workers to cover up for him. This particular absence may have led to his contract's not being renewed in June that year. Although Faulkner was never very happy working in Hollywood, his job at Fox had become his chief means of support. His most recent novel, *Pylon,* had sold about 7,500 copies, not bad considering the economy of the country, but it did not produce even a small portion of the money he needed to maintain, in addition to his own family, the family of his recently deceased brother, his mother and, from time to time, other family members. He made some money by writing short stories for the magazines, but this income was unpredictable; only the weekly paychecks at Fox were dependable.

The importance of his job to him is obvious — Faulkner would never have deliberately entered what his biographers have described as self-chosen "drinking cycles." As they portray these cycles, Faulkner's drinking problems arose as a response to some inner emotional turmoil or anguish. But Faulkner drank under any and all circumstances, good, bad or indifferent. His behavior had only one explanation: he was an alcoholic. By 1936 and 1937 he could never be sure what might happen to him after two or three drinks. This new condition was very different from the past, when his powers of recovery were legendary; now, with increasing regularity he was winding up in hospitals for extended treatment.

Nevertheless, Faulkner did not consider giving up alcohol, for most of the time nothing much happened, and he could convince himself that, by and large, he was still a social drinker. In his Hollywood years, he would usually retire at a relatively late hour, rise at first dawn to work on, for example, the final portion of *Absalom, Absalom!* and follow this up with a full day's work at the studio — an amazing feat of energy, but Faulkner was nothing if not amazing in much of what he did. He could follow this regimen with apparent rigidity for months on end. He allowed himself two or three drinks before dinner, but every few months or so these would become four or five, or even more. After a night or two like this, he would feel such agony that he had to turn back to his old cure, the morning drink followed by several drinks at lunch, and then several more at dinner. Within a few days all his control was gone: he was now drinking just to "stay in place." By this time the withdrawal agonies were so great that he couldn't stop; within a week or so his friends were required to take him to the hospital.

Faulkner remained baffled for the rest of his life about what had happened to his body, unaware that, in addition to normal aging, both his metabolism and the cells of his body had undergone changes on account of drinking over the years which made him extremely vulnerable to alcohol. When he left Oxford for a combined business and pleasure trip to New York in October of 1937, he discovered that lost jobs and hospitalizations were not the only things he might experience through his newfound difficulties with alcohol.

New York had always been a dangerous place for Faulkner when he was drinking heavily; he'd experienced prolonged episodes there in 1928, 1931 and 1933. He was often in the company of people who recalled his times in New York well enough to write about them. On this occasion Sherwood Anderson, Faulkner's literary mentor from his New Orleans days in the mid-twenties, and Meta Carpenter saw Faulkner a number of times during his three-week visit. He was there mainly to get the last details straightened out in connection with the forthcoming publication of *The Unvanquished* and also hoped to get a contract and an advance for the book that became *The Wild Palms*. Random House was his new publisher and this was his first visit to its offices, not yet located in the beautiful quarters it shared for many years with the Archdiocese of New York, in the Villard mansion on Madison Avenue. The Random House of 1937 was in a new building on East Fifty-seventh Street between Fifth and

Madison. In the first few days he spent time with the three partners in the firm, Robert Haas, Donald Klopfer and Bennett Cerf, as well as with a deposed partner, Harrison Smith, who had been his editor and publisher on all the books from *Sartoris* through *Absalom, Absalom!* Within the course of the same few days Faulkner would come in contact with a surprisingly large group of friends, both old and new, including Saxe Commins, who edited a good many of the later books. Faulkner had not been present in New York for the publication of *Absalom, Absalom!* the previous year; now a number of his New York friends made up for it by throwing parties and also wined and dined him for a week or more.

The usual happened. After ten days or so, Faulkner simply disappeared from everyone's sight. There was no response from his room at the Algonquin Hotel. A New York friend, the boating enthusiast and writer Jim Devine, finally forced open the door and found Faulkner face down on the carpet, naked except for a pair of shorts. The windows of the room were open despite the chill fall air. Closer examination of Faulkner's body revealed that he had suffered a deep third-degree burn the size of a man's palm in the middle of his lower back. Devine lifted Faulkner onto the bed and called a doctor friend, who placed a temporary dressing on the wound. He also prescribed a dose of the evil-smelling drug that Don Birnam encountered at Bellevue Hospital, in the pages of Charles Jackson's *Lost Weekend*. Paraldehyde, a specific for severe alcohol withdrawal, worked as well for Faulkner as for the fictional Birnam: he was able to sleep without interruption for fourteen hours, a big step toward sobering up. The wound, however, pained him terribly and, despite numerous skin grafts and other medical procedures, would continue to plague him for the rest of his life.

The next day Faulkner explained what had happened. While sitting on the toilet, half comatose with drink and wearing only shorts, he had apparently passed out and fallen back on an exposed steam pipe located directly behind the toilet. The sheer weight of his body kept it pressing back on the pipe, but he had drunk so much he didn't feel a thing. He had no idea how long he'd lain on the floor.

Meta Carpenter, then recently married to Wolfgang Rebner, had returned to New York after a visit with his parents in Germany. Some days before the accident Faulkner had called her and all three had a pleasant lunch; she had been eager for her husband to meet Faulkner. At some point during his torturous recovery, the Rebners entered Faulkner's room at the Algonquin; they too had been unable to make contact with him. As she tells the story in her book, *A Loving Gentleman,* the Rebners found a nude Faulkner on the bed, who mumbled to her that he had begun drinking *this time* because of her "belonging to someone else." It is doubtful that she believed this, but it is clear that Faulkner felt that he must somehow supply a rationale for his behavior. At Faulkner's invitation, the Rebners returned a few days later to have dinner in his room, but left when they saw how much pain he was suffering.

During severe alcohol withdrawal, time passes slowly and sleep becomes next to impossible without paraldehyde. Devine spent as much time as he could with his recovering friend but he needed help. Sherwood Anderson assisted by coming to the room and talking to Faulkner for hours on end. A week or so earlier, at a cocktail party, Faulkner had apparently tried to convince Anderson that their friendship was still alive; Anderson's behavior at this time indicates that it was. In a few days Anderson wrote to his wife about his friend's difficulties:

> Bill Faulkner has been through a big drunk, for a week. The poor chap is an alcoholic. A friend [Devine] had been sticking to him and trying to straighten him out but the friend was exhausted. Bill had been wandering — nude — about the hotel corridors.
>
> We got Dr. Joe up there and he gave Bill something to make him sleep. They hope to get him off for home . . . today.

When "Dr. Joe" had his first conversation with his sobered patient, he could not resist asking him, "Why did you do it?"

He could not comprehend how any human being could allow himself to get into such a painful situation. Faulkner is reported to have stuck out his jaw at the doctor and responded with a resounding "Because I like to!" This seeming bravado was echoed in the words with which he answered a similar question, this time addressed to him by his publisher. When Bennett Cerf asked why he would want to spend a vacation under a doctor's care, Faulkner's reply was truculent: "Bennett, it was *my* vacation."

Faulkner was just under forty at the time of his severe burn at the Algonquin Hotel. In 1937, after three recent hospitalizations, the first bout of D.T.'s and now this crippling accident, Faulkner might have been expected to realize that he was in the grip of something that was going to become worse. Actually, his disease was going to damage him in ways that far transcended the pains of general incapacity and hospitals: he would soon find it harder and harder to write, the thing that had always come so naturally to him, the thing that had defined his life. The questions that must be asked are, How could he have become enmeshed so inexorably? Why *did* he continue drinking? What had he gotten from drink in the past? What hope had he of continuing to get it?

2

> Like other people who became adults during prohi-
> bition, and like Hammett himself, [Lillian Hellman]
> thought of drinking and alcoholism as romantic,
> even chic.
>
>   — Diane Johnson, "Obsessed," *Vanity Fair,* 1985

OVER GENERATIONS the members of the Falkner family, especially the men, drank heavily; nearly all of them were alcoholics, and William Faulkner may have been predisposed to
become an alcoholic. The cultural environments in which he ma-
tured — the local one of a small town in the Deep South and
the literary one of New Orleans — placed great store in drinking
and contributed heavily to Faulkner's involvement with alcohol.
But along with these environmental factors was the genetic leg-
acy from all those drinking Falkners. Faulkner's great-grand-
father ("the Old Colonel") was most likely an alcoholic, while
his son, J.W.T. Falkner, as well as his son, Murry, were both
alcoholics. So too were all of the novelist's brothers, John,
Murry and Dean. William and his brothers were the fourth generation known to be alcoholic. And in that family the women
were not entirely spared: Willie Medora, one of the Old Colonel's children, appeared to share in the affliction and is reported
to have been treated for a bad case of the shakes with some of
her nephew Murry's whiskey. She had suddenly been deprived
of her daily dose of Prunella, one of the countless "medications" women drank in those years for every known com-
plaint; the constant element in all of them was alcohol, 50 to 80
proof. All in all, alcoholism was truly the family disease of the
Falkners, as they were known until William Faulkner added
the *u.*

The Old Colonel, William Clark Falkner, whom his great-
grandson renamed Sartoris in his fiction, gained fame in his life-

time not entirely by heroic deeds on behalf of the Confederacy. He was also a man of letters who wrote a wide variety of books, including a novel, *The White Rose of Memphis,* that was enough of a seller in its day to require thirty-five printings. From early on, young William Faulkner patterned himself on the Old Colonel, once telling his third-grade teacher, "I want to be a writer like my great-granddaddy." According to one of the younger novelist's biographers, the Old Colonel wrote, like his namesake, at night, while his body servant, Nathan, "[supplied] him with the bourbon whiskey which he consumed in large amounts."

J.W.T. Falkner, known as the Young Colonel to distinguish him from his father, drank so much that his family was often required to take him to Memphis for the renowned Keeley Cure, once a popular remedy for alcoholism. Holding sway for decades, the treatment consisted of injecting the alcoholic with a solution of double chloride of gold, which purportedly caused a lasting repugnance to spirits in any form. Like all aversion therapies, the long-term results of the Keeley Cure were nil: the moment the patient began to feel better, he or she resumed drinking. The only real benefit of the cure was the opportunity to sober up and dry out, which is probably all friends and family hoped to accomplish. Aversion therapies for alcoholism are not treatments resigned to the past. They keep reappearing in different guises, most recently in England during the 1950s and 1960s, when psychologists there hit on the idea of showing alcoholics how they actually looked when they were drunk. This was accomplished by secretly filming their activities when under the influence of the alcohol supplied them by the hospital authorities. The therapists believed that seeing themselves as others saw them when drunk would turn alcoholics off drinking permanently; the results were no better than those of "the Keeley."

J.W.T. Falkner's son, Murry, the father of the novelist, began to pay his own visits to the Keeley at an early age. The three oldest Faulkner boys, including William, would assist their mother in the task of getting their father to Memphis, thus gain-ing an awareness of the realities of alcoholism while still children. All the Faulkner boys grew up in a culture that regarded drinking as an integral part of life — a man's life, that is, for there were few women drinkers, and female alcoholism was universally condemned. The general thinking of the day approved of men drinking; some of them could hold their liquor and others couldn't and required treatment from time to time. Abstinence was taken up only as a last resort. In a sense, the drying-out periods of heavy drinkers were looked upon as a sort of dues that were to be paid for feeling splendid while imbibing. Once they were paid in full, the drinker could resume in good conscience. Murry's second son, named after him, related in a family memoir that his father had stopped drinking some time in the 1920s — "simply decided he had had enough." This was the considered judgment of his son, who stopped his drinking in the mid-1950s at about age fifty-five; he was the only one of the four Faulkner sons to stop.

Faulkner's pedigree placed him from birth in a highly vulnerable position in relation to alcohol. Such a familial background supports both a genetic and an environmental or cultural basis for the transmission of alcoholism to family members. In Faulkner's case both factors were operative. His alcoholism can be "explained" only in part by pointing out all those other alcoholic Falkners. The other factor was the culture of which they were all a part. Alcohol was a constant in that culture, and Faulkner's earliest memory of drinking was the consumption of what were called "heeltaps," that is, the unfinished portions of drinks served on social occasions. Finishing off the heeltaps appears to have been a part of growing up in the Deep South, at least for little boys of ten to twelve. Consuming a half dozen or so of these heeltaps might have given a child of that age the same feeling as drinking a bottle of vanilla extract. At any rate, Faulkner's initial exposure to alcohol occurred at an early age.

Faulkner recalled that his regular drinking began while attending the annual deer hunts organized by his friend Phil Stone's father, "General" James Stone, at Batesville in Delta country. The hunts were noted for the amount of liquor con-sumed; Faulkner started downing his share at about age fifteen. But it was not until he was in his early twenties that anything particularly remarkable was reported about his drinking habits. As I've previously mentioned, he liked to make up stories about his exploits with the Canadian Flying Corps, and nearly all of them have a strong alcohol content. One of his favorites was a yarn about cracking up a plane while drinking heavily and then landing it upside down on top of a hangar, with considerable damage to both plane and pilot. This story became the founda-tion for the limp he affected during his early twenties and that he was still maintaining in New Orleans in late 1924 when he first met Sherwood Anderson.

Three years earlier he spent several months trying his luck in New York, with the aid of the Mississippi writer Stark Young, whom Faulkner had known since he was seventeen. Young was also born in Oxford, graduated from the University of Missis-sippi and taught at Texas and Amherst. Phil Stone, Faulkner's mentor at the time, had brought the two together, and Young played an important role in the early career of Faulkner, whose first verses Young had taken the time to read and criticize. Al-though considerable attention has been devoted to Phil Stone's influence on the youthful Faulkner, Stark Young's contribution to his development has been unjustly ignored. There is much evidence to suppose that what Faulkner obtained from Phil Stone came secondhand from Stark Young. At any rate, Young possessed a degree of intellectual sophistication that Stone never achieved. In the twenties and thirties Young was a literary figure of considerable importance. A friend of Eugene O'Neill's and Edmund Wilson's, he was the drama critic of The New Repub-lic, as well as a translator of Chekhov; his novel of the ante-bellum South, So Red the Rose, was a best seller in 1934.

With the sum of $60 in his pocket, Faulkner set forth for New York in late 1921 with the idea of staying rent-free with Young until he could begin earning some kind of living. Young found a job for him in Lord & Taylor's Doubleday Book Shop for $11 a week, but Faulkner rapidly sickened of life in the city and returned home to Oxford. Seventeen years after the visit, Young recalled being shocked by how much liquor his guest consumed. Very much the same feeling was expressed by the novelist Hamilton Basso, who remembered Faulkner's "astonishing capacity for hard drink." Sounding just a bit embarrassed for bringing the matter up, Basso went on to say:

> Let us get this latter talent over with immediately. Faulkner drank. We have heard many stories and probably will hear many more. I would only point out that the large body of his work . . . could not have been produced by a crock.

But it was. What both Young and Basso were talking about was Faulkner's amazing tolerance for alcohol.

Alcohol tolerance is a measure of the body's ability to metabolize or oxidize liquor, a physiological process that occurs in the liver. It enables alcoholics to process larger amounts of alcohol far more efficiently and rapidly than nonalcoholics. Tolerance is also achieved by the adaptation of the central nervous system to the toxic effects of liquor. Alcohol tolerance is not learned, but simply attained by steady drinking, and is usually established rather quickly. Nonalcoholics often develop a degree of tolerance, which may be either high or low, at an early age. It remains fixed until the onset of mid-life. Alcoholics, however, tend to develop an early but vastly greater tolerance, which is often noted for its sharp and dramatic rise.

By the age of twenty-seven William Faulkner had achieved a mighty tolerance that nearly everyone noticed, so much so that he began to need to explain it, if not to himself, then at least to others. When he arrived for an extended stay in New Orleans at the end of 1924, Faulkner had created a rationale for his continual heavy drinking. He had already composed a tale that might set people at their ease; Sherwood Anderson may have been among the first to hear it.

By 1924, after publishing *Winesburg, Ohio* and *Horses and Men,* Anderson was in the front rank of American writers, with only Willa Cather, Theodore Dreiser, and the young Sinclair Lewis as his rivals. It is not surprising that Faulkner would have wished to meet Anderson. The encounter was arranged by Anderson's second wife, Elizabeth Prall, who had been Faulkner's boss at the short-lived job in New York. Faulkner had recently written his first book, *The Marble Faun,* a volume of poems whose publication was underwritten by Phil Stone. Published by a quasi-vanity house in Boston, it sank like the proverbial stone in the pond, but at least it had given him the satisfaction of being a published author. In wishing to make contact with Anderson, Faulkner may have been obeying the same impulse that had made Hemingway seek out Anderson in Chicago three years earlier. Both younger men recognized that Anderson was then the leading figure in the vernacular tradition in American writing, which began with Mark Twain. Faulkner and Hemingway discovered in Anderson a liberating influence that permitted them to create their own styles.

Anderson and Faulkner became instant friends; they told each other endless tall tales about an imaginary Al Jackson as they walked together every night along the docks of New Orleans and through the streets of the old French Quarter; drink was always present in these exhibitions of storytelling prowess. A year later Anderson decided to use many of Faulkner's personal characteristics as the basis for a story/sketch called "A Meeting South," which he published in 1925. For over five years Faulkner had been telling everyone he knew about his nonexistent wartime flying experiences; Sherwood Anderson was no exception. Calling Faulkner David, a visiting younger friend, Anderson begins his narrative by supplying details that justify his character's overwhelming compulsion to drink:

> He told me the story of his ill-fortune — a crack-up in an airplane — with a very gentlemanly little smile on his very sensitive, rather thin lips. Such things happened. He might well have been speaking of another. I liked his tone and I liked him. . . . When we went down the stairs from my apartment I noticed that he was a cripple. The slight limp, the look of pain that occasionally

drifted over his face, the little laugh that was intended to be jolly, but did not quite achieve its purpose . . .

It soon becomes clear that David requires what was forbidden to Americans during the 1920s:

> I felt at once that he would be wanting a drink and . . . even in Prohibition times such things can be managed. We achieved several and my own head became somewhat shaky but I could see that what we had taken had not affected him.

When the supply runs out, David is able to replenish it:

> He produced a bottle from his hip pocket. It was so large I was amazed. How had it happened that the carrying of so large a bottle had not made him look deformed? His body was very small and delicately built.

David explains to Anderson that the whiskey in his bottle had been manufactured by the servants "on his father's plantation somewhere over in Alabama."

Anderson takes his young visitor to the home of Aunt Sally, an older woman, a local "character" from the Quarter who had once run a brothel. David tells them about his gift for drinking. "I didn't always have it. It is a thing built up." He then relates the story of his plane crash on the Western Front, which involved broken legs, a torn scalp, and long-lasting, unendurable pain.

> "The nerves of my leg and of my face have never quit hurting. . . ." I got it. No wonder he carried his drinks so well. When I understood, I wanted to keep on drinking with him. . . . The point was that he never slept, could not sleep, except when he was a little drunk.

Toward the end of the story, David tells Aunt Sally about the silver plate that had been "set under the skin" of his left cheek. He then explains to Anderson and his hostess that he can only fall asleep outdoors, and proceeds to do so only after consuming more of Aunt Sally's whiskey.

Faulkner always made it clear that he had very little use for the dull, flat truth of everyday life ("I don't have much patience with facts"), and his making up a completely false history of aerial combat was very much a part of this tendency. The story he concocted for Sherwood Anderson served this purpose admirably: besides eliciting sympathy, it also disarmed those who might well have been concerned about the huge amounts he imbibed; a man in desperate pain needs all the drink he can get.

But these events were taking place in the middle of the Prohibition era, when millions of Americans were determined to drink as much as they could on any and all occasions. Historians of the period have established that many people considered the breaking of the Volstead Act entirely justifiable, and some regarded it as a personal declaration of independence and the assertion of a free spirit. It is surely noteworthy that women only started to drink openly when it had become illegal to do so. Drinkers were proud of the amount they could consume and, oddly enough, of the terrible aftereffects the booze produced; one of the recurring phrases of the time was "Boy, did I tie one on last night!"

After 1920 many Americans began to drink whatever they could obtain as long as it promised a high degree of intoxication. All the writers discussed in this book reached their artistic maturity during this period when drinking became something of a duty as well as a pleasure. It was the age of bad liquor. No one has written more memorably about what Americans drank during the twenties and thirties than Herbert Asbury, whose account remains unrivaled:

> Farm hands in the Middle West drank a fluid drawn from the bottom of a silo, where silage had rotted and fermented for perhaps several years. No viler beverage can be imagined. . . . In Maryland drinkers who didn't care much what happened guzzled a drink called Old Horsey, which is exactly the way it is said to have smelled. Bootleggers in Baltimore sold, especially to oystermen, a liquor known as Scat Whiskey. It cost five or six dollars a bottle. Most of this stuff was made on a farm near Baltimore,

where bootleggers had set up a big still which turned out one thousand gallons of hootch a day for several years. Instead of the copper which is the only safe metal through which to run alcohol vapors, the still was equipped with lead coils, as were thousands of other moonshine plants throughout the country. The acids in the distillate picked up the lead.... Scat Whiskey was loaded with it. A popular drink on the Philadelphia waterfront was a terrible thing variously known as Happy Sally and Jump Steady. It sold for fifty cents a half pint. Most of it was made in a section of South Philadelphia called Moonshine Valley, which also produced Soda Pop Moon. This was sold in soda pop bottles for three dollars a quart, and analyses showed that it contained isopropyl alcohol, a violent poison.... In Chicago many speakeasies sold a very dark concoction called Yack Yack Bourbon, which was loaded with iodine, burnt sugar, and other flavoring matter. In 1923 enterprising bootleggers bottled this stuff and sold it in Chicago hotels, especially to southerners, who are very fond of bourbon.... Probably the worst drink that appeared during Prohibition was fluid extract of Jamaica ginger, popularly known as Jake, which was about 90 percent alcohol.... In many states drugstores sold Jake to all comers for thirty to fifty cents for a two-ounce bottle, and bootleggers peddled it at about the same prices. The principal buyers were poor people, and boys and girls, who couldn't afford more than one drink at a time and wanted something that started them off with a bang. Since it was too strong to be guzzled straight, Jake was usually mixed with ginger ale.... As far as is known, nobody died from drinking it, but even small quantities nearly always caused a terrible form of paralysis.

Nearly all the liquor sold in the United States during Prohibition was bad in one way or another. Out of a batch of 480,000 gallons of confiscated liquor seized in New York City, 98 percent contained poisons. Many drinkers did not live to tell any sort of tale: sixty people died of wood alcohol poisoning in New York in 1928 — forty-two in October alone. You had to be careful, but all the care in the world told you little about what you were drinking in the age of the "noble experiment."

Faulkner and his friends in New Orleans took their form of

care by making their own booze. In his memoir of their days together in 1925, the artist William Spratling presented a picture of how they did it in the Vieux Carré:

> The favorite drink at that time was Pernod, made right there in New Orleans and it cost six dollars a bottle. We made it up in great pitchers for all our parties. We also made gin in the bathtub using five-gallon cans of Cuban alcohol and adding the proper little bottle of Juniper essence, which you could buy at the corner store. We then rolled it in barrels across the floor of the attic to aerate it. Without this aeration, this gin would taste rather flat.

Spratling, who accompanied Faulkner on his first visit to Europe, has also left us with a picture of Faulkner's working habits as he typed out the pages of his first novel, *Soldier's Pay*. Spratling describes a working morning:

> Faulkner, of course, drank constantly, though I must add that I don't think I ever saw him really drunk — perhaps a little vague, but never sloppy. In the morning, once I was out of bed, Bill would already be out on the balcony with a drink, usually alcohol and water, banging away at his typewriter; this was every morning.

As if he anticipated a strong reaction to this revelation, Spratling immediately followed it with: "I think that what dominated him was the ideas in his head and not the alcohol."

In addition to his familial vulnerability to alcohol, as well as the force of the prevailing liquorish atmosphere of the twenties, Faulkner's drinking pattern was influenced by other factors — so many, in fact, that one might think he was doomed to drink alcoholically. There was the simple fact of his shyness: he found he got along with people a lot better with the relaxed feeling that drink gave him. His friend Jim Devine said that liquor served to "warm him up." Many who knew Faulkner felt he used alcohol to oil the wheels of social behavior. Without it he often appeared strained and ill at ease.

Like many other drinkers, Faulkner tried to assure a safe supply by buying whiskey in wholesale quantities from bootleggers who presumably imported it from various places in the Caribbean. Once he was forced to draw a bank draft for $200 against his then publisher, Horace Liveright, for this purpose. In a 1927 letter, he told Liveright why he suddenly needed the money:

> It was a case of dire necessity. Its quite a yarn. I had just purchased twenty-five gallons of whisky, brought it home and buried it in the garden. Two days later I went to Memphis, lost over three hundred dollars on a wheel, and gave a check for it. I had had about one-fifty in bank, and I knew I could dispose of my whisky and raise the balance with only the minor risk of being had by the law for peddling it. So I came home in about three days, found that one of our niggers had smelled the whisky out, dug it up, sold a little and had been caught and told where the rest of it was. So I lost all of it.
>
> I had to have the money to meet my check. . . . So I had to do something for temporary relief. Thank you again for honoring the draft. I shan't do that again; certainly not without asking your leave first.

Unlike Jack London and Scott Fitzgerald, who eventually found they could write *only* when they were drinking, Faulkner drank while he wrote right from the start. His extraordinary tolerance for alcohol allowed him to write superlatively well for a decade or more, an ability he shared with two of his contemporaries, Eugene O'Neill and Hart Crane. This was not the case with either Fitzgerald or Hemingway in their earlier years as writers: even small amounts of alcohol made Fitzgerald quite drunk, while Hemingway always believed that he could and should keep his drinking time apart from his writing. But Faulkner kept an indeterminate combination of alcohol and water beside him as he filled the pages with his minuscule script. This would not make him drunk, at least not until he reached his mid-thirties. He drank just enough, it would appear, to instill in himself the mood or the way of looking at things that he believed he needed. In time, this ability to write and drink concurrently and productively left Faulkner. He began to resemble both Jack London and

Fitzgerald in his later years; alcohol became the necessary fuel to get the creative engine going.

Faulkner made no bones about his drinking habits while working, praising the merits of whiskey to nearly everyone he met as the sovereign cure for all problems. Some of his public utterances at this time arose out of a desire to shock, but there is no doubt that he was telling the truth about the supply of liquor on his writing table. Some writers are deeply disturbed about the presence of alcohol in the creative process. They think, probably correctly, that the use of alcohol while writing produces fuzzy thinking and a distorted view of the world. In their view, it is manifestly impossible for any artist to produce anything of value while under the influence. But since the time of De Quincey and Baudelaire, we have grown to know that such rules are not inflexible. There *are* exceptions and Faulkner is clearly one of them.

What did Faulkner obtain from drink that he couldn't have found sober? We obviously don't know the answer, but one can guess that he found in alcohol what a number of other great talents have sought in drugs: an altered state of consciousness that permits the artists a freedom they don't believe they possess in sobriety. The fact that this freedom is illusory is beside the point; many artists have convinced themselves that they obtain it in no other way. The ability to create successfully when drinking is a rare one indeed. Raymond Carver commented that he, for one, was not helped by alcohol when he tried to mix it with writing. "Nothing good came of it. I never wrote so much as a line that was worth a nickel when I was under the influence of alcohol." Legions of writers have tried the drinking-writing combination with predictable failure; most writers require all the stamina and sobriety they can muster to turn out publishable material; alcohol is usually fatal to writing. But Faulkner seems to have led a charmed life in the years of his major achievements.

Perhaps his belief that he needed whiskey in order to write was confirmed by his admiration for Baudelaire, Swinburne, and Verlaine, all of whom affirmed the liberating effects of alcohol on the poet. All three were alcoholic.

The rationale, which can be traced back to the Romans, is simple: poets are deeply inhibited by their environment and need to throw off its constrictions in order to express themselves with true passion. Without the ecstasy and fervor produced by drinking, the writing will remain earthbound and sterile. Faulkner used the work of these men as the models on which he based all his early verse; for years he regarded himself primarily as a poet.

When Faulkner spoke of his first attempts at poetry, he freely admitted a great debt, saying that at the age of sixteen he discovered Swinburne: "Or rather, Swinburne discovered me, springing from some tortured undergrowth of my adolescence, like a highwayman, making me his slave." His admiration for the strange little red-headed English poet left its mark on his style, especially in the early and late books, with nymphs, satyrs and fauns appearing in many of the novels. There were other similarities between these two small men of great dignity: they shared a common passion for alcohol and for one of the most celebrated drinkers in English literature, Dickens's Mrs. Sarah Gamp; both men loved to quote her at length. Both maintained a rigid body posture that involved holding their backs so straight they seemed likely to fall over backward. When drunk, they liked to insist that they could repeat every word spoken in the preceding few hours and would actually do so. More important, Faulkner, like Swinburne, exhibited an overwhelming fluency with words and a lush, incantatory style with its ever-present danger of using words just for the sake of the sound. Faulkner found it advisable to throw the lushness aside when he began to write the books we now think his best. But in subsequent years, he would return to the extreme floridity, monotony and lack of precision that characterized the later Swinburne.

Swinburne was forced to give up riotous drinking at the age of forty-two for reasons of health, and in 1879 he went to live with a self-appointed protector, Theodore Watts-Dunton, whose main goal was to keep Swinburne from drinking himself to death. Except for a daily beer, Swinburne abstained for his last thirty years, but his poetic talent faded; he continued to write in huge quantities, but little of it had the vitality of the earlier work. These facts about Swinburne were widely known in the twenties, and it is likely that Faulkner would have shared Conrad Aiken's views, as reported by Aiken's second wife, Clarissa Lorenz, who attempted to control his drinking:

> "Don't try to change me," he said, though I was only trying to preserve him, and not in alcohol either. He reminded me that all good writers drank: "A poet without alcohol is no real poet. Swinburne's personality disintegrated, and his creative flow was dammed up when Watts-Dunton banned liquor."

It was perhaps Baudelaire who carried his love for intoxication further than the others:

> Always be drunk. That is all: it is *the* question. You want to stop Time crushing your shoulders, bending you double, so get drunk — militantly.
>
> How? Use wine, poetry, or virtue, use your imagination. Just get drunk.
>
> And if occasionally, on the steps of a palace, a grassy ditch in the bleak loneliness of your room, you come to, your drunkenness diminished or gone, ask wind, wave, star, bird, clock, everything that turns, that sings, that speaks, and ask the time; and wind, wave, star, bird, clock will reply: "Time to get drunk! Rather than be the martyred slave of Time, get drunk perpetually! Use wine, poetry, or virtue, use your imagination."

Here Baudelaire sees the artist as one who vanquishes time by the creation of his art; it will outlive him, and therein lies his victory. Many of Faulkner's characters echo this desire to escape the burden of time, as when young Quentin Compson, in *The Sound and the Fury,* recalls the day his father gave him his grandfather's watch:

> Quentin, I give you the mausoleum of all hope and desire; it's rather excruciatingly apt that you will use it to gain the reducto absurdum of all human experience. . . . I give it to you not that you may remember time, but that you might forget it now and then for a moment and not spend all your breath trying to conquer it.

If Faulkner had any lingering doubt about the beneficial combination of drink and writing, it could easily have been dissolved by reflecting on Baudelaire's testimony or Swinburne's career. But there was no need: by 1925 alcohol and writing were at the center of his life.

3

God damn! Why do I do it!?
— Faulkner, 1944

UNTIL WELL INTO his late twenties, Faulkner was known in his hometown of Oxford, Mississippi, as "Count No 'Count," a name he earned from his neighbors because, by their reckoning, he "didn't do anything," at least in the sense of holding down a steady job. To them, Faulkner was that scruffy young man who continued to wear his military uniform around town for five or six years after the war, was frequently unshaven and just as often smelled of whiskey. Having been given the job of local postmaster, he failed to perform his duties and was dismissed. The only thing he could do, apparently, was write. And drink.

The "No 'Count" label lingered on for years, despite the fact that he had begun the construction of an astonishing body of work. Between 1928 and 1941 he wrote ten novels that make him arguably the leading American novelist of this century, an amazing burst of creation that is unparalleled in American writing. A great deal of this furious output was accomplished against strong odds. By and large, Faulkner's novels were for the discerning few, and his courage in continuing to write them in a climate of public indifference is worthy of the highest praise. Even more remarkable is the fact that these books were written when their creator was in the early stage of alcoholism, the one in which liquor is the proverbial good friend and nothing seems amiss. Until 1928, if he had hangovers, they were bearable; as yet there were none of the other signs of alcohol withdrawal. By that time Faulkner had completed his first three apprentice novels, *Soldier's Pay, Mosquitoes* and *Sartoris,* and had begun to work on the book that made him a world figure, *The Sound and the Fury.*

Over the years, the degree of Faulkner's truthfulness in discussing his drinking was erratic, but at least some of the stories he told in the early days were due to his impatience with facts: he frequently stated that "any writer is a congenital liar to begin with or he wouldn't take up writing." He was always something of a "humbug artist," in the sense that you could never be sure if he was telling the truth. His practice of dissembling turned up regularly, as when he told a friend in Pascagoula in 1927 the story he had told Anderson in 1924, that he drank "because he had a silver plate in his head." But four years later, when asked by his cousin Sallie where he picked up the revolting material in *Sanctuary,* Faulkner replied, "Sallie Murry, I get a lot of it when I'm drunk." Here one doesn't know if he was just being evasive or pulling her leg to shock her. But when he told his French translator, Maurice Coindreau, that he "kept his whiskey within reach" when writing *The Sound and the Fury,* it is clear that he meant what he said.

Or did he? Could Faulkner's repeated assertions that he drank while he wrote — always good copy for an interview — be simply another tall tale? Considering the superb quality of the work up to 1942, it is tempting to think so. How he was able to write such a succession of amazing books under these circumstances is a tantalizing puzzle.

Faulkner's first three novels remain bound to their time; they have little of the literary quality of *The Sound and the Fury* or the books of the following decade. While it is true that *Sartoris* sets forth the particulars of the imaginary county that would occupy him for the next thirty years, it does not rise very much in quality over the first two. How Faulkner could transcend his previous work so completely in his revolutionary fourth novel will always remain a mystery. Perhaps the only clue is the few observations he made in a 1933 preface about the origins of the book, indicating that he started it differently:

> When I began the book I had no plan at all. I wasn't even writing a book. . . . I had written three novels with progressively decreasing ease and pleasure, and reward or emolument. The third one (*Sartoris*) was shopped about for three years during which I sent it from publisher to publisher with a kind of stubborn and fading hope of at least justifying the paper I had used and the time I had spent writing it. This hope must have died at last, because one day it suddenly seemed as if a door had clapped silently shut forever between me and all the publishers' addresses and booklists and I said to myself, "Now I can write. Now I can just write." Whereupon I, who had three brothers and no sisters and was destined to lose my first daughter in infancy, began to write about a little girl.

The little girl was Caddy Compson, and in deciding to write about her from the viewpoints of her three brothers, Faulkner created an extraordinarily rich and complex work of art, which began with the youngest of the four Compson children:

> I just began to write about a brother and sister splashing one another in the brook and the sister fell and wet her clothing and the smallest brother cried, thinking that the sister was conquered or perhaps hurt. Or perhaps he knew that he was the baby and that she would quit whatever water battles to comfort him. When she did so, when she quit the water fight and stooped in her wet garments above him, the entire story, which is all told by that same brother in the first section, seemed to explode on the paper before me.

Powerfully moved by this image, Faulkner next produced the concept of Benjy Compson, the idiot for whom time did not exist:

> And that Benjy must never grow beyond this moment; that for him all knowing must begin and end with that fierce, panting, paused and stooping wet figure which smelled like trees.

Characteristically, Faulkner chose to relate in later years a modified version of how he had begun *The Sound and the Fury,* although its details were present in the 1933 preface. The later explanation also dealt with wet undergarments but focused on the image of the three Compson boys, along with their black playmates, staring up at Caddy's wet drawers as she climbed a tree in the deepening twilight to see what was happening at the funeral being conducted in their home.

I have set forth the details of this vision, if it can be called that, because it reveals a peculiarity of Faulkner's approach to writing, whereby he often regarded himself as merely the re-corder of *things that have already happened.* He seemed to see himself as a catalyst between the events and the page before him. When asked why he did not supply names for characters such as the reporter in *Pylon* or the Tall Convict in *The Wild Palms,* he would say that he had never been able to catch them. This ability to use the creative power of a single image occurred again in 1931, when he began *Light in August* with the vision of Lena Grove walking the hot, dusty roads of Mississippi looking for the father of the child she is bearing. It may be that Faulkner, in his role as "transcriber," believed that his particular powers of imagination flourished best when he was in an elevated state; in this heightened awareness he could permit his deepest feelings to come forth — hence alcohol. He was not alone in thinking this way. After sobering up in the last few months of his life, John Berryman made some entries in his journal that cast light on the need both Faulkner and he had had for alcohol while writing:

> So long as I considered myself as the medium of (arena for) my powers, sobriety was out of the question. . . . The even deeper delusion that my art *depended* on my drinking, or at least was *connected* with it, could not be attackt directly. Too far down. The cover had to be exploded off.

Faulkner had exaggerated: *Sartoris* had not in fact been shopped around for three years; twelve months after its completion it had reached the desk of Harrison Smith, who was both senior editor and advertising manager for Harcourt, Brace in New York. Smith was extremely influential in the history of Faulkner's career, functioning as editor, publisher, banker, confidant and, most important, admirer from 1928 to 1936. He was to publish seven of Faulkner's novels — most of his best work — and five of these under his own imprints. The relationship began as a comedy of errors: Smith believed *Sartoris* was the work of Ben Wasson, a young Mississippian who had become Faulkner's literary agent in New York. When the battered manuscript reached Smith minus its title page, he called Wasson in to talk over terms for publication. When Faulkner was revealed as the author, Smith informed Wasson that his firm would be willing to take the book on if it was cut; shortening the book was the wish of Alfred Harcourt, who thought there was just too much in it for one novel. Wasson agreed to make the cuts and suggested that Faulkner come up to New York to oversee them. So Faulkner arrived in September 1928, bearing the unfinished manuscript of *The Sound and the Fury*, which he had begun that spring.

Faulkner's second extended visit to the city was important because his friendship with Smith became strong enough to guarantee that this new publisher would issue nearly everything he wrote, a comforting assurance for a writer whose books were a series of literary experiments. Smith already had considerable experience in publishing the innovative: he was the acquisitions editor for all of Virginia Woolf's books in America after 1922. He had noted the slow, steady growth of her fame and sales and was prepared to take on Faulkner, who might have seemed too risky for other publishing houses. Smith possessed a measure of literary sophistication that was uncommon in New York publishing at the time. But there was something else about him that Faulkner liked. Witty, soft-spoken and relaxed, Smith did not appear to be a businessman; it may have been this aspect of his personality that Faulkner was thinking of when he described Smith to a newspaper interviewer in 1931 as "the one man in the North I can trust." The fact of the matter was that Smith published books because he liked them, thinking that if he did, the audience would follow in time. Smith once told me that he was so impressed by the physical appearance of a section of Faulkner's handwritten manuscript of *The Sound and the Fury* that he felt it was partly responsible for his decision to take on the book; anyone who labored this carefully must be a dedicated craftsman.

There were also old friends to see in New York, Hamilton Basso and William Spratling from New Orleans, but there were new ones as well, Smith's boating friend Jim Devine in particular. In these early days Faulkner detested wearing shoes, both at home and in society, and removed them on every occasion he could. Shoeless, sipping bootleg whiskey, he liked to tell his new friends tall tales along the lines of those that became "Spotted Horses," and equally spurious ones about the events of his own life. One of these concerned the two children he had fathered in New Orleans. Walt Whitman told a similar story for many years: neither was true.

After moving in and out of various apartments, as guest and renter, he secured a tiny one for himself in order to finish the revision of *The Sound and the Fury.* After Faulkner dropped out of sight for several days, Jim Devine and his friend Leon Scales came around to check up; knocking on the door produced only silence. Peeking through the transom, they saw Faulkner lying unconscious on the floor, surrounded by empty gin bottles. This is the first recorded instance of Faulkner's losing control of his drinking. He had now begun nonstop consumption, the kind that in just a few years would require hospitalization. The two friends dragged Faulkner to Devine's apartment near Morningside Heights; Faulkner had eaten nothing for days and was very weak. But at thirty-one he still had the resiliency of youth and was himself again in just a few days.

Ben Wasson records in his book *Count No'Count* that when Faulkner left him the manuscript of *The Sound and the Fury,* in late October 1928, to send over to Harrison Smith, he told him, "Read this, bud, it's a real son of a bitch." Wasson is not always reliable as a source of information, but this sounds authentic. Less so is the remark he also ascribed to Faulkner: "This one's the greatest I'll ever write." In any event, Wasson dutifully delivered the manuscript to the Harcourt offices, and another comedy of errors ensued. Faulkner was sending Smith the book on a personal basis rather than as a regular submission to the firm, because he knew by then that Smith was just about to announce the formation of his own publishing company, Jonathan Cape and Harrison Smith; Faulkner's novel would look very good on Smith's first list. Smith left Harcourt at the end of December and started operations on his own, leaving the manuscript of *The Sound and the Fury* behind. Absent-mindedness was one of Smith's qualities that some found endearing while others considered it maddening. When the book was supposed to enter the production phase, Smith couldn't find it. Ben Wasson remembered where it was, and Smith sent Wasson, who was now working for him as an editor, to pick up the manuscript, and the book was soon on its way to publication. Faulkner left New York in early December to begin the novel that would give him his first taste of fame: *Sanctuary*.

Besides completing *Sanctuary*, Faulkner wrote *As I Lay Dying* in 1929 and married his childhood sweetheart, Estelle Oldham Franklin. Nearly two years older than Faulkner, Estelle bore some resemblance to Zelda Fitzgerald: she suffered severe depressions, attempted suicide and was an alcoholic. Both were Southern belles who were brought up to believe they deserved only the best and to accept nothing less; both women had occasion to wonder if their marriages came up to their expectations. They were married to men of great literary talent but with whom they felt a need to compete. Like Zelda, Estelle wrote a full-length novel and then destroyed it in a fury, to her husband's dismay, after only two rejections. Her feeling seems to have been that if two publishers up there in New York thought it no good, it probably wasn't. Again, like Zelda, Estelle had been the most popular girl in town. There were many who considered her the best-dressed girl in Mississippi. Slender, later anorectic, with bright, piercing eyes, Estelle had a flirtatious manner that never perished.

She may have exaggerated when she told Joseph Blotner that she had decided to marry Faulkner when she was seven, but there is no doubt that they were childhood sweethearts. A decade later Estelle and Faulkner attempted to carry out her plan when still in their late teens. Estelle's parents prevented the marriage by finding a far more suitable choice for her, Cornell Franklin, an up-and-coming young lawyer, who married her and took her to Shanghai. The marriage foundered, and by 1929 Estelle was back home in Oxford, accompanied by her two children, Malcolm and Victoria, ready to resume her involvement with her darling Billy, who appears to have developed mixed feelings about her.

Although Estelle never suffered hospitalization for her emotional problems, she had more than her share. In a remarkable letter that Faulkner wrote to Harrison Smith asking for a loan, he alludes to qualities not commonly sought after in a wife:

> Hal, I want $500.00. I am going to be married. Both want to and have to. THIS PART IS CONFIDENTIAL, UTTERLY. For my honor and the sanity — I believe life — of a woman. This is not bunk; neither am I being sucked in. We grew up together and I don't think she could fool me this way; that is, make me believe that her mental condition, her nerves, are this far gone. And no question of pregna[n]cy: that would hardly move me.

So with borrowed money (from Smith or relatives, we don't know) Faulkner became a husband and the father of two small children.

What home life with the Faulkners could have been like early in their marriage was recalled for me by Tony Buttitta, who visited Faulkner in Oxford in January 1932. Faulkner had bought the old Shegog place, which he transformed into his Rowanoak, mostly by means of his own physical labor. The house was then a gaunt, moldering ruin without electricity; dust, dirt and exposed lathing were everywhere. After staying one night in the house, Buttitta elected to spend the rest of his visit in a local hotel. One evening he was invited to dinner, and he tells of the strange scene of a formal meal served by two black servants, their napkins at the ready, in the semidarkness of the dilapidated dining room. Estelle was present that night for dinner, although she had refused to live in the house until it was ready for her and had been staying with her parents.

After dinner the Faulkners continued to drink, an activity they had begun long before the meal. Buttitta recalls that Estelle was haggard, her hair in disarray, as she hurled a steady stream of complaints about Faulkner's conduct, especially his apparent refusal to go to Hollywood to work as a scriptwriter. "He won't go, I know he just won't." She repeated over and over, "I want to go to Hollywood, I want to go to Hollywood!" She rose to her feet and began to dance around the room with an imaginary partner in the flickering light cast by the kerosene lamps. What impressed Buttitta most vividly about that chill evening in front of the fireplace was that Faulkner paid no attention whatever to Estelle's behavior. He ignored her completely the entire time, and scarcely a word passed between them; it was as if she weren't there, as if she didn't exist. Faulkner felt that Estelle "has never had any regard or respect for my work, has always looked on it as a hobby, like collecting stamps." At one time Faulkner had loved her deeply, but their alcoholism and his extramarital affairs took their toll. Eventually he came to regard her not exactly as a wife but certainly as "family"; that is, as someone so close that he could never leave her.

Faulkner used his firsthand knowledge of drinking rather sparingly in his writing. Unlike Hemingway and Fitzgerald, whose fiction is filled with heavy drinkers, Faulkner wrote about far fewer such characters. When he did deal with alcoholism, however, there was a great difference in technique. Faulkner sometimes placed the reader in the drinker's mind, as when he describes Gowan Stevens, in *Sanctuary,* telling the local college boys how well he learned to drink up in Virginia. After a night of drinking, Gowan samples the local brew, finds it on the weak side and begins to throw it back like water:

> "Look out, fellow," the third said. Gowan filled the glass level full and lifted it and emptied it steadily. He remembered setting the glass down carefully, then he became aware simultaneously of open air, of a chill gray freshness and an engine panting on a siding at the head of a dark string of cars, and that he was trying to tell someone that he had learned to drink like a gentleman. He was still trying to tell them, in a cramped dark place smelling of ammonia and creosote.

Probably no novelist until Faulkner had so convincingly handled the eerie passage of time in the mind of a drinker, in which one moment is succeeded by another many minutes or hours later, with nothing between them.

Tradition has always had it that *Sanctuary* became a best seller that lifted him from the ranks of poverty, but this wasn't so: a little over 12,000 copies were sold, and this did not make a best seller even in the Depression days of 1931. The book had a modest success, largely because of the coup of Louise Bonino, Harrison Smith's publicity manager, in getting Alexander Woollcott to review it on his popular radio program. Smith thought that it was worth paying Woollcott's under-the-table price of $500 to publicize the work of a man whose books were then selling fewer than 2,000 copies. But the book did make Faulkner a celebrity of sorts among the taste makers in New York, so that magazine editors suddenly started to buy some of his old stories. He began to be talked about as far away as Paris, where Allen Tate gave Hemingway's copy of *Sanctuary* to John Peale Bishop to read. One of the results of Faulkner's newfound fame was an invitation to a conference of prominent Southern writers held in Charlottesville at the University of Virginia in October 1931. When he agreed to appear there, Faulkner began a ten-week odyssey through Virginia, Florida, North Carolina and New York, most of which he spent drinking far beyond his tolerance.

The guests at Charlottesville included nearly every Southern writer of note — James Branch Cabell and Ellen Glasgow attended, although it was the absent Thomas Wolfe that Faulkner most probably would have wanted to meet. Sherwood Anderson was there and, as if fated to record all of Faulkner's less than shining hours, noted in a letter to Laura Lou Carpenter that "Bill Faulkner had arrived and got drunk. From time to time he appeared, got drunk again immediately, & disappeared. He kept asking everyone for drinks. If they didn't give him any, he drank his own."

There were others at the conference who noticed his great thirst, among them Caroline Gordon, who reported that Faulkner's response to the question "What do you think, Mr. Faulkner?" was simply "I think I'll shorely get a little drink in three, four minutes."

At no time in his life was Faulkner interested in literary shop talk: it bored him profoundly, and he had come to Virginia only because Harrison Smith bought him the railway ticket and gave him some expense money. He went out of his way to tell an acquaintance at the conference that he "didn't give a damn about Ellen Glasgow." Shortly after the conference, she received a note from Faulkner's old Oxford friend Stark Young: "I hear that Bill Faulkner was somewhat *in absentia* in many ways. Not a bad move: it will convince most of the authors there that he is all the more of a genius, especially those that live in New York." Young's quip clearly shows that excessive drinking had become, as Lillian Hellman put it, "romantic, even chic" in literary circles and for many was a sure sign of writing talent.

As Anderson stated, Faulkner spent nearly all of his time in Virginia either drunk or passed out; Smith also attended the conference and may have regretted buying that ticket. But Faulkner was never combative when drunk: unlike Hemingway and Fitzgerald, who became increasingly abusive, Faulkner usually liked to recite some of his favorite poems, nearly always choosing Shakespeare's "The Phoenix and the Turtle."

When Faulkner arrived in New York after the conference, he walked into a situation he had never faced before. Lordly and even regal in later years, he was still shy and retiring in 1931, but he had suddenly become a valued person to invite to lunch or to have drinks with. He entered a feverish round of social engagements with literary people all over New York and made some new friends (perhaps acquaintances is more accurate), among them Dashiell Hammett, Lillian Hellman, Nathanael West, Dorothy Parker, Alfred and Blanche Knopf, Bennett Cerf and Donald Klopfer of Random House. The sage of Baltimore, H. L. Mencken, even invited him to come down to that city for dinner, an invitation he accepted.

He did a lot of drinking (and passing out) around town. Louise Bonino, who later worked for Random House for many years, told me of opening the door to her Sheridan Square apartment one night at this time to see a weaving, barely conscious Faulkner, who had but a single question for her: "Miss Louise, could I, right now, take a short nap?" She obliged by leading him to her bedroom, where he passed out immediately but in about three or four hours was awake again, ready to keep his next appointment. Drunk or sober, Faulkner was always extremely courteous to both men and women; Bonino recalled that over the years he always propositioned her by asking, "Miss Louise, can I sleep with you tonight?" He accepted her regular refusals with gentlemanly ease.

When drinking and away from home, Faulkner took a stronger interest in women than he could in Oxford. During this New York visit was when he saw something of the attractive young writer Leane Zugsmith, whom he had met in his 1928 Liveright days. The early books of the witty Kentucky-born novelist had also been published by that firm, and her later ones by Harrison Smith and then Random House. Friendly with Hammett, James T. Farrell and most of the left-wing writers of the time, Zugsmith appeared regularly on picket lines during strikes and wrote her version of the new proletarian fiction. It was Louise Bonino's view that Zugsmith's political zeal prevented any deepening of feeling between her and Faulkner. The same problem may well have arisen in his friendships with Hammett and Hellman — Faulkner was uninterested in politics.

In the midst of all the drinking and socializing, something unexpected was going on that concerned him seriously. His publisher, Harrison Smith, had just been thrown out of the firm he had launched so recently. His disaffected English partner, Jonathan Cape (who held the controlling interest in the firm), had not much liked the books Smith had published on his own, particularly those of William Faulkner. Smith's end of the business had gone badly and was close to bankruptcy, confirming what Cape had believed for some time, that Smith had no commercial judgment as a publisher. With what some have called a sense of revenge, Cape put the firm in liquidation in order to ensure Smith's not getting back any of his investment. In addition, Cape refused to disburse to his American authors the monies he owed them, while paying his English ones. Faulkner received not a penny of the $4,000 owed him for *Sanctuary* — his advance had been $200. The full extent of the financial debacle reached him the following year when, having counted on this money and being on the verge of falling into serious debt, he was forced to accept MGM's offer of $500 a week and began a twenty-year career as a Hollywood scriptwriter.

Cape may have had some personal animosity toward Faulkner, if the apocryphal story is true that during their one recorded meeting Cape confronted Faulkner with a difficult passage in *As I Lay Dying* and asked him what it meant. A flippant Faulkner affected not to recall the meaning because he had been "too corned up" when he wrote it.

While Smith was attempting to set up a new firm, he was faced with a new problem: what to do with Faulkner here in New York. Since he now went out and drank so much, might he just sign a contract with a rival publisher — Knopf or Viking? Smith, aware that Faulkner had brought along with him the unfinished manuscript of *Light in August* and was showing it to people, embarked on a bizarre solution: he suggested that Milton Abernethy, who had come to New York with Faulkner and Smith in the drive up from Virginia, take the by now sodden Faulkner on a boat trip down to Jacksonville, Florida. Young Abernethy, the editor and co-founder, with Tony Buttitta, of

Contempo, a Chapel Hill literary magazine, was delighted to spend time with Faulkner, even to become his nursemaid. They embarked together and Faulkner drank steadily for the entire trip. Abernethy decided to take his charge up to Chapel Hill, where Faulkner spent a few days sobering up. Nearly a week later, with Smith established in a new firm of his own, Faulkner returned to New York to continue his interrupted social rounds. One aftermath of the Chapel Hill stay was Faulkner's giving Abernethy and Buttitta a number of poems he had brought along on his trip, as well as a terrible short story that they immediately printed in an all-Faulkner issue of their magazine. Giving away material for nothing infuriated Smith, and when Abernethy attempted to publish a limited edition of some of the poems, Smith lost his patience and castigated Faulkner, who replied: "I'm sorry. I didn't realize at the time what I had got into. Goddam the paper and goddam me for getting mixed up with it and goddam you for sending me off with that pirate in the shape I was in."

Faulkner's continued heavy drinking at this time created another problem, which bore long-term consequences. It arose innocently enough in a four-page introduction that Faulkner wrote for the Modern Library edition of *Sanctuary* — a piece commissioned by the firm's president, Bennett Cerf. Having a title included in the Modern Library in the thirties, forties and fifties was a great honor, a sure sign that one had arrived. Cerf's decision to request the material was standard practice for the series, but what Faulkner wrote for him was not. These four pages contained a good deal of arrogance and posturing, as well as a seeming contempt for the reader. The introduction soon acquired a notoriety that cost Faulkner a good measure of the critical support he sorely needed; it served only to alienate many people. Possibly writing when drunk, he told his prospective readers, "This book was written three years ago. To me it is a cheap idea, because it was deliberately conceived to make money." In a harder-than-nails style that tried to outdo Hemingway, Faulkner related the story of his career to date and produced a mixture of truth and lies that has taken decades to unravel. He stated that he wrote *Sanctuary* in three weeks — in truth it took four months — and that he set down *As I Lay Dying* "in six weeks, without changing a word." We now know that he did revise *As I Lay Dying*. His assertion that he wrote the book while working as a coal passer in a power plant was short of the truth. He *did* work in a power plant, but his job was supervising those men with the shovels. But it was the "writing for money" aspect that alienated the literary establishment.

After relating how he revised the original galleys of *Sanctuary,* he went on:

> So I tore the galleys down and rewrote the book. It had been already set up once, so I had to pay for the privilege of rewriting it, trying to make out of it something which would not shame *The Sound and the Fury* and *As I Lay Dying* too much and I made a fair job and I hope you will buy it and tell your friends and I hope they will buy it too.

The last twenty-five words particularly raised the ire of the critics. Bennett Cerf's copy of the manuscript of this introduction has its author's dedication — a strange one, written in Faulkner's tiniest script: "Fuck you Bennett," perhaps an indication that he regretted ever writing it. It was one thing to write novels at home with "whiskey within reach," but writing introductions to them in New York was something else, something that left scars. Oddly enough, Scott Fitzgerald, three years later, wrote *his* Modern Library introduction to *The Great Gatsby* in a less than sober state and offered to pay Cerf for the privilege of rewriting it and having it reset.

The 1931 New York trip became the prototype of all the ones to follow for the next thirty years, except that after 1937 most of them culminated in hospitalization.

It is common for many alcoholics at a certain stage of their drinking, often in their late thirties, to place curbs on their consumption, either by cutting back or by abstaining completely for a few months, or even a year or more. Some event, an alcohol-provoked disaster or fiasco of some sort, or complaints from employers, wives and children — any of these can lead to such a curb in the regular drinking pattern of alcoholics. They are attempting to convince themselves they are not alcoholic by demonstrating their control over their drinking — if they can drink "normally" for a few months, or abstain altogether, doesn't it prove that they cannot be considered alcoholics? What inevitably occurs is that the moment the interdiction is lifted, there is a return to the drinking pattern that was interrupted where the alcoholic left off, and the disease proceeds apace.

It was not until 1933, at the age of thirty-six, that Faulkner saw any need to place a restriction on his drinking. At the time of the death of his first child, Alabama, in early 1931, he had refused a drink when offered one, saying, "This is the one time I'm not going to do it." But the abstention was brief, and he continued to drink in his usual manner. In 1933 certain events may have given him cause to think his drinking was getting out of hand. It is also likely that he began to find it progressively harder to drink and write at the same time. His body required ever more alcohol to satisfy his increased tolerance. Managing this mixture — dangerous from the start — became increasingly difficult to accomplish, and if he wasn't careful, drinking this way could lead to an extended bout.

When Harrison Smith came down to Oxford in November 1933 for the christening of Faulkner's daughter, Jill, all went well during a social week, but after Smith took a side trip to New Orleans, he returned to Oxford to find his major author in the middle of a drinking episode similar to the ones described earlier. Smith left for New York without finishing whatever business he'd wished to discuss. Perhaps his sudden departure caused Faulkner to fly to New York the following week in his Waco plane, the one he had purchased that year from the money earned at MGM. Bennett Cerf gave a cocktail party for him and invited all his New York friends. The party was a failure: the guest of honor arrived very late and passed out almost immediately. This visit became a shortened version of what had happened in 1931. He expressed contrition over his conduct, writing to Cerf a week or so later:

> I'm mighty sorry I made more or less of a fiasco of my part of the afternoon at your place. I was sick. It had started coming on soon after I got to New York, and I made the mistake of trying to carry on on liquor until I could get back home. That was the reason I was so near blotto, though it is no excuse.

The note of worry about what he'd done and what people might think about it was echoed in a letter to Smith that he concluded with "I'm still sober and still writing. On the wagon since November now."

Estelle told Faulkner's first biographer, Joseph Blotner, that this was about the time he "gave up alcohol for a year in order to show he could do it." We have no way of knowing just how long he remained abstinent, but by February 1934 he arrived hung over at the home of Roark Bradford, a once-popular novelist, in New Orleans after a night of heavy drinking. Faulkner told Smith in August of that year that he looked forward to seeing him again in Oxford in November: "I will be sober (I have not had a drink since you left)." These attempts to reassure Smith indicate that Faulkner was aware his publisher had become increasingly apprehensive about what was happening to him.

When Faulkner wrote *Pylon* in the last few months of 1934, he displayed a detailed knowledge of alcohol withdrawal. It is clear that both the mechanic, Jiggs, and the never-named "Reporter" are alcoholic; Jiggs, for example, cannot begin his day's work on the plane until he has had his morning drink. (The characters in this novel drink perhaps even more than do those in Hemingway's *The Sun Also Rises*.) In addition, Jiggs also suffers from the shakes:

> Schumann watched him set the water glass down, where it chattered again on the table before he released it, and then with both

hands attempt to raise the other one to his lips. As the glass approached Jiggs' whole head began to jerk so that he could not make contact with his mouth, the rim of the glass clicking against his teeth while he tried to still it. "Jesus," he said quietly. . . . "Maybe if you wont look at me I can drink it."

By the time Faulkner returned to New York again in October 1935, the "nondrinking year" was over, and he now prided himself on his newly gained talent for moderation. He wrote to Estelle: "I drink in a very moderate way, two whiskeys before supper and no more, and I am actually enjoying drinks now, and everyone is amazed at my temperateness." But this attempt to drink normally was short-lived. Meta Carpenter relates that Faulkner was drunk the second time she met him, in Hollywood that December when they were both working for Howard Hawks at Twentieth Century–Fox. As I've indicated earlier, this episode was soon followed by the series of increasingly severe ones that required several hospitalizations.

Alcohol withdrawal at a detoxification institution is an unpleasant experience that Faulkner endured dozens of times. A withdrawal takes a minimum of two or three days but may extend to a week or more in serious cases; the age and general health of the patient have much to do with the duration of the treatment. Patients often arrive at the hospital unconscious or in delirium, frequently suffering from tachycardia (rapid or irregular pulse). They are usually weak from malnutrition, caused by not eating for days or weeks, and disoriented: many patients do not know the day of the week or even the month. After an examination, a physician administers various drugs — vitamin B for their poor nutritional state and Dilantin to prevent the onset of convulsive seizures and D.T.'s — and prescribes tranquilizers that are taken at regular intervals throughout the day. These replace the alcohol to which the system has become accustomed. Before tranquilizers became available, when Faulkner visited Towne's Hospital in New York, carefully doled out drinks were served to bring the patient down.

Detoxification is a severely trying time. Nothing much happens; it's all a waiting process while the body is being slowly weaned from alcohol. Patients pace restlessly up and down the corridors, smoking endless cigarettes and drinking coffee from paper cups. There is a terrible apathy in the air: everybody is waiting to feel better. The patients are served a high-protein diet that is aimed at restoring the body's functions. Although they may not have eaten for a week or more, they have little or no appetite for days. During withdrawal, patients find it difficult to sleep; even with sedation, three or four hours is the most they can expect for the first days. The main thing they anticipate is the administration of medication. They spend a lot of time thinking, particularly about what has brought them to the hospital. What is going on in the outside world of home and work? How many people know about their plight and, more important, what are they going to do about it? Such thoughts can induce terrible anxiety in the mind of the alcoholic. A patient such as Faulkner, with a shaky job at Fox, worried continuously: Will they suspend my contract?

Although it is clear that 1933 and 1934 saw Faulkner begin to express concern over his drinking and that *Pylon*, published in 1935, shows a marked falling off in quality from the four novels that preceded it, *Absalom, Absalom!*, of 1936, shows a remarkable return to the level of the earlier books. (It is noteworthy that *Pylon* contains, page for page, more heavy drinking than any of his other novels.) He had begun *Absalom, Absalom!* early in 1934 but had abandoned it for a time to write *Pylon* later that year. He finished *Pylon* in a little over a month — he was telling the truth this time — and then went on with *Absalom, Absalom!* both at home and in Hollywood while working on scripts five and a half days a week at Twentieth Century–Fox. During this period he underwent hemorrhages and several hospitalizations for drinking, not to mention dozens of hangovers, but was capable of writing one of the great American novels. His ability to write with such power under such killing circumstances is little short of miraculous. He was nearly forty at the time of its completion and had preserved his creativity at full force longer than might have been expected — far longer than any of his noted contemporaries who were also alcoholic.

4

I am the best in America, by God.
— Faulkner, 1939

MOST PRESENT-DAY DEFINITIONS of alcoholism include the drinker's loss of control over his drinking. According to most recorded instances, Faulkner fell easily into this pattern after the mid-1930s, but there are friends and relatives who believe that he was nevertheless capable of a measure of control, some even going so far as to say he *willed* any number of his bouts. This belief was based on his predictable recital of some favorite poem, usually by Shakespeare, during the day or two preceding the drinking. His family interpreted these recitals as his way of warning them that he was about to begin a period of heavy drinking. But this is not at all the same as demonstrating control over alcohol, for once started, Faulkner couldn't stop, and he deeply regretted these episodes that disabled him for days. He may well have intended to drink only for a day or two, but he had no idea how much he would drink or where it might take him. When he returned to sobriety, often confined to a hospital bed, he would be full of remorse and more than once stated: "Don't ask me why I do it. If I knew, I wouldn't do it."

If Faulkner had been able to stop, these episodes would never have taken place; the cost was far too high for that. What sent him into these periods of around-the-clock drinking was the loss of control suffered by many alcoholics in the middle stage of the disease. At this point their tolerance declines as their withdrawal symptoms increase, which means simply that once Faulkner started drinking heavily, the pain of stopping was too much to bear, and he continued until hospitalized. Why alcoholics lose their earlier control is largely the effect of the aging process — even moderate drinkers cannot drink in later years as much as they did when younger. If the pain of these episodes was so great, why didn't Faulkner quit for good? It is clear that he thought the price not that excessive, that a life without alcohol was no life at all.

As for the "control" he exhibited in ordinary social situations, Faulkner, like many alcoholics, could drink normally when necessary, utilizing a self-imposed braking system of limiting himself to two or three drinks. Normal drinkers do not have to concern themselves this seriously with just how much they consume; alcoholics, however, require these curbs in order to avoid an extensive episode and inevitable collapse. The alcoholic's desire to drink without inhibition returns in time — weeks or months later — with increasing strength. By 1937 Faulkner required a daily infusion of alcohol to feel "normal"; without it he would become ill, nervous and depressed.

The later, uncontrollable drunks extending for a week or ten days caused considerable anxiety and sometimes pain to members of Faulkner's immediate family. Estelle's own periods of extended drinking became a problem; both adult Faulkners fell down the stairway of their home more than once, while her son, Malcolm, began to exhibit signs of alcoholism in his twenties. Faulkner's daughter, Jill, perhaps felt the greatest pain. She bitterly recalled her attempt to stop her father once he'd embarked on a spree:

> It was just before my birthday and I knew that Pappy was getting ready to start on one of these bouts. I went to him — the only time I ever did — and said, "Please don't start drinking." And he was already well on his way, and he turned to me and said, "You

know, no one remembers Shakespeare's child." I never asked him again.

In time his family, as well as the friends he had, learned to accept Faulkner's alcoholism as a central part of his life; apparently, no one could imagine him without liquor.

Faulkner had few friends. Despite its grand name, there was very little social life at Rowanoak, and as for friends in Oxford, there really weren't any to speak of. By the beginning of the 1940s, his two decades of friendship with the intellectual mentor of his youth, Phil Stone, had come to an end, in part because of Faulkner's outgrowing him, as well as Stone's gradual but definite decline into madness. Faulkner would terminate friendships of many years' duration for reasons that remain obscure; his immense pride was quick to respond to any slight, real or imaginary. Ben Wasson and his Hollywood screenwriter friend A. I. "Buzz" Bezzerides never knew why Faulkner refused to see them again. Faulkner's lordly arrogance, which took the form of a reserve that often approached rudeness, prevented his forming deep friendships. He was hard to know and there were many who found him enigmatic. Despite Meta Carpenter's love for him, she admits that he always "remained a cipher" to her: she never really knew what he thought about anything. Much of the time he seemed detached and preoccupied, or as Bezzerides claimed, "You always had a feeling that he was not really there; he was in his head somewhere." (He may have been right. Faulkner spent many of his waking hours composing in his head what he would soon be writing on paper.) As evidence, Bezzerides tells a tale, difficult to believe, about what happened one night when Faulkner passed out on the floor of his house in Hollywood. When Bezzerides lifted his guest up, he heard a faint murmur arising from his lips and then listened carefully as whole paragraphs came forth, paragraphs that he would later recognize as part of what Faulkner was working on at the time. Faulkner was never boisterous when drunk, given to fighting or smashing up the furniture. His physical appearance in Hollywood was probably best described by the producer-screenwriter Gene Markey, who called him "a handsome, trim, well-dressed little man with the grave air of a High Court Justice." The grave air would never quite leave him, even when he was passing out.

After his terrible burn in late 1937, Faulkner returned to Oxford, where he produced four books — three novels and a collection of short stories — at the rate of one a year. The novels, *The Wild Palms, The Hamlet* and *Go Down, Moses,* show him writing at very nearly the top of his form, certainly legitimizing his remark about being the best in America. He was all of that, but none of these books earned enough to keep him afloat financially. Work on the novels was constantly interrupted by what he called "boiling the pot," writing stories for *The Saturday Evening Post.* Most of the time the *Post* found them too dense or "too good," and they were published in *Harper's* and *Scribner's* magazines or in *The American Mercury,* which paid him only a quarter as much as the *Post.* His desperate need for money arose not only from having to support his family of five; he was also the sole provider for his mother, his brother Dean's young widow and child and, occasionally, his brother John and his family. Without these constant drains on his pocket, Faulkner might have been able to avoid his longish periods of employment in Hollywood, but his financial commitments kept him returning there for over a decade.

· When not writing or drinking, Faulkner had two other ways he spent his time: flying and hunting. He took up flying in 1933 by buying his own small plane with the money he'd earned at MGM. Just as accident-prone in the air as Hemingway was with firearms, Faulkner kept narrowly avoiding disaster until he finally quit flying altogether in 1946, after a near calamity when he approached the ground so low that a crash was imminent and his nephew Jimmy had to seize the controls and land the plane. It is more than likely that his reflexes, not too good to begin with, had suffered damage from liquor. As a friend had once told him, "You can't drink and fly, Bill." Although flying had given him great pleasure, it was not going to interfere with his drinking.

Hunting had been a rich experience in his youth, supplying him with the background to write his superb stories about the struggle between man and beast. But after the late 1930s his interest was confined to the annual deer hunt conducted each November in the area around Batesville. The hunters entered the deep woods — the last, ever-decreasing piece of wilderness left in Mississippi — with a good supply of bourbon. On one such occasion, in 1940, Faulkner had to be rushed home from the hunt, unconscious and hemorrhaging from the amount he'd drunk. In the years of his great fame he gave up big woods hunting completely and replaced it with the fashionable Virginia version of fox hunting.

After the completion of *Go Down, Moses,* his last book of distinction, in December 1941, Faulkner was disconcerted to find that editors in New York had begun to reject his short stories with regularity. He became alarmed enough the following June to write to his agent, Harold Ober: "I seem to have touched bottom as earning goes . . . 1 story out of 6 since January. . . . I've got to get away from here and earn more money." A few days earlier he'd told Ober why his new stories had stopped selling: "I know what the trouble is in what I write now. I have been here for three years now for lack of money and I am stale." He mentioned this feeling of staleness when he wrote to Bennett Cerf of Random House the next day, stressing his imminent financial collapse: "Right now, I can't move at all. I have 60c in my pocket, and that is literally all. I finished a story and sent in it yesterday, but with no real hope it will sell." His finances worsened so much that he was forced to borrow $100 from Ober to prevent the electricity from being turned off; by the end of June 1942 Faulkner owed his grocer $600 and had taken to avoiding his many creditors on the town square in Oxford.

Some of the stories written at this time were clearly bad by any definition — "Snow" and "Knight's Gambit" in particular — and indicate what was to come, but to ascribe their failure to sell to his staleness seems strange when considered in light of where he proposed to go to escape it: Hollywood, a place he actively disliked. The phrase "taking a geographical cure" is widely used by participants in the Alcoholics Anonymous program to mean the common practice of alcoholics' traveling to a new place, hoping that by doing so they will avoid the deepening despair caused by their increased drinking. They believe that in a different location things are bound to improve. This geographical cure is no more effective than "the Keeley," but many alcoholics travel for this reason, consciously or unconsciously. It is entirely possible that Faulkner had this idea when he began to implore Ober to get him *any* screenwriting job ("I will take anything above $100.00"), but it is more likely that it was his deepening financial plight that drove him to such a low estimate of his market value as a screenwriter. His figure of one hundred a week may seem odd after the thousand he received from Twentieth Century–Fox in 1936, but the news of his drinking, especially the time he spent away from work recovering from his bouts, had come to the attention of all the major studios, including Warner Brothers, who nevertheless offered him a seven-year contract. The contract contained yearly options attached to very small increments in pay, and the deal would be worse after two agents took their commissions from the rock-bottom salary of $300 per week. He had, in a sense, been blacklisted by the industry, and the offer reflected this fact. But he accepted it without hesitation and began an unhappy three years in which he wrote (with a single exception) nothing but screenplays and treatments.

In Hollywood he resumed his old affair with Meta Carpenter, who was now divorced from Wolfgang Rebner. She recalls this period of their relationship as being based on far more realistic grounds than those prevailing during their first days together in the late 1930s, even to the point of her realizing there was little chance of Faulkner's divorcing Estelle:

> The knowledge for me that it was never going to work in terms of being married to Faulkner changed the color and the depth of

it. I knew that I still cared and he indicated he still cared for me, but somehow if you realize that it's never going to have an end, that only today counts, or next weekend or whatever is left, then that moment out of all time, and history and space, becomes terribly important. And so it carries with it a different kind of excitement. It isn't something brand new that you think is going to lead to paradise.

Faulkner attempted to make sure that Meta saw little of him when he was incapacitated, but she had a few glimpses, especially the night of "the Jerries," which terrified her.

Buzz Bezzerides, author of *They Drive by Night* and at the time a screenwriter at Warner Brothers, invited Faulkner to be his house guest for extended visits during the three years Faulkner worked for Warners. This was wartime Hollywood and housing was very scarce; he spent six months in 1944 and four in 1945 staying with Bezzerides. They were an odd couple: Bezzerides talked nearly all the time while Faulkner rarely had a word to say. When not boarding with Bezzerides, he lived at the slightly seedy Highland Hotel, not far from the center of Hollywood but still an hour's bus ride from the studio. In 1944 he rented a house for several months and brought Estelle and Jill out to spend time with him, but even bringing his "home" to California failed to cheer him. His worries about wasting his time for a low salary at Warner Brothers continued to disturb him, but he had no alternative: "I shan't jeopardize my position with the studio though, as I apparently cannot make enough money at anything else and must resign myself to being a part-time script writer at least."

But he repeatedly jeopardized his job. Meta and Buzz agree about the drinking side of the Faulkner they knew in these years: he was a hard worker who took his writing tasks seriously and who drank his nightly two or three drinks with no apparent ill effects and then went on (or up) to bed. But every few weeks or so the story was different — the usual one of nonstop drinking, D.T.'s and the ensuing hospitalization. Both friends could occasionally account for the "motivation" of the drinking cycle, but there were just as many times when they had no clue. The simple truth was that Faulkner could restrain himself only just so long before exploding with several days of drinking that would cost him a week or more away from work. He once narrowly avoided being caught drunk at the studio, an event that could have led to the cancellation of his contract. Back in 1936 it had been Howard Hawks who quietly spirited Faulkner home from Fox when drunk, and now it was Meta and Buzz who performed this function at Warner Brothers by removing him bodily after he had passed out in his office.

Faulkner began to find it increasingly necessary to depend on people to take care of him not only when he was incapacitated but at other times as well. Bezzerides feels that Faulkner "used" people to maintain himself in life — his friends supplied him with free bed and board and chauffeur service and carted him off to the half-dozen hospitals in which Faulkner spent time recovering during these years. When he awakened to the agony of a hangover and began the slow, days-long path to recovery, Faulkner would behave like an animal in a cage, repeating over and over, "You gotta get me outa here, you gotta get me outa here!" Bezzerides witnessed more of the distasteful side of Faulkner's drinking than anyone else at the time and has his theories about how and why his guest drank so much:

> When he didn't want to get drunk, he could drink any amount and it didn't matter, but when he wanted to get drunk, the liquor would begin to take effect and he couldn't stop drinking. He didn't drink just to drink; always it was to escape something.

What Bezzerides had observed was the puzzling phenomenon that the same amount of alcohol produces very different effects on the same man at different times. Bezzerides was convinced that Faulkner was capable of exercising "will power" over his drinking when it is quite clear that he could not predict or choose the results.

Once, when the subject of these killing drunks arose between them after a hospitalization, Faulkner smashed his fist into his palm, shouting, "God dammit! Why do I do it? Why do I do it?" His host responded with the advice that many at the time believed was the only kind you could give to an alcoholic: "If you really want to know why you do it, you'd go to a good psychologist and sit down and talk to him because if you want to know, you can find out." Buzz's reply reduced Faulkner to complete and lasting silence on the subject. Forty years after this conversation, Bezzerides still seems angry at Faulkner for not following his advice. But psychologists have made little headway against alcoholism, either then or now; Faulkner would have been wasting his money.

By 1944 Faulkner had become sufficiently frightened of losing his job at Warner Brothers to resort to a stratagem that would guarantee his getting to the office on Monday morning, the day that was most problematic. Perhaps having read about W. C. Fields and his similar situation in his last days at Paramount, Faulkner hired a male nurse, a Mr. Nielson, to follow him around town and administer just enough drinks to keep him high but not enough to plunge him into a major drunk. Faulkner worked out some sort of rationing system in advance, and Mr. Nielson carried a bottle of bourbon in a medical-looking black bag. Whenever Faulkner felt the need, he would request a supply and perhaps argue awhile until the nurse obliged him. This solution was abandoned almost immediately because it was totally impractical; once begun, the cycle had little chance of being interrupted.

In time, alcoholism succeeds in invading virtually every part of a person's life, and Faulkner was no exception. His age (forty-five in 1942) had precluded his seeing active service in World War II. All his efforts to secure a commission failed, and he had resigned himself to reading about the war in the papers when Harold Ober managed to get the Army Air Corps interested in paying Faulkner to write a book for them about their overseas operations. This task would entail a tour of duty in one or more of the combat zones. Faulkner was delighted at the prospect of escaping the drudgery of writing unproduced screenplays about the war and, while on leave of absence from Warners, agreed to drive up to the Memphis airport to confer with an Air Corps major. When he arrived, he was, in his own words, "tight," and the assignment fell through with no further discussion.

As I have recounted in *Some Time in the Sun,* Faulkner participated in the writing of at least three films of merit at this time: *To Have and Have Not, The Big Sleep* and *The Southerner.* The first two were directed by his friend Howard Hawks, the director with whom he'd worked at MGM in 1932–33 and at Fox in 1935–36. His Warner Brothers salary paid him for the first two, while the scenes he wrote for Jean Renoir's *Southerner* were done as moonlighting without credit. Outside these three, none of Faulkner's dozen or more scripts and treatments was used, including such ambitious war projects as *The de Gaulle Story, The Life and Death of a Bomber* and, with Howard Hawks, *Battle Cry.* The first and third of these have recently been published in book form, and they presage the style that Faulkner was to use in the next decade.

Although he probably had only a fleeting awareness of it, the Faulkner who spent three years writing these screenplays in Hollywood had largely dried up as a creative writer of the first class. Virtually everything he would publish in the last fourteen years of his life was material that he created and decided to write about prior to 1942. His work published after that date was written on the basis of commitments made mainly to himself in order to complete his chronicle of Yoknapatawpha County, his "Golden Book," or his "own little postage stamp of native soil," as he sometimes called it. His correspondence with his agents and publishers, again prior to 1942, contains the titles and plots for *Intruder in the Dust*; *Requiem for a Nun*; the final two volumes of his Snopes chronicle, *The Town* and *The Mansion*; and his very last book, *The Reivers.* The only extended work that Faulkner was to create out of new material was a book that had its origin in a notion the director Henry Hathaway and the producer William Bacher had had for a screenplay about Christ and his twelve apostles returning to earth as a corporal and his squad during World War I. Bacher hired Faulkner to write a screen treatment of the story. It was never filmed but became, after nine years, *A Fable,* which Faulkner hoped would be his "magnum o," his masterpiece.

5

Well, I'm doing something different now, so different that I am writing and rewriting, weighing every word, which I never did before; I used to bang it on like an apprentice paper hanger and never look back.
— Faulkner to Bennett Cerf and Robert Haas, January 10, 1945

I . . . write so slowly now that it alarms me sometimes; now and then I think the stuff is no good, which is the reason it takes so long.
— Faulkner to Robert Haas, October 3, 1947

FAULKNER once told one of his editors, Robert Linscott, "I reckon I wrote *The Sound and the Fury* for fun." This statement cannot describe the way he wrote what I have called his personal albatross, the novel that required nine years of on-again-off-again toil, mostly off. After the abrogation of his contract with Warner Brothers early in 1946 to work on *A Fable,* the following years were marked by increasingly severe symptoms of alcoholism, producing his first convulsive seizures and memory loss, and by electroshock therapy. Apparently convinced he had used up all his material about life in Mississippi, Faulkner turned to writing a huge allegory about the Passion of Christ reenacted on the Western Front, a book profoundly alien to his talent, as he was intermittently aware. He told its publisher,

"Now and then I think the stuff is no good." Making a break with his past, he felt that he would have to write the ambitious work with a care and patience that were new to him; he would no longer "bang it on," but would weigh every word, unlike the Faulkner of the thirties, who wrote with superb self-confidence and amazing speed.

Alcoholics are often given to grandiosity accompanied by a loss of common sense, a combination that can be fatal to any writer. At its inception, the writing of *A Fable* appeared manageable. Faulkner told Robert Haas in May 1946 that four months "might do it"; one year later he told Ober that "it will take another year, probably two." After 1946, except for the funds from an occasional brief stint at screenwriting, his chief source of income was the $500 per month advanced him on the book by Random House. His feelings about the project vacillated widely; after telling Haas that "the stuff is no good," he turned about in the same letter and said, "There's nothing wrong with this book; I am just getting older and dont write fast anymore." It is a distinct possibility that Faulkner might even have abandoned it, especially when he began having strong doubts about the value of what he was writing. At one point he gave his publisher the chance to back out: "I dont know how much longer . . . any time Random H. feels this has gone far enough, so do I."

As his difficulties mounted, he became willing to stop work on the book whenever anything else offered: more scripts in Hollywood, writing *Intruder in the Dust* and, finally, the play/novel *Requiem for a Nun*. It is clear that after a certain point he thought of *A Fable* as something he *had* to finish, viewing it as a task that would give him his final freedom: "I shall be through, can break the pencil." At forty-nine he began to believe that his talent was exhausted, telling a creative-writing class at the university in Oxford in April 1947: "I feel I'm written out. I don't think I'll write much more."

Besides the intractable nature of his material, there were two important events causing the long delays. The first was the rapid composition of *Intruder in the Dust* in three months — perhaps undertaken as a respite from "the big book" — and its publication in October 1948. The book sold more than anything he'd ever written — 25,000 copies — largely because of the critical interest in his work created by the reception of Malcolm Cowley's *Portable Faulkner* in 1946. *Intruder in the Dust* was sold to MGM for $50,000, a sum that relaxed any pressure he may have felt about being on Random House's "cuff for a long time now." The second event, tied closely to the first, was his being awarded the Nobel Prize in literature only two years later, which made him an international celebrity and irrevocably changed his life. From then on, he was never again in desperate straits over money. Not only were his early books beginning to be in demand, but his publisher was hungry for new material. He would supply it, but with (save a few exceptions) little of the joy of the past, the joy he'd had in writing just "for fun."

In the years following the Nobel Prize, Faulkner developed what was close to a mania for privacy, especially where reporters and interviewers were concerned. It is not fanciful to think that his alcoholism had something to do with this near obsession: alcoholics worry about what people are thinking about them. They are particularly concerned about people's knowing how much they drink. In this regard, Faulkner chose to telephone Memphis, seventy miles from Oxford, to order his liquor. He could have gotten it from the local bootlegger — Mississippi was a dry state in the 1950s — only seventeen miles from town, but this would have given his townspeople information he didn't want them to have.

When he arrived in New York for the publication of *Intruder in the Dust,* he found himself lionized by the New York literary establishment that had ignored him for so long. The beleaguered Faulkner now assumed a new role with interviewers. He told them, "I'm just a writer. Not a literary man," or more often than not he said he was "just a farmer," as if he were determined to relinquish the status of writer that he'd worked so hard for twenty-five years to attain. Some think this was a harmless affectation on Faulkner's part, but he seems to have been hinting that he no longer wished to be *judged* as a writer.

The adulation continued for several days until he dropped out of sight: he was repeating what had happened to him on his 1931 and 1937 visits by drinking without letup for three days and eating nothing. The man to whom Faulkner owed so much for his current vogue, Malcolm Cowley, had arranged a lunch date with him at the Algonquin Hotel and, after failing to reach him, was admitted to his room. Duplicating Sherwood Anderson's function in 1937, Cowley kept the torpid Faulkner company for several hours, then left the room, not knowing what to do with him. Two of Faulkner's friends, the *New York Times* critic Harvey Breit and the actress Ruth Ford, convinced that his life was in danger, went into action by summoning an ambulance, which took Faulkner to the Fieldston Sanitorium in Riverdale, a place that did a brisk business in detoxification. After the first day of incarceration, Faulkner repeated to Breit what he'd told Bezzerides: "You gotta get me out of here!" Eager to oblige, Breit persuaded Cowley to accept Faulkner as his house guest in Sherman, Connecticut, for the several days necessary to dry him out. Faulkner accepted the invitation and spent three days in the country, where Cowley and his wife administered weak drinks and beer at carefully spaced intervals of every two or three hours. Although he did not identify Faulkner by name at the time, Cowley described this tapering off in a piece he wrote called "The Natural History of the American Writer":

> I know two distinguished novelists who have never stopped [drinking]. One of them [Faulkner] is among the true alcoholics who shouldn't take a drink for the rest of their lives. That is the one rule solidly founded on experience: once a man becomes alcoholic he can never resist taking a second drink if he has taken the first. This novelist, however, has an almost inhuman pride and will power. Coming out of a spree that has almost killed him, he takes a drink every two hours (with the sweat standing out on his forehead as the moment approaches, but he doesn't cheat the

clock), then in a few days he is back on the schedule that should be impossible for a man in his position: one cocktail before lunch, two before dinner, and not another drink all day.

Cowley here describes the "will power" that Faulkner possessed on a day-to-day basis: the kind that inevitably was followed by an uncontrollable period of drinking that had become life-threatening. Cowley summed up alcoholism among American writers, and by implication Faulkner's, as a "defect of character," the familiar but benighted idea of the disease as primarily a moral problem. Both Faulkner and Cowley were ignorant about alcoholism, especially in their common belief in the efficacy of will power. Unlike Faulkner, however, Cowley understood that alcoholics must not drink at all.

That the personality of alcoholics suffers severe changes as they age admits of little doubt. After a time alcoholics are so concerned about the effects of the disease on themselves that their attention is often devoted to just being able to keep going in the never-ending struggle with hangovers and blackouts, in addition to the burden of guilt and remorse that goes with all this. The sheer terror of leading an alcoholic life can easily cause an obliteration of moral distinctions: alcoholics can no longer afford to make them when they are distracted by the effects of the last drinks they've had or concerned about where the next ones are coming from. Examples of Faulkner's decline in this area have been mentioned, such as his reply to his daughter's plea about her birthday, but there were to be many others. When Bezzerides and his wife spent a week in Oxford on their single visit there, he encountered behavior in his friend that seemed out of keeping with the man he knew in Hollywood. After an evening of drinking,

> we all sat outside talking, getting tipsy. Soon we went to our various bedrooms. I was always very aware of that sliding door that separated Faulkner and his wife lying in their bed from us lying in ours, but there was no sign of embarrassment by anybody. But, on this night, I awoke about two or three o'clock in the morning, and I heard the fierce, vicious whisper of Estelle's

voice: "Don't touch me, Bill, I don't want you to touch me. Don't you touch me." I woke up my wife, and she heard Estelle's protest, and in the middle of all this, there was a sound I'll never forget: that sharp, intense striking of a hand against flesh. He had apparently slapped her face. Just to hear that slap inflicted pain; and then silence. Shortly after that, we became aware of a sexual encounter on the other side of the door. . . . Next morning, Estelle was as cheerful as she could possibly be when we sat down to eat with her and Bill. Breakfast was served as if nothing had happened. Later that morning we prepared to leave.

They saw each other only once again. Whether he felt shame at what had taken place is unknown, but Faulkner made no further effort to see his Hollywood host of long standing, despite Bezzerides's attempts to re-establish contact.

In the years immediately following the Nobel Prize and his trip to Stockholm, Faulkner suffered his initial convulsive seizures and underwent electroshock therapy. What led up to them was a period in which he wrote little and traveled a lot. Paris was a favorite place to which he returned a number of times, and it was there that he claiméd he'd fallen from a horse while riding in the Bois de Boulogne in the spring of 1952. This story may not be true, but there was no doubt about the agonizing pains he felt in his back. On examination, these proved to derive from a series of fractures he'd suffered over the years, some of them produced by his repeated falling down the stairs of his home. His remedy for pain was the oldest painkiller, alcohol, which he now consumed in even larger amounts. In the past he'd had to manufacture reasons for his heavy consumption: his younger brother's death in an air crash, Meta's marriage to Wolfgang Rebner and his contractual difficulties at Warner Brothers. Now his heavy burden of pain gave him what amounted to a license to drink without guilt.

In September 1952, after a week of steady drinking, Faulkner tried to taper off without success and in the midst of doing so suffered his first convulsive seizure and was rushed to the Gartly-

Ramsay Hospital, a psychiatric institution in Memphis, where he experienced a second seizure before his discharge a week later. Convulsive seizures are common in advanced cases of alcoholism and often lead to cardiac arrest. They are caused by the too sudden withdrawal of alcohol from the system and can be avoided by the administration of Dilantin, a drug that some epileptics take daily. Faulkner's system was now so saturated with alcohol that it was taking ever stronger means to detoxify him. The beer and weak drinks that sufficed in the past were insufficient; much more powerful medication was required, the kind that only hospitals could safely supply.

By present-day standards, little was known about alcoholism in the early 1950s, and one cannot in good conscience criticize the doctors who kept discharging Faulkner from their hospitals with a bottle of sleeping pills and their best wishes. Physicians were then far more diffident about telling their patients they were alcoholics; calling Faulkner one would have been tantamount to insulting him. After all, only "bums" were alcoholics. He was now in his mid-fifties, and his extended bouts began to trouble him emotionally as never before. I have chosen to use the term "alcoholic depression" to describe the terrible, debilitating despair caused by chronic drinking episodes, with all the accompanying remorse and guilt. The term must not be confused with clinical depression. Unlike the latter, the emotional state of an alcoholic can usually be stabilized after a few months of sobriety. It is frequently the case, however, that physicians confuse the alcoholic variety with the clinical and prescribe treatment inappropriate for alcoholism. Alcoholic depression or despair was a likely prospect for a drinker like Faulkner. Indeed, he suffered so seriously from it that he received electroshock. Some of Faulkner's feelings about himself just prior to being taken to the Gartly-Ramsay Hospital can be seen in a letter he wrote to Else Johnson, one of the three women he became close to in his later years:

> Though probably the great trouble is unhappiness here, have lost heart for everything, farming and all, have not worked in a year

now, stupid existence seeing what remains of life going to support parasites who do not even have the grace to be sycophants. Am tired, I suppose. Should either command myself to feel better, or change life itself, which I may do; if you should hear harsh things of me, dont believe all of them.

Along with his general unhappiness, Faulkner now kept up a steady pattern of denial that he was still a writer. He responded to a friend's question about the critical reception of Hemingway's *Across the River and into the Trees* by telling him that "Hemingway ... should be a farmer like me and just write on the side." This disclaimer about his newly defined role indicates how strongly he wanted to deny his profession. From 1919 through the end of the forties, Faulkner never failed to identify himself as either a poet or a writer; now, as a farmer, he could regard himself as out of the competition, finished. For a writer like Faulkner to take such a radical stance, in which there is nothing ahead to accomplish, was undoubtedly threatening to his psychological balance, as we can see by what happened shortly after his discharge from the Gartly-Ramsay. Within just a week or so he began to drink uncontrollably, and this time Estelle turned for help to Saxe Commins, Faulkner's Random House editor, who flew down from New York to see what he could do. Commins reported his findings to his employers, Cerf and Haas, his letter to them beginning ominously by mentioning "a harrowing night":

My first glimpse of Bill made me realize how accurately they [Estelle and the family] had reported on his condition. He was lying on the couch in the drawing room in a stupor. His face is covered with bruises and contusions. His pajamas had slipped down and I could see how battered his body is. He greeted me mumblingly and incoherently, saying, "I need you. Get me beer!"

We carried him to the bathroom and up to bed. Then began a long vigil. Every few minutes he had to be carried to the bathroom and since he has little control of his functions, it was a disagreeable as well as pathetic office we had to perform. We placated him with a few tins of beer.

Commins struck a grim note when he gave his opinion about what was "wrong" with Faulkner:

> The fact is that Bill has deteriorated shockingly both in body and mind. He can neither take care of himself or think with any coherence at all. This may be only evidence of his condition in a state of acute alcoholism. But I believe it goes much deeper and is real disintegration.

Commins echoed this feeling in a letter to his wife, stating that it was "more than a case of acute alcoholism. It was a complete disintegration of a man." Commins could not comprehend that Faulkner's collapse was due solely to his alcoholism: he believed that there had to be "something else" behind the drinking. After doubting that it could be done, Commins managed to get Faulkner back to the Gartly-Ramsay, where he was detoxified after a week, demonstrating again his tremendous physical resilience; two bouts like these, involving convulsive seizures, would have been sufficient to kill many men. When Faulkner arrived at his home in Oxford, he encountered a predicament that he described to Commins:

> Hell's to pay here now. While I was hors de combat, E[stelle] opened and read Joan Williams' letters to me. Now E. is drunk, and I am trying to nurse her before Malcolm sends her to a hospital which costs like fury and does no good unless you make an effort yourself. I can't really blame her, certainly can't criticise her, I am even sorry for her, even if people who will open and read another's private and personal letters, do deserve what they get.

Estelle's discovery that Faulkner was having an affair placed the couple on the verge of divorce, a situation that persisted for at least a year. In his letter to Commins, Faulkner discussed his plight and asked for help:

> Never can I remember ever being so unhappy and downhearted and despaired. I have done no work in a year, am living on my fat, will begin soon to worry about money, and I do not believe I can work here. I must get away. I want to come up to Princeton, per your invitation, and finish the big book [A Fable].

He told Joan Williams, who was a young would-be writer from Memphis, pretty much the same thing: "I am too unhappy here now, never in my life have I ever been so unhappy and depressed." Leaving Oxford for New York and Princeton in the midst of his marital difficulties may appear to have been another attempt at the "geographical cure," which worked no better in New York than in Hollywood.

Within a month after his arrival in Princeton he drank so much that he had to be admitted to a hospital, this time the Westhill Sanitorium in Riverdale. Here he was given six electroshock treatments by Dr. Eric Mosse, who probably believed his patient was in clinical depression. One of the unfortunate side effects of electroshock is its tendency to cause memory loss, sometimes only briefly but occasionally for longer periods. The therapy is of no value whatsoever for alcoholics: they are generally ready for another drink the moment they're feeling better. Yet, within another week Faulkner was back in Saxe Commins's office at Random House, working away at *A Fable*.

Despite his unreliability about the truth, Faulkner could be nakedly honest with those for whom he cared. After returning to Oxford for the 1952 Christmas holiday, he wrote Joan Williams about the trouble he was having finishing his "big book."

> What I expected seems to have happened. I have run dry. . . . It began three days ago, what I put on paper now is not right and I cant get down what I know is right. I cant work here. . . . I will be able to do nothing until I get away.

When he returned to New York he wrote again to Williams, and this letter is perhaps the most revealing about what had happened to his ability to write:

> I was wrong. The work, the mss. is going again. Not as it should, in a fine ecstatic rush like the orgasm we spoke of at Hal's [Harrison Smith] that night. This is done by simple will power; I doubt if I can keep it up too long. But it's nice to know that I still can do that: can write anything I want to, whenever I want to, by simple will, concentration, that I can still do that. But goddamn it, I want to do it for fun again like I used to: not just to prove to bill f. that I still can.

There is surely something tragic about a great writer's admission that all the joy he has taken in writing is gone and that only the sheer power of his will keeps him working.

His drinking in New York was as disastrous as it had been in Mississippi: he was hospitalized twice in February 1953. After his admission to Doctors Hospital he was attended by a Dr. Melchionna, whom Faulkner told about his recent blackouts, three of them, one lasting two whole days. Blackouts are a frightening consequence of advanced alcoholism. Blackout victims will shockingly come to full consciousness after a drinking episode, unable to recall a single detail of what has happened to them for the past few hours or, quite frequently, entire days. There have been recorded instances of blackouts lasting for two and three weeks. You can well imagine the horror and dread in the mind of the blackout victim. But if you encounter someone in a blackout, you cannot detect that he or she is functioning in that way. The victim may even drive a car in this condition and not cause an accident. The memory of what *did* occur during the period of the blackout cannot be retrieved, even under the stimulus of drugs or hypnosis. There is no adequate medical explanation of the phenomenon.

Predictably, Faulkner did not ascribe his blackouts to his drinking but rather to the aftereffects of his fall from a horse in Paris during the previous year. Although alcohol had brought him to Doctors Hospital, as well as to all the others, the diagnosis of alcoholism was never made. Instead, the doctor prescribed a number of physical tests that were both expensive and time-consuming. They showed that Faulkner had nothing wrong with him, an astounding fact in view of his having recently been observed (according to Monique Soloman) consuming twenty-three martinis in a single day. Since he was not considered physically ill, the doctors assumed Faulkner had a psychological problem and was capable of being treated by analysis. He was referred to Dr. S. B. Wortis, the chairman of the Department of Psychiatry and Neurology at the New York University medical school, and paid several visits to his office. The doctor subjected his patient to a little analytic probing; Faulkner resisted all his efforts stoically and the doctor soon concluded his treatment by telling Faulkner that he should "stop drinking for three or four months." As might have been expected, Dr. Wortis gave Faulkner a bottle of sleeping pills.

6

> Never ask me why. I don't know the answer. If I did, I wouldn't do it.
> — Faulkner, 1956

> If I can't lead a normal life I'd just as soon be dead.
> — Faulkner, 1957

FAULKNER kept himself busy during his last years, but writing books played only a small part in his life. He took up sailing, on Lake Sardis in Mississippi, to replace the flying and hunting of his earlier days and continued to pursue his unprofitable farming activities. Because of his worldwide fame, his rate of pay for writing film and TV scripts in the 1950s was far higher than in his earlier time in Hollywood, especially the ones he wrote for Howard Hawks. He became a great traveler for the State Department, presenting himself as an American ambassador of good will to enthusiastic audiences in Brazil and Japan. For a shy, nonpublic man who loved his privacy and fought hard to preserve it, his success was astonishing. He concluded two love affairs (with Joan Williams and Jean Stein) and decided not to divorce Estelle, or it may have been Estelle who decided to remain with the man she'd known for forty years. He became a Virginia gentleman and rode to hounds. He endured a series of dangerous falls from horses, and his drinking became more life-threatening than ever.

Nineteen fifty-three was a dangerous year for him. After a dismal beginning, with two hospitalizations in February in New York, he forced himself back to work on *A Fable*. Why hadn't he abandoned this book about which he felt so ambivalent? Perhaps because by this time Random House had given him so much in advances that the financial burden of failing to finish would have been as heavy as the moral one: he *had* to complete it. And by September of 1953 he believed he had. When he looked up from the last page he was in an empty house. Estelle and Jill were in Mexico on vacation, and there was no one else around to tell the good news. Feeling powerfully euphoric, he had himself driven down to Greenville to see his literary agent from the thirties, Ben Wasson.

When he arrived, he repeatedly told Wasson and his friends that he had with him the manuscript of what he considered his greatest work, showing them a bulging briefcase containing hundreds of pages. In a strange celebratory mood among people who were largely strangers to him, Faulkner freely discussed the huge book. This was a new Faulkner, contrasting strongly with the writer of the twenties and thirties who had tossed the manuscript of *The Sound and the Fury* to Wasson, telling him only, "Read this, bud, it's a real sonofabitch." In those days he had resolutely refused to discuss the meaning of his work; now he became the helpful explicator of this immense pile of pages that had occupied him for nine unhappy years. After a night of heavy drinking, he suffered a bad fall that produced a bloody gash on his head; Wasson began to consider how to get his drunken friend back home to Oxford and decided to drive him there in the company of some young friends of his, the Keatings, whom Faulkner liked. Unconscious when he departed Greenville, Faulkner left the manuscript in Wasson's home, duplicating what he had done in 1936 when he left the *Absalom, Absalom!* manuscript with friends under similar circumstances.

At Rowanoak Wasson was forced to undertake the nursing services performed by Commins the previous year. After three days and nights of drinking, Faulkner was a sick man: "His skin was yellowish and beneath his eyes were dark smudges." The next day was worse:

> Bill had apparently fallen from the sofa and lay beside it. He was unwashed and no one had cleaned him. It was an ugly sight. His face looked even more mask-like than it had the day before and his skin had now become ashen.

Hospitalization was again the only recourse, and he was readmitted to the Gartly-Ramsay in Memphis. Drinking episodes like this one, coming on the heels of the completion of long novels such as *Absalom, Absalom!* and *A Fable*, seem to support the view that Faulkner went on his binges because of the triggering pressure produced by the exaltation he felt when the work was finished, similar to the feelings experienced by Virginia Woolf when she finished a book. It is certain, however, that Faulkner began most of his bouts with no particular pressure whatever; his alcoholism was sufficient to produce them.

When he recovered, a discovery awaited him: he wasn't quite finished with *A Fable* after all. He went to New York and spent several weeks revising the manuscript before finally completing it for good in November 1953. By that time Joan Williams had broken off their relationship, although not their friendship. Her grounds were based on the disparity in their ages (thirty-one years), but it is likely that his drinking played a part as well: alcoholism is not beneficial for maintaining sexual relationships unless both parties are alcoholic.

In December he left for Paris to join Howard Hawks to work on the script of *Land of the Pharaohs,* which became perhaps the worst film Hawks ever directed. It is an amazing sign of Hawks's abiding trust in Faulkner that even when the principal writer on his new project arrived in a semiconscious condition at the director's Paris hotel, supported by two gendarmes — Faulkner had passed out in Montmartre — Hawks let it pass. Several such incidents occurred during the many months of work the script required in Paris, St. Moritz, Rome and Cairo. Word about Faulkner's errant behavior became common knowledge in Hollywood: Nunnally Johnson, one of Faulkner's producers in the thirties, once told me:

> Bill needed the money and if Hawks wanted to give it to him, why not? Hawks even enlisted Faulkner to work on a script about the building of the pyramids or some such nonsense, and engaged the late Harry Kurnitz to work with him on it. (Faulkner always had to have a collaborator [on his screenplays] or it was unlikely that he would have written anything at all.) That was a real saga, Faulkner and his bourbon and Harry Kurnitz and Egypt, but apparently Bill wrote no more in The Land of the Pharaohs than he did in Zanuckland.

While attempting to discover how pharaohs talked — a project doomed to failure, as Johnson suggests — Faulkner met and began his affair in Paris with Jean Stein. But many other disquieting episodes took place before Hawks finally gave up and allowed Faulkner to leave for home. Loyal as ever, he gave Faulkner full credit for very little work, allowing his name to appear on screen with Kurnitz's and Harold Jack Bloom's.

From about 1955 on, Faulkner was widely regarded in the United States as the greatest living American writer, a view that was shared in France, Germany, Sweden and Italy. He had earned this stature by the power and originality of the work written before 1942; now in his final years he was still producing new work but its force, or as he often put it himself, the "fire," was gone. He was using his "will power" to write these later books, the same will power he unsuccessfully tried to use to control his drinking. Faulkner was never completely deceived about the erosion of his talent, coming back to it again and again in his letters to Jean Stein and Commins. In January of 1956, after he had begun The Town, he wrote Stein about his doubts, despite her liking the material he had sent her:

> I still feel, as I did last year, that perhaps I have written myself out and all that remains now is the empty craftsmanship — no fire, force, passion anymore in the words and sentences. But as

long as it pleases you, I will have to go on; I want to believe I am wrong you see.

He was just as glum with Commins at about the same time:

> The Snopes manuscript is going pretty good. I still have the feeling that I am written out though, and all remaining is the craftmanship, no fire, force. My judgement may be extinct also, so I will go on with this until I know it is no good. I may even finish it without knowing it is bad, or admitting it at least.

Most of us feel that Faulkner had ample reason to fear that he'd lost the magic that enhanced his early books. If we ask what kind of work he produced in these later years, the answer is painful: *A Fable* is a labored and pretentious allegory, crippled by endless ranting; it is Faulkner's only completely dull novel; many find it unreadable. Both *The Town* (1957) and *The Mansion* (1959) continue the Snopes family saga begun so brilliantly in *The Hamlet* of 1940, but these concluding books seem to have been written by a different person, a tamed writer rather than the demonic one of the first novel. The new ones are, in the words of Irving Howe, "the work of a man no longer driven, who must now drive himself." They lack dramatic tension, and everything in the narratives is filtered through the consciousness of peripheral characters who are rhetoricians first and last. In earlier days Faulkner had often used this technique, but with the great difference that Mr. Compson and his son Quentin, for example, are as interesting in themselves as the characters they discuss.

But Faulkner's talent was so great that even in disarray it could still turn out novels of a quality far superior to that of the later work of some of his contemporaries. I am thinking of the opening sections of *The Mansion*, which serve as a tantalizing reminder of how good he had been in his prime. As late as 1961, in his sixty-fourth year, he suddenly discovered that he'd become "hot again," as he put it, and wrote *The Reivers*, a book filled with many familiar characters and situations from the past, but now combined again with unmistakable charm. Unlike other

writers of the time, he suffered no permanent delusions about the worth of some of his later work, telling a Brazilian reporter, "I confess honestly that *A Fable* does not please me."

Through the late 1950s Faulkner was hospitalized every three or four months for drinking. The worst episode occurred in March 1956 and brought a new and even more dangerous threat to his life. After drinking for some days, he began to vomit blood and lost consciousness. He was rushed to the Baptist Hospital in Memphis, where he received blood transfusions and was placed in an oxygen tent. The hemorrhaging continued. With perhaps the thought that his brother was dying, Murry Falkner journeyed to the hospital from his FBI job in Mobile, Alabama. Faulkner's doctor coaxed Murry into telling his famous brother that the time had come for him to stop drinking for good: his life was now in real danger. When told this news, Faulkner is reported to have declared to his brother that a life without alcohol was no life at all. Several years earlier, in Rome, Lauren Bacall had asked him why he drank so much. His answer to that question has some bearing on what he later told his brother: "When I have one martini I feel bigger, wiser, taller. When I have a second, I feel superlative. When I have more there's no holding me." There's not much one can reply to such feelings. To Faulkner the dreaded thing was a life without liquor.

Since Faulkner wrote so much and so well before reaching forty-five, need we concern ourselves about his decline after that age? Is it possible that he might have continued writing at his best if he hadn't drunk so much? Any answers to these questions are bound to be conjectural. After all, some writers do dry up creatively without ever tasting a drop. But it is a fact that a high percentage of the major American writers of this century have suffered from alcoholism. The creative decline usually begins in the writer's late thirties. Faulkner, perhaps because of the immensity of his talent, lasted longer than any of the rest. But this was not the case with the great English and European writers of the last century, who did not drink alcoholically and who continued to write powerfully long beyond the modern American ones: Tolstoy wrote *Anna Karenina* at fifty, Dickens *Our Mutual Friend* at fifty-three, Dostoevsky *The Brothers Karamazov* at fifty-nine and Henry James, a transplanted American, *The Ambassadors* at fifty-six. Thomas Mann wrote *Doctor Faustus* at seventy-two.

Faulkner's affair with Jean Stein came to an end early in 1957, apparently for the same reason that caused the breakup with Joan Williams. After this time, Faulkner appeared resigned to his life with Estelle and made no move to break away. His last years were spent in part as the writer-in-residence in Charlottesville at the University of Virginia, a task he enjoyed. Life there was enhanced by the proximity of fox-hunting country, and he took up the sport again with gusto. It was here in Albemarle County that Faulkner attempted to duplicate Thomas Sutphen's dream, in *Absalom, Absalom!*, of owning a huge estate commensurate with his success, the yearning that was articulated in the great phrase "where a more fortunate one would have had a house." The house in question was a mansion on an estate of over 250 acres and cost many hundreds of thousands of dollars, but Faulkner lined up the support of Donald Klopfer of Random House and Linton Massey, a wealthy Virginian, to meet the purchase price.

But the great move away from Mississippi, the final cutting of his roots, was never to be. Back home in Oxford, in the middle of June 1962, he suffered a terrible blow as a result of being once again thrown from his horse while riding alone. The horse threw him with such force that Faulkner took the full impact on his back, producing a shock that left him unconscious for a time. When Estelle picked him up in a car and brought him home, he insisted on remounting his horse and putting it through its paces: no horse was going to dominate William Faulkner.

Besides his back pain, he felt tired and began to have strong premonitions of death; some noticed that he'd aged more in these last months than he had during the past three or four years, and photographs confirm it. He began his last spell of drinking on July 3, 1962, but it was a far shorter episode than most. Consuming a fifth and a half in a day, he agreed to leave for Wright's Sanitorium, the very first of his drying-out places, the one he'd gone to in 1936. Although he complained of chest pains, he was treated only for his alcoholism. He spoke confusedly of military ranks and flickered in and out of full consciousness. Seven hours after admission, he suffered a massive coronary occlusion that killed him in his sixty-fifth year.

Faulkner created an extraordinary social milieu and a galaxy of memorable characters unmatched in our literature. It will probably remain a mystery how the creator of Yoknapatawpha County, and Dilsey and her Compsons, Addie Bundren, Joe Christmas, Jiggs, Flem Snopes and Lukas Beauchamp could have achieved so much in little more than a decade of sustained output. No man or woman in our literature accomplished more than Faulkner in a body of work written, as he once said, "in the agony and sweat of the human spirit." Faulkner's achievement is surely all the more remarkable in that so much of it was produced under the sway of the alcohol he loved so much.

Fitzgerald

✧

"BLUER SKIES SOMEWHERE"

1

I was never disposed to accept the present but always striving to change it, better it, or even sometimes destroy it. There were always far horizons that were more golden, bluer skies somewhere.

— Fitzgerald, April 1938

My 3rd novel, if I ever write another, will I am sure be black as death with gloom. I should like to sit down with ½ dozen chosen companions and drink myself to death but I am sick alike of life, liquor and literature.

— Fitzgerald to Maxwell Perkins, August 1921

FITZGERALD would appear to have always been ashamed of his parents, seeing them as seldom as possible after leaving home in St. Paul for school and the East. They were old as parents went, even by 1896 standards, when Scott, their first child to survive, was born to Edward, then forty-three, and his wife, Mollie McQuillan, thirty-six. Scott's mother was a vague, eccentric woman much given to reading the sentimental literature of the time; her manner of dressing provoked comment about its drabness. Fitzgerald's father produced a strong but mixed impression on his young son. Always described as a small, dap-

Fitzgerald with Adrienne Monnier in Paris, 1929

per man who dressed beautifully in sharp contrast with his dowdy wife, Edward has been characterized as a born loser so deeply in love with the beloved Confederacy of his youth in Maryland that he lacked the vitality to succeed in the world of trade. After failing in all his business enterprises, he obtained employment at the age of forty-five in the wholesale grocery trade with the firm of Procter & Gamble in Buffalo, New York, and later on in Syracuse.

People said that Edward drank "more than was good for him." He once embarrassed the nine-year-old Scott by attempting to play baseball with him in the backyard of their home while under the influence. Three years later, in 1908, Edward was suddenly dismissed from his job after ten years of service with the company. We have no idea what he did or didn't do, but it is quite possible that his drinking had something, if not everything, to do with his being let go at the age of fifty-five. If a man is fired this late, especially in those days, the chances of finding new employment are usually slight. Edward was no exception, and he never worked another day for the rest of his seventy-seven years; Mollie's family became the providers for the Fitzgeralds.

One could easily assume that Edward was an alcoholic and that his son, like William Faulkner and Eugene O'Neill, inherited a vulnerability to the disease, but we don't know enough about Edward or his forebears to make such an assumption. Nor can we make any safe assertions about Mollie's side of the family; her brothers possessed, however, a reputation for being heavy drinkers. In any case, from 1908 the family fortunes were overtly in the hands of Mollie, who was unsympathetic to her son's early literary ambitions, once going so far as to destroy some of his compositions. But the dire implications of the firing produced in Scott an enduring conflict of feeling about his father, which was tempered by the fact that it was Edward who instilled in the young Fitzgerald a deep love for literature and self-expression. Edward once wrote a letter to his lonely young son, who was spending a miserable time at a summer camp: "I enclose $1.00. Spend it liberally, generously, carefully, judiciously, sensibly. Get from it pleasure, wisdom, health and experience." What Fitzgerald certainly did get from his parents was a lifelong preoccupation with money and the security it was reported to bring.

Fitzgerald seemed to regard Princeton as more of a club than a college; while there he threw most of his considerable energy into writing stories for the *Nassau Lit* and musical comedies for performance by the Triangle Club. Girls, always the best-looking ones, and literature were at the center of his emotional life during his college years. It was at this time that Fitzgerald discovered, according to Andrew Turnbull, the most eloquent of his biographers, that certain types of literature, especially the poems of Keats and Francis Thompson, provided a special kind of intoxication for him. His most notable achievement at Princeton was his apprenticeship in literature, much aided by two of his closest friends at school: the now neglected novelist John Peale Bishop and Edmund Wilson, both of whose tastes he greatly admired. While still at Princeton, Fitzgerald developed all the characteristics of the writing style that was to make him famous at twenty-four.

Besides the style, Fitzgerald offered the American reading public something new in 1920: young girls who smoked cigarettes, drank cocktails and allowed themselves to be kissed by lots of boys. The sex in *This Side of Paradise* was confined to the kissing; Fitzgerald was to remain extremely conservative in his handling of sexual relations. But these elements were enough to launch a successful career on the basis of a sale of over 40,000 copies, immediately establishing its author as a writer who could supply lightweight, romantic fiction for *The Saturday Evening Post* with dispatch. His identity became fixed as the creator of the Jazz Age, an honor he would in time come to regret. His second novel, *The Beautiful and Damned*, coming two years after the first, is part self-portrait of his marriage with Zelda, part social satire of "smart" New Yorkers like George Jean Nathan. Its hero, Anthony Patch, becomes an alcoholic; his drinking is explained by his "wish to sustain 'the old illusion that truth and beauty [are] in some way intertwined.'" It was all mostly talk, showing no improvement over *Paradise,* and sold not quite as well as the first book. Both novels contain a great deal of period charm, a quality that dates quickly; they are nearly unreadable today. It was only with the third novel, *The Great Gatsby,* that Fitzgerald wrote a book of genuine merit.

Fitzgerald and Zelda had trouble with drinking right from the start. In the early days it took very little to make them drunk; after riotous misconduct at parties, they passed out very quickly and were put to bed by their hosts, who rapidly grew accustomed to such behavior. It took a far longer time for Fitzgerald to develop even a passable tolerance for alcohol than it did for any of the other writers discussed here. At no time did he display the fabled capacity of Faulkner and Hemingway, both of whom could easily outdrink nearly everyone they ever met.

It was in the early 1920s in New York, in Great Neck, in Paris and on the Riviera that the Fitzgeralds created the aura of personal audacity that attracted the readers of three immensely successful biographies in the fifties and sixties: Arthur Mizener's, Turnbull's and Nancy Milford's. All three books sold far better than did the novels written by their legendary subjects. These books created half-mythical personages whose doings continue to move us in complex ways. From the beginning there were two sides to the Fitzgeralds: the drunken pranksters who combined a fierce, aggressive energy in pursuit of their fun along with a serious side concerned with a devotion to the art of writing. The prankster side made the couple resemble a Broadway comedy team — or so Louise Brooks recalled them — accustomed to setting each other off in their favorite routines: stripping at the Follies, diving into the Plaza Hotel fountain and boiling all the party guests' watches in tomato soup. When sober, Fitzgerald was the serious young man of letters whose burgeoning career was boosted by the attention Edmund Wilson gave him in the pages of *Vanity Fair.* It is the clash of these two styles, along with Scott's failed career, Zelda's madness and the two really good novels that emerged from it all, that has kept the Fitzgeralds alive in our imagination.

When meeting people for the first time in the early 1920s, Fitzgerald often introduced himself with "I'm very glad to meet you, sir — you know I'm an alcoholic." This seems to have been done to shock. Although he may have had some worries about his drinking, it is unlikely that he took it that seriously. By openly proclaiming that he was beginning to have trouble with alcohol, he may have hoped to turn the matter into a kind of joke. At any rate, it gave "them" something to think about, another way of getting their attention, like his habit of hurling ashtrays across the room at parties. The printed word, however, was a different matter. When Edmund Wilson discussed his heavy drinking in a critical article he was writing for *Vanity Fair*, Fitzgerald demurred and the offending passage was removed — he wished nothing to appear in print that might harm him professionally.

As early as 1922 he began to have trouble with Zelda over the time he required for his writing. She had not yet taken up painting or dancing and found her role as wife unsatisfactory — it was not until the late twenties that she began to publish stories and articles, most of them appearing under the name of her husband. At no time was housekeeping her métier; the Fitzgeralds' living quarters were frequently described by their friends as messy. She lived for parties, and when Fitzgerald's work intervened she became resentful, a situation in which he could produce work only with great difficulty. Alec McKaig, a close friend of the couple's during the early twenties, kept a diary that depicted their domestic life: "[The apartment] looks like a pig sty. If she's there Fitz can't work — she bothers him — if she's not there he can't work — worried what she might do."

Although both Fitzgeralds drank incessantly, Zelda's capacity for alcohol became greater than Scott's. What worried him most was what she might do when drinking by herself. She had naturally high spirits, which many men took to be sexually provocative. For him to get down to writing, a period of abstinence was required. One of these, of eight days' duration, made McKaig remark that Fitzgerald "talks as if it were a century." He was glum about the couple's prospects: "God knows where the two of them are going to end up."

The answer was Europe, for their second visit, the most truly productive one for him as a writer. In April of 1924, perhaps aware that he was digging a pit for himself in New York with its endless parties, Fitzgerald and Zelda went to St. Raphael, where he began writing *Gatsby* sometime in May, completing it at the end of October. His revisions of the manuscript were completed in Rome, where, while drunk, he incurred the wrath of the Italian police, who beat him severely before imprisoning him for the night — the experience he gave Dick Diver in *Tender Is the Night*. It appears that he abstained from drinking while actually writing *Gatsby* and the two novels that preceded it; not until about 1928 did Fitzgerald begin to combine alcohol with writing. While working on *Paradise* he drank hundreds of Cokes; he switched to coffee for *The Beautiful and Damned*.

2

My work is the only thing that makes me happy — except to be a little tight — and for those two indulgences I pay a big price in mental and physical hangovers.
— Fitzgerald to Maxwell Perkins, December 1925

If you don't mind, though, you are the best damn friend I have. And not just — oh hell — I can't write this but I feel very strongly on the subject.
— Hemingway to Fitzgerald, March 1927

AMONG FITZGERALD'S friendships with men, that with Hemingway was perhaps the most emotionally and intellectually rewarding. Despite ups and downs it continued for fifteen years. For a man like Hemingway, who eventually broke with virtually everyone he ever knew, the keeping of a signed photograph of Fitzgerald in his bedroom at Finca Vigía in Cuba during the late 1950s surely indicates that his regard for Fitzgerald had continued long after his death. Although some ambivalence appears in his portrait of Fitzgerald in *A Moveable Feast,* some of the original affection for him can be observed there. As for Fitzgerald, he continued to care about Hemingway and his writing long after he'd lost contact with so many of the friends he'd alienated while drinking, or as he noted in 1928: "*wrecked myself with dozens of people.*" No friendship ever meant as much to him.

Hemingway described Fitzgerald's drinking capacity in *A Moveable Feast.* It was a vivid recollection of their first meeting, at the Dingo bar in Paris in early 1925:

> As he sat there at the bar holding the glass of champagne the skin seemed to tighten over his face until all the puffiness was gone and then it drew tighter until the face was like a death's head. The eyes sank and began to look dead and the lips were drawn tight and the color left the face so that it was the color of used candle wax.

Although Fitzgerald had consumed only a third of a bottle of champagne with the Princeton baseball star Dunc Chaplin and his new friend Hemingway that evening it was enough to make him ask embarrassing questions, babble foolishly and even pass out — he had to be sent home in a cab. Hemingway proceeds to tell of a less stressful drinking session only a few days later. This time Fitzgerald was perfectly capable of drinking two Scotch and sodas with no ill effects. Current knowledge of alcoholism would suggest that at their first meeting Fitzgerald had been in the midst of a drinking cycle, perhaps stretching over several days, in which he had absorbed so much alcohol into his system that it required just two or three weak drinks to make him unconscious and cause him to suffer a blackout: the next day he had no memory of what had happened that night. By the time of their next drinking session, Fitzgerald's basic tolerance, although still quite low, had returned and he could easily drink far more than he could on the first occasion. Hemingway observed that "there was no chemical change in him. . . . I watched for it, but it did not come and he . . . did nothing embarrassing, made no speeches, and acted as a normal, intelligent and charming person."

If Hemingway felt reassured by Fitzgerald's ability to handle two strong whiskeys, he was rapidly disabused of such feelings in the next few weeks. In the course of a car trip from Lyons to Paris later that year, both writers drank several bottles of a light, white French wine, which Hemingway discovered "could cause chemical changes in Scott that turned him into a fool." Since the car had no top, sudden heavy showers soaked both men to the skin. In the early evening they stopped at a hotel along the way. Convinced that he had suffered a dangerous chill, Fitzgerald consumed several whiskeys with lemon in order to fight off what he regarded as a life-threatening situation. As they ate dinner together that night in the hotel restaurant, Fitzgerald passed out at the table with his face in his hands. It was then that Hemingway decided that Fitzgerald was extraordinarily sensitive to alcohol. He attempted to place both of them on a regimen of light drinking for the duration of the trip to Paris.

There were similarities between the absurd car trip and their first meeting at the Dingo bar. Fitzgerald had been drinking before he met Hemingway in Lyons and was again most likely caught up in a drinking cycle in which a little went a long way. In his account of the beginnings of their friendship Hemingway had observed three of the classic signs of alcoholism: Fitzgerald tended to deny that he had any trouble with alcohol, he was prone to sudden, unexpected blackouts and, as the months passed, his tolerance for alcohol was abnormally low, although he was working hard to increase it. At twenty-nine Fitzgerald was clearly an alcoholic, but he had been one long before he met Ernest Hemingway.

It all began with those drinks at the Dingo bar, with alcohol remaining a constant element. Although Hemingway noted in *A Moveable Feast* that he'd quickly realized his new friend could not drink *anything* safely, his drinking behavior with Fitzgerald in the 1920s shows that it took some time for him to believe it; a nondrinking Fitzgerald would have been a contradiction in terms. Heavy drinking in the twenties and thirties was reckoned by many to be one sure sign of dedication to the arts. Then, as never again, the expression "good writers are drinking writers" was believed to embody the truth that real creativity thrived on liquor. Until this time Fitzgerald had kept drinking apart from his writing. His particular misfortune now was to make a friend of Hemingway, who drank huge amounts all the time and yet wrote powerfully. There was another factor: many people thought Hemingway equated an ability to drink with manliness; if you couldn't hold your liquor, your manhood might come under suspicion. Together these two factors, creativity and sexual identity, were sufficiently strong guarantees that Fitzgerald would, in some measure, attempt to keep up with Hemingway.

Of all the writers in this book, Fitzgerald displayed the least aptitude for drinking. Until well into the mid-1920s he continued to astonish his friends by the extremely small amounts it took to make him roaring drunk. Louis Bromfield, a popular novelist of the period who had literary ambitions that were scorned by both Fitzgerald and Hemingway, recalled that

> [Scott] simply couldn't drink. One cocktail and he was off. It seemed to affect him as much as five or six drinks affected Hemingway or myself. Immediately he was out of control and there was only one end . . . , that he became thoroughly drunk, and like many Irishmen, when he became drunk he usually became very disagreeable and rude and quarrelsome, as if all his resentments were released at once.

Hemingway undoubtedly believed drinking was a skill you had to learn, just as you would any other. In his view it was something of a social grace, and if you were incapable of doing it well, you probably shouldn't do it at all. Apparently, Fitzgerald

accepted this notion and kept attempting to build up his tolerance by continuing to drink when it was clear that he really
couldn't. At no time in his life did Fitzgerald ever attain a normal
tolerance for alcohol, although he never stopped trying to ex-
pand it.

Besides admiring all the obviously attractive things about
Hemingway — his extraordinary sensitivity, physical vitality,
charm and wit — Fitzgerald perceived that besides himself, the
war hero from Oak Park, Illinois, was then writing the best
prose of any young American writer. A mutual admiration society quickly developed once Hemingway had read *Gatsby*.
Within a week or so of their first meeting at the Dingo they
began seeing each other on a daily basis, meetings that always
involved alcohol.

It was literature that kept them friends. Throughout his life,
Fitzgerald loved the role of teacher, and Hemingway became his
star pupil in the art of taking care of oneself in the literary jungle
both men saw themselves inhabiting. Since Fitzgerald had published three novels and two collections of stories, was three years
older than his pupil and earned as much as $20,000 a year (to-
day equivalent to at least eight times that amount), he taught
Hemingway some of the insider information he'd picked up in
the past five years. Because he steered Hemingway to Max Perkins at Scribners and followed that up by advising Hemingway
to cut the dullish first two chapters from the manuscript of *The
Sun Also Rises*, the book made a smashing debut for Hemingway in the autumn of 1926. Selling 23,000 copies in its first year,
it was followed three years later by *A Farewell to Arms*, which
passed 80,000 copies. By 1930, in a curious reversal of roles, the
pupil clearly had outdistanced his teacher, not only in sales but
in the estimation of those critics both novelists worried so much
about. Only five years after his first U.S. publication, Hemingway was the uncrowned king of the younger American writers,
while Fitzgerald was settling into the long decline that marked
his career during the thirties.

Despite their mutual admiration, their ways of achieving success were fundamentally opposed. Although by 1925 Hemingway had published only two short volumes of stories whose combined sales were less than a thousand copies, he told Fitzgerald that he was in pursuit of literary fame in his own way and intended to pay no attention to the demands of the marketplace. In order that no contamination might interfere with his literary goal — "to write the kind of prose that doesn't go bad" — he'd quit his lucrative newspaper work and had to publish his early stories in the only places that would accept them, the small literary magazines in Paris and Berlin, which left him and his wife, Hadley, living on a subsistence level. But his method paid off handsomely: within five years *A Farewell to Arms* had sold twice as much as anything Fitzgerald would ever publish in his lifetime.

The Hemingway method, writing your best and hoping that an audience would develop in time, was unacceptable and perhaps incomprehensible to Fitzgerald. He had started at the very top of the market in 1919 when *The Saturday Evening Post* had accepted his story "Head and Shoulders," and he was not about to retreat from the world of the $2,500 per story they were paying him in 1925: one could live in a lordly style on the kind of money Fitzgerald was earning. He became obsessive about his money-making ability and maintained his *Ledger,* which listed, Hemingway noted,

> all of the stories he had published in it year after year with the prices he had received for them and also the amounts received for any motion picture sales, and the sales and royalties of his books. They were all noted as carefully as the log of a ship and Scott showed them to both of us [Hadley was with Hemingway] with impersonal pride as though he were the curator of a museum. Scott was nervous and hospitable and he showed us his accounts of his earnings as though they had been the view. There was no view.

Hemingway believed that Fitzgerald had not been able to finish the strange novel about Francis Melarkey that he'd begun in

1925 — the book that concerned a young American on the Riviera who kills his mother — because of being intimidated by the effusive reviews that *The Great Gatsby* had received, in addition to letters filled with praise. There were two in particular, the first from Gilbert Seldes, the author of *The Seven Lively Arts* and a noted taste maker. Seldes wrote Fitzgerald, telling him that "For God's sake . . . don't be persuaded not to go on with this, your real line of genius. I hope you're writing another already and that it is as good." Another letter, this time from his Princeton friend John Peale Bishop, told him much the same but more emphatically:

> Gatsby is a new character in fiction. . . . You have everything ahead of you; Gatsby definitely admits you to importance. For god's sake take your new place seriously. Scrutinize your own impressions, distrusting your facility which will continue to work anyhow.

That facility was for turning out his *Post* stories. They provided Fitzgerald with the money to maintain his expensive tastes, which, he made it clear to Perkins in an April 1925 letter, he had no intention of changing: "I can't reduce our scale of living and I can't stand this financial insecurity." He had a curious fancy about his place in the world of money, once telling the Canadian novelist Morley Callaghan that he was, in a sense, a millionaire, since he was living on the interest generated by his capital — that is, his talent. The publication of *Gatsby* could be seen as an incursion on that capital, for its sales of 23,000 copies barely served to earn back the advances he'd been paid by Scribners. In the same letter, he told Perkins about his literary intentions:

> Now I shall write some cheap [stories] until I've accumulated enough for my next novel. When that is finished and published I'll wait and see. If it will support me with no more intervals of trash I'll go on as a novelist. If not I'm going to quit, come home, go to Hollywood and learn the movie business.

In the late 1920s, in Paris and on the Riviera, as well as back in his new home, Ellerslie, in Delaware, Fitzgerald talked a lot about his new novel, showing parts of it to his friends, including Hemingway, all of whom admired it greatly. But he made comparatively little progress for two reasons: his increasing alcoholism and the fear that he would eventually publish a book that would not live up to *Gatsby*. After endless rounds of all-night parties that ended only when he'd passed out more than once, Fitzgerald would force himself into a regimen of no drinking for a week or so while he turned out a *Post* story. When he had sent the story off to New York, he would then resume what had become his normal life. The result was little or no serious work for weeks or months on end. The novelist Joseph Hergesheimer summed it up when he said, "Scott could write and didn't; couldn't drink but did." The *Ledger* entries for 1925 — "Zelda painting, me drinking" and "Self disgust. Health gone" — as well as the one for September 1928 that begins with the word "Ominous" underlined three times and followed by "No real progress," pretty much echo Hergesheimer's view of what Fitzgerald was doing with his talent.

When the Fitzgeralds returned from their third European trip in September of 1928 to resume living at Ellerslie, Fitzgerald noted in his *Ledger* that he was "back again in a blaze of work *and* liquor." It was from this time on that he began to use alcohol in order to assist him with his writing. He now regarded drink not as the depressant it is but rather as a stimulant that would spark his creative energies. He was facing a worsening situation: the morning dilemma in which he regularly awakened with all the fear and dread of a terrible hangover. Should he write with the hangover or just have a few to get things going? He made the second choice and kept on making it at an ever increasing cost to his work.

The poet Allen Tate first met Fitzgerald in Paris, at a party given at the apartment of their friend John Peale Bishop in 1929. The Fitzgeralds arrived late, as usual. When Zelda did appear, Bishop introduced her to Tate, who found her captivating and far better looking than her photographs ever indicated. He was too shy to ask her where her famous husband was. Later, when Tate was still wondering about Fitzgerald's whereabouts, Bishop explained to him that Fitzgerald would be along soon, that he "was in the kitchen hiding his gin." Bishop added that Fitzgerald liked to increase the strength of his martinis without being observed. When Bishop introduced Tate to Fitzgerald, Scott's first question was the usual "icebreaker" he asked in those days: "Do you enjoy sleeping with your wife?" Tate thought he had misunderstood and asked him to repeat the question; Fitzgerald obliged him. Tate's reply was "It's none of your damned business." Having smashed that piece of formal ice, the two men began to talk about the state of contemporary letters.

Fitzgerald's determination to finish a novel that might easily prove to be unpopular — the one about "the boy who killed his mother" — became agonizing: he was unable to give up the book as hopeless and move on to something else, as Hemingway did with his unfinished novel about young Jimmy Breen. In September of 1929 he wrote Hemingway a despairing letter about his lack of progress that concluded with "Perhaps the house will burn down with this mss. and preferably me in it." He then added a postscript in which he bragged about his continuing ability to command top dollar in the commercial story market: "Here's a last flicker of the old cheap pride: the *Post* now pays the old whore $4000 a screw. But now it's because she's mastered the 40 positions — in her youth one was enough." Hemingway responded wittily and, as it turned out, all too prophetically:

> (They never raise an old whore's price — She may know 850 positions — They cut her price all the same — So either you arent old or not a whore or both) The stories arent whoring, they're just bad judgement — you could have and can make enough to live on writing novels. You damned fool. Go on and write the novel.

He concluded by apologizing for his bluntness, "because I felt so bad that you were feeling low — am so damned fond of you and whenever you try to tell anybody anything about working or 'life' it is always bloody platitudes —" He would have served the friendship more honestly if he had told Fitzgerald that the *Post* stories were indeed whoring. What he did not know was that only eight years later Fitzgerald, just like the imaginary lady with the 850 positions, would wind up by having his price cut to $250 per story.

By the time of Zelda's breakdown and confinement to the Prangins Psychiatric Clinic in Switzerland in the spring of 1930, Fitzgerald had entered the kind of nervous, alcoholic despair that has its victims needing to start some days with a drink or two, and then a few more until they pass out, to reawaken with such a hangover and agitation that only another drink can calm them down. The cycle continues, day after day, often filled with recriminations about how it all began — who was to blame for this misery? While still a patient at the clinic, Zelda sent Scott long letters, raising the issue of how they had "ruined each other." He told her, in a letter he may or may not have mailed, "We ruined ourselves — I have never honestly thought that we ruined each other." Zelda may have been clinically mad at the time, but she was perceptive enough to realize that alcohol was the thread running through the past ten years of their marriage and that it had led to her breakdown and his despair of ever writing anything worthwhile again. In a remarkable letter that runs to over eight thousand words, Zelda chronicles the story of their marriage, beginning with their arrival in New York and continuing to her collapse:

> — and Rome and your friends from the British Embassy and your drinking, drinking. . . . We drank always and finally came to France because there were always too many people in the house. . . . You drank all the time and some man called up the hospital about a row you had had . . . and the summer passed, one party after another. . . . There were too many people and too many things to do: every-day there was something and our house was always full. . . . We lived in the rue Vaugirard. You were constantly drunk. You didn't work and were dragged home at night by taxi-drivers when you came home at all. . . . What was I to

do? You got up for lunch. You made no advances toward me and complained that I was un-responsive. You were literally eternally drunk the whole summer. . . . You know the real reason you couldn't work was because you were always out half the night and you were sick and you drank constantly. . . . You disgraced yourself at the Barry's party, on the yacht at Monte Carlo, at the casino with Gerald and Dotty. Many nights you didn't come home. . . . You were miserable about your lung, and because you had wasted the summer, but you didn't stop drinking.

In her letter Zelda indicated Fitzgerald's sexual indifference to her, suggesting that it was caused by his impotence: "Twice you left my bed saying 'I can't. Don't you understand' — I didn't." She concluded with the heartbreaking admission that "it was wrong, of coure [sic], to love my teacher [Lubov Egorova, her ballet teacher] when I should have loved you. But I didn't have you to love — not since long before I loved her."

Fitzgerald's reaction to Zelda's doctors at the clinic is equally remarkable but for different reasons. Apparently Zelda told them that alcohol had played a major part in her collapse. When confronted with the news that the physicians attending his wife thought it might also be good for him to give up alcohol, Fitzgerald went into a paroxysm of denial, telling Dr. Oscar Forel that it was Zelda who had made him start drinking with any regularity: "We went on hard drinking parties together sometimes but the regular use of wine and apperatives [sic] was something that I dreaded but she encouraged because she found I was more cheerful then and allowed her to drink more."

The mere idea of giving up liquor filled him with a horror that he dramatized by explaining to the doctor:

> Two years ago in America I noticed that when we stopped all drinking for three weeks or so, which happened many times, I immediately had dark circles under my eyes, was listless and disinclined to work.

He went on to say that he felt that his health was giving out and that he had great difficulty in obtaining adequate life insurance coverage. He downplayed his drinking in a way the doctor could have foreseen if he had known much about alcoholism.

> *I found that a moderate amount of wine, a pint at each meal made all the difference in how I felt. When that was available the dark circles disappeared, the coffee didn't give me excema or beat in my head all night.*

Although it is clear from his actions at the time that he didn't mean a word of it, he discussed with Dr. Forel the possibility of giving up liquor for six months — liquor was here defined as "strong drink" — and Fitzgerald made it plain his abstinence would be a limited one:

> Bind myself to forswear wine forever I cannot. My vision of the world at its brightest is such that life without the use of its amentities [*sic*] is impossible. . . . *The fact that I have abused liquor is something to be paid for with suffering and death perhaps but not with renunciation. For me it would be as illogical as permanently giving up sex because I caught a disease.* . . . I cannot consider one pint of wine at the days end as anything but one of the rights of man.

He concluded his torrent of rationalization for Dr. Forel by raising the question of what would happen if he *did* give up drinking — wouldn't that be a tacit admission that all of Zelda's emotional problems were due to his alcoholism? Wouldn't that "justify" her conduct and therefore condemn him to a life of asceticism? Alcoholics are masters of self-deception, and Fitzgerald's letter is characteristic of how far one can go in attempting to defend the desire to continue drinking whatever the cost. It is possible that Fitzgerald believed he could live with his pint of wine, although at thirty-four his system was no doubt accustomed to far larger amounts — a switch to wine was an impossible solution to his problem. The doctor was apparently swayed, however, and dropped the issue.

3

Drinking increased. Things go not so well.
— *Ledger*, September 1932

Me caring about no one and nothing.
— *Ledger*, April 1936

IN THE SINGLE DECADE left to him, Fitzgerald began to suffer increasing pain from the severe medical consequences of his disease. Until about the age of thirty-five he had always been able to end his two- or three-day drinking episodes with no need for extended sedation or hospitalization. Then he discovered —just as Faulkner did after 1936 — that alcoholics, as they grow older, require ever larger amounts of alcohol to make them feel "normal." Morning drinks may become a regular part of daily life, as does the chronic insomnia they suffer which requires still more alcohol. Many alcoholics in their late thirties and beyond find their tolerance accelerating wildly, often leading them into nonstop binges that can be ended only by detoxification in a hospital.

After Zelda's release from the Prangins Clinic in September of 1931, the couple returned to America for good; the rapidly falling dollar made living in Europe no longer desirable. Fitzgerald may also have felt that his years of living abroad had much to do with his inability to finish his Melarkey novel. The Fitzgeralds rented a house in Zelda's hometown of Montgomery, Alabama, for the winter. But there was an interruption in their time there: Irving Thalberg of MGM agreed to pay $1,200 a week for Fitzgerald's services in Hollywood to write what he called "smart lines" for the Jean Harlow film *Red-Headed Woman*. He worked for five weeks on the script without completing it. His drunken behavior at a party given by Thalberg's wife, Norma Shearer, appears to have been responsible for his leaving the studio by "mutual agreement," as MGM's files report the event.

When he returned to Alabama, Zelda suffered her second major collapse; Fitzgerald had her admitted to the Phipps Psychiatric Clinic at Johns Hopkins Hospital in Baltimore in early 1932. In May he rented La Paix, a house just outside the city and owned by the Turnbull family, a huge, rambling, furnished mansion filled with Victorian bric-a-brac. Here Fitzgerald, armed with the $6,000 he'd received from MGM, began a determined effort to bring his long-unfinished novel to a conclusion. Abandoning the matricide theme of the earlier drafts, he recast some of the old material into a manuscript he now called "The Drunkard's Holiday," which drew heavily on Zelda's breakdown and the field of psychiatry. While Zelda was confined to the clinic in 1932, she wrote her only published novel, *Save Me the Waltz*. After its publication, in the same year as its completion, she began another book, possibly about Nijinsky but also dealing with her own psychiatric history.

This choice of subject infuriated Fitzgerald, who felt she was intruding into his domain, since his novel was to be one of the first American works of fiction to depict psychotherapy. After Zelda's release from the Phipps Clinic, they continued to quarrel bitterly over his attempts to control what she wrote. But while an inpatient, Zelda had been under the care of Dr. Adolf Meyer and Dr. Mildred Squires, who had encouraged her with her novel. Dr. Meyer was a leading authority on schizophrenia, and his chief aide was Dr. Thomas R. Rennie, who went on to become one of the founders of the Payne-Whitney Psychiatric Clinic in New York. He later won worldwide fame for administering the groundbreaking project Mental Health in the Metropolis. Doctors Meyer and Rennie were more difficult to deceive than Dr. Forel in Switzerland; both men knew that a contributory factor in Zelda's breakdowns was the alcoholism she shared with her husband. The doctors realized that if he stopped drinking there would be a far likelier chance of her recovery; they believed he needed treatment as much as she did.

But Fitzgerald resented any delving into his psyche, especially any that might threaten his drinking, telling Dr. Meyer in a draft of a letter:

> The witness is weary of strong drink and until very recently he had the matter well in hand for four years and has it in hand at the moment, and needs no help in the matter being normally frightened by the purely physical consequences of it.

He concluded that he might consider stopping, "but only under conditions that seem improbable — Zelda suddenly a helpmate or even divorced and insane." This reply was a justification of his drinking on the grounds that he was married to a madwoman. This placed the responsibility for his continued drinking squarely on Zelda.

He took an extremely hard line about this on an occasion in May of 1933 when he and Zelda, in the presence of Dr. Rennie, discussed their sexual and marital problems. Fitzgerald became quite aggressive, telling the doctor, "The first time I met her I saw she was a drunkard." When her right to write as she pleased came up, Fitzgerald summed up precisely what he required of her: "I want you to do what I say," or, in other words, stop trying to compete with me. She retorted that if he was really as good as he said he was — he'd told them he was the highest-paid short story writer in the world — why was he afraid of a little third-rater like her?

Fitzgerald was angered by her references to his drinking. "I am perfectly determined that I am going to take three or four drinks a day." He then offered the doctor and Zelda his by now familiar rationale that if he did stop drinking, it would appear that "her family and herself would always think that that was an acknowledgment that I was responsible for her insanity." It is clear from reading the 114-page transcript of this three-way talk that Zelda was perfectly lucid in everything she said, especially about the main problem that had plagued their marriage. When she was asked by Fitzgerald what had caused him to think that he had ruined his life, her answer was right on target. "I think the cause of it is your drinking. That is what I think is the cause of it." They then discussed his sexual inadequacies, and Fitzgerald said to Zelda: "Our sexual relations were very pleasant and all that until I got the idea you were ditching me. They were all very nice to then, weren't they?" Her reply demonstrated that she had lost none of her wit: "Well, I am glad you considered them satisfactory."

It is not uncommon for alcoholics to display an avid curiosity about the drinking habits of their friends. Hemingway exhibited a continuing fascination for Fitzgerald's drinking and the effect it had on his work. When Fitzgerald died, Hemingway switched his attention to the alcoholic behavior of Faulkner. Fitzgerald's target of inquiry in this area was Ring Lardner, whom he recognized as one of the "brotherhood of the intemperate." He frequently asked Max Perkins about Lardner's health, and nearly always there was a question about how much he was drinking. The cause of such curiosity arises most likely from the alcoholic's wish to compare himself with other drinkers, perhaps making him feel, "There, you see, I'm not (yet) that bad!" Fitzgerald was aware of his own and Hemingway's interest in how alcohol was affecting them. At the beginning of 1933 he wrote Perkins that he was "going on the water wagon" in the very near future:

> But don't tell Ernest because he has long convinced himself that I am an incurable alcoholic, due to the fact that we almost always meet on parties. I am *his* alcoholic just like Ring is mine and do not want to disillusion him.

The letter indicates that Fitzgerald was still refusing to consider himself a "real" alcoholic. By this time, however, his addiction was so far advanced that it would have been painful for him to stop. The chances of remaining on that water wagon for long were indeed faint.

4

Hard times begin for me now. Slow but sure.
— *Ledger,* 1933

I use up my health making money + then my money
in recovering health. . . . Dont answer — there isn't
any answer If there was I'd have thought of it long
ago.
— Fitzgerald to Harold Ober, December 1933

DRINKING HAD BECOME the central point of Fitzgerald's existence, the one thing around which everything else revolved, including the constant problem of Zelda's instability and his sudden difficulties in selling his stories. By 1933 his daily gin drinking had begun to affect him so severely that home remedies no longer sufficed to sober him up. Just as Faulkner did in 1936, Fitzgerald began to spend time in the hospital — Johns Hopkins — for periodic withdrawals, each stay running between three and seven days. There were two of these in 1933, two more in 1934 and another four in the next two years. Besides the expense of these visits, he lost valuable time from completing what became *Tender Is the Night,* as well as from turning out the commercial stories that had been his main source of income for over a decade.

Efforts were made to get him to stop drinking, most of them originating with the various doctors to whom he went for treatment, not only for the shakes and D.T.'s but also for the recurring lung problems to which he was subject — a malady that he often used to cover up the far more threatening one of his drinking. One doctor in New York tried diminishing Fitzgerald's gin intake. The doctor told him he would die unless he stopped and gave him a one-gill (one-quarter pint) measuring cup in which to imbibe his new daily ration. Fitzgerald took the train home, armed with the cup and a full quart of gin. When he reached Baltimore

> he stopped off to see his old friend, John Biggs, now a distinguished judge. He was so obviously ill that Judge Biggs took him out to his home in the country. Sitting on the lawn Fitzgerald began to talk, and carefully, gill by gill, finished the quart.

Despite the increasingly unpleasant things that were happening to him, Fitzgerald was determined to keep drinking no matter what the price; he was not only addicted but it had become too important for him to stop. Why? Why *does* a man of intelligence continue a course of action that leaves him weak and shaken day after day, drained of his bodily strength and surely possessing the knowledge that he is close to losing his creative powers? It is possible that by this time a life without alcohol would have been, for Fitzgerald, no real life. James Thurber, another alcoholic, once recalled spending a long night of drinking and talking in New York with Fitzgerald just before the publication of *Tender Is the Night* in April of 1934. Thurber ascribed his new friend's drinking to a wide variety of causes, refusing to recognize him as what he termed a "natural alcoholic."

> [Fitzgerald] began to use liquor for posture and gesture, like almost any other writer of the 1920's, but by the time he was forty he had found or invented ten or twelve reasons for keeping it up. (Most writers have only four or five.) . . . The most persistent of these was that his creative vitality demanded stimulation if it was to continue to operate. . . . But when Fitzgerald began to drink because he thought he had to, in order to write, he was lost.

To his dying day Fitzgerald believed that no one could smell gin on his breath; for this reason and for the immediate high it supplied, it remained his favorite drink. "Priming the pump" with gin became his standard procedure to get himself started writing — one or two just to get things moving was the goal, but unless he took great care in rationing out his supply, he could easily slip past any semblance of sobriety and little would be written that day. When he lost control and began around-the-clock drinking, he had the choice of going to the hospital or attempting to taper off with beer; sometimes he would consume as much as thirty twelve-ounce bottles a day. He was perhaps only hazily aware that this amount was equal in potency to about a fifth and a half of gin. The only real difference between the gin and the beer was that he did not pass out as rapidly from the beer and managed, somehow, to send off finished pages to his agent, Harold Ober, in New York. During this Baltimore period (1932 through the end of 1934) Fitzgerald was nearly always either drinking or painfully hung over.

Besides the hangovers, he was plagued by persistent insomnia, a malady often accompanying alcoholism. After only two or three hours of sleep, he required Benzedrine tablets to get him out of bed. After a tortured night he would enter a daylight world in which his body would scream for the release supplied by a few drinks, hence the difficulty of sticking to his rationed amount. Like many alcoholics, he smoked continuously (he "ate" his cigarettes, Turnbull reports), and his diet was usually confined to those items which would appeal to a man with little appetite for food: deviled ham, scrambled eggs and chocolate fudge cookies. Both the smoking and the diet were bound to endanger his cardiovascular system. There were days when the sheer awfulness of his life became so great that he resolved to stop drinking altogether, but these intentions were short-lived: the addiction was far too powerful.

It was in October of 1933 that he finally wrote the concluding pages of *Tender Is the Night,* the book that he began to refer to as his "Testament of Faith," referring to its protagonist's concern with ideals. The months preceding publication were frenzied ones: in addition to all the normal tasks of seeing a book through the press, Fitzgerald's job was doubled because he was working on another version of the novel, the mildly expurgated *Scribner's Magazine* text. Always a tireless reviser, Fitzgerald carried out many changes in both versions simultaneously, demanding and getting new sets of galleys on which to make his feverish corrections right up to the last moment. He would appear at the Scribners building on Fifth Avenue in New York before it opened, waiting to be admitted so he could go over the latest batch of proofs he'd worked on the previous night. Sometimes he'd arrive still high from the night before, his speech slurred but anxious to complete the work in time. In the midst of all this turmoil, Zelda had her third major breakdown and was admitted to Craig House in Beacon, New York; the additional excitement produced by the exhibition of her paintings in New York may have contributed to her collapse.

Andrew Turnbull observed that "the man who began [*Tender Is the Night*] in 1925, who had fashioned the beautiful barbarism of its opening sequences, wasn't the same man who completed it in 1933." Turnbull's view is confirmed when one realizes how far superior the earlier chapters — the reworking of material originally written in France during the twenties — are to the last third of the book, which its author later said was written "on stimulant." Fitzgerald believed that alcohol had marred the work:

> A short story can be written on a bottle, but for a novel you need the mental speed that enables you to keep the whole pattern in your head and ruthlessly sacrifice the sideshows. . . . If a mind is slowed up ever so little it lives in the individual part of a book rather than in a book as a whole; memory is dulled. I would give anything if I hadn't had to write Part III of *Tender Is the Night* entirely on stimulant. If I had one more crack at it cold sober I believe it might have made a great difference.

Considering the circumstances under which the book finally came forth after eight years in the making, it is miraculously good despite its many faults.

In relating the story of Dick Diver, the brilliant young psychiatrist who married his wealthy patient, the schizophrenic Nicole Warren, Fitzgerald drew heavily on the raw materials of his current situation with Zelda. In the novel, Nicole feeds on Dick's vitality — a kind of spiritual vampirism — and is cured of her illness. In doing so she robs him of his will to live a healthy, productive life. In a state of psychic exhaustion, Diver begins to drink heavily and destroys his career. When Nicole's cure has been completed, the marriage is over and the alcoholic doctor, now an empty vessel, is dismissed by her family. It is apparent that Fitzgerald, by using alcohol as both cause *and* effect in the creation of Diver's malaise, was drawing a parallel between his fictional couple and Zelda and himself.

From the time of the novel's first publication, many readers have wondered what caused the relatively sudden crack-up in Dr. Diver's life. One critic saw it as arising from "his desire to please, in his egotism, and in his romantic view of life." All this is perfectly true, but left out is the unacknowledged fact of Dick's alcoholism, the disease that Fitzgerald apparently could not (or would not) ascribe to his protagonist until the very end of the book, although he permits us to observe that nearly all of Dick's troubles — professional and marital — have alcohol behind them. Thus the "official" alcoholic in the novel is Abe North, the character that Fitzgerald based on Ring Lardner. By deflecting the disease away from Dick Diver and toward his friend, Fitzgerald could safely distance himself from it.

A persistent myth about *Tender Is the Night* is that it was a critical and financial disaster. Neither is true: the book received a wide range of reviews and most of them were good. As for the sales figures (13,000), they compare favorably with those of other prominent literary novelists who published books at this time: Dos Passos's *1919* sold 9,000 copies; Faulkner's *Light in August* outsold his *Sanctuary* with 14,000 copies; and Hemingway's short story collection *Winner Take Nothing* sold 12,500. All these figures would have been proportionally higher if the Depression had not had such a dampening effect on sales — people stop buying books before they stop buying automobiles. With the exception of Hemingway, who sold widely in all markets almost from the beginning, these writers had no best sellers as did Edna Ferber and Sinclair Lewis, whose books never sold fewer than 100,000 copies. It is likely that the main reason Fitzgerald regarded *Tender Is the Night* as a failure was that he'd accepted so much in the way of advances from Scribners over the years that the book needed to sell nearly 30,000 copies to get him out of their debt.

He frequently resorted to lying in order to conceal the truth about his drinking, especially from his literary friends who might have heard rumors that he'd become a hopeless drunk in a dingy old house on the outskirts of Baltimore. When Malcolm Cowley visited him in May of 1933, just a few months before he finished the novel, Fitzgerald kept his guest from New York up until the small hours. At thirty-seven, the Fitzgerald that Cowley observed at La Paix was still a handsome man, but his skin had taken on a gray pallor and he had developed a drinker's paunch. Fitzgerald held forth on the contemporary literary scene with that donnish delight that he never lost whenever he related the latest insider gossip to an awakened curiosity. His own was boundless: Who's up, who's down? What *about* the proletarian novel? For a man in a literary backwater, Cowley's visit was a welcome diversion from the huge pile of pages that constituted his novel.

Supplying Cowley with a pint of bootleg whiskey, Fitzgerald told his guest that he himself was on the wagon and drinking only water; he kept disappearing from time to time to replenish his glass in the kitchen. Sometime after two in the morning, Fitzgerald became truculent — especially when he discovered that Cowley had never read *Gatsby* — but smiled suddenly and then, rather in the spirit of a naughty child who has chosen to tell the whole truth at last, confessed that he'd been drinking gin the entire evening! Cowley wasn't quite sure how to react to the news, and went sleepily off to bed.

5

The D.T.'s and the nice nurse.
— *Ledger*, June 1934

The nice nurse. Then drinking.
— *Ledger*, July 1934

EVERYTHING GOT WORSE. Hemingway had been right: the "old whore" was forced to lower his prices. By the mid-thirties, Fitzgerald's price for his magazine stories started to drop steadily, partly because of the economic depression but mainly because his stories began to arrive at his agent's office lacking the craftsmanship and surface polish that *The Saturday Evening Post*'s editors had grown to expect. It became progressively harder to sell them.

Ober noticed that Fitzgerald's familiar old ability to write smooth, well-constructed commercial fiction was being eroded by an increasing carelessness about details of plot and characterization. Until 1933 his stories were admittedly mechanically contrived, but they possessed a sureness of expression that pleased the *Post*'s readers — they were attentive to a thoroughgoing consistency of detail, however, and would accept no less. The magazine's editors began to send Ober lists of items that had to be fixed before they would buy a story; when they did, the price descended from $4,000 to $3,000. Ober and his associates started submitting their own critiques to Fitzgerald *before* they delivered a story to the *Post*, hoping thereby to increase the chance of a sale.

Lowering the price at the *Post* was bad enough, but the magazine rejected more and more of the stories; Ober sold some to *Redbook, Liberty* and *McCall's* for $2,500 and sometimes less. By the end of 1934 he was selling Fitzgerald's stories on a regular basis to the recently launched *Esquire*. Arnold Gingrich, the editor, would publish virtually anything Fitzgerald submitted, but the $250 they paid was not enough to support him, and he continued to regard the *Post* as his primary market. Whenever Ober confronted Fitzgerald with his drinking as the source of this falling-off in performance, he would reply, "The assumption that all my troubles are due to drink is a little too easy." He took an even stronger line of defense against his sister-in-law, Rosalind Sayre: "To say that my conclusions have ever been influenced by drink is as absurd as to think that Grant's '64 and '65 campaigns were influenced by the fact that he needed stimulant and used it."

Turning out incompetently written magazine stories endangered Fitzgerald's ability to earn a living, but his writing difficulties turned up in work that, while commercial in intent, represented something else entirely. In 1934 he wrote a series of four stories about medieval France in the eighth century, "Count of Darkness," which had as their hero Philippe, who, in some private way known only to Fitzgerald, was based on Hemingway. He intended to write another half-dozen episodes and then weld them together to create a novel that Scribners would publish. Multiple rejections followed their submission; the editor who finally bought the series, Edwin Balmer, admitted that his superiors at *Redbook* thought he'd lost his reason when he took them on. These stories represent the lowest point of Fitzgerald's career. There is an amateurish quality about the writing that makes it difficult to believe he wrote them. Even more shocking is the fact that Maxwell Perkins genuinely liked the Philippe stories. Perhaps both men were swayed by the huge popularity being enjoyed by historical fiction in 1934.

He invented a new kind of dialogue for his characters to speak in this eighth century of his, a curious combination of tough-guy crime talk out of the pulps and a kind of western/southern quality — a language intending to show that past and present weren't all that different. The result was ludicrous; one example may suggest the flavor. When Philippe is in a threatening mood, he slaps his enemy's face and says, "Answer me like that one

more time and I'll let daylight through you." It is clear that Fitzgerald, at least for the moment, had lost his critical judgment
about his own work, so much so that later, in 1939, he actually
remained indecisive about whether to finish the series or proceed
with *The Last Tycoon*. At thirty-seven, he could no longer distinguish between the worst sort of hack fiction and the work
that made him first rate.

Besides his talent, he was now capable of losing what was left
of his personal dignity. In 1934 he decided to write a musical
comedy, and in order to obtain a sense of what young America
was thinking about, he enlisted the collaborative services of the
seventeen-year-old future comedian Garry Moore, then a senior
at the local high school. Moore had appeared in Zelda's play
Scandalabra and Fitzgerald was impressed with his talent. Fitzgerald was then living on a maintenance diet of gin, supplying
himself with either one or two ounces every hour; sometimes he
would cheat and double the dosage. Toward the end of their
collaboration on the play, Moore made the serious error of
bringing along with him his pretty fifteen-year-old sister. Within
a half hour of her arrival, Fitzgerald had begun to pursue her
around the living room; both Moores fled the house and that
was the end of their work together. When Moore told me about
this incident, he still wasn't sure how he felt about it — it seemed
to him both comic and tragic.

Harold Ober continued to show remarkable patience and tolerance for a client whose material became progressively harder
to sell. At one point in 1933 he wrote Fitzgerald:

> I think we have made a mistake in sending your recent stories to
> the *Post* in a very hurried fashion and I think it has been a mis-
> take to let them know that we were in such a hurry about a
> decision. . . . We have caused the wrong psychological effect on
> a possible buyer.

A year later he commented on his client's increasing inability to
deliver promised material on time:

Up to a couple of years ago if you had sent me word that a story would arrive on a certain date, I would have been as certain that the story would arrive as that the sun would rise the next day. . . . [Now] I have no faith at all that it will come.

Ober's anger rose when he advised Fitzgerald to stop communicating with editors on his own:

Sometimes I think it would be better if you would take the telephone out of your house entirely. . . . You are apt to use [it] when you are not in your most rational state of mind and when you do call anyone up in that way it only adds to the legend that has always been ready to crop out — that you are never sober.

Ober knew whereof he spoke, for Fitzgerald had started calling people at strange hours, eager to discuss projects of doubtful value; these calls endangered his professional standing as a writer. He not only called Irving Thalberg of MGM late at night but once sent him a telegram about a film project:

. . . HAVE . . . I THINK AN EXTRAORDINARY IDEA FOR AN ORIGINAL STOP AM IN NO POSITION TO COME TO COAST AT PRESENT NOR CAN I DEVELOP THE IDEA MYSELF TO ANY COMPLETE EXTENT BECAUSE OF OTHER CIRCUMSTANCES STOP HAVE YOU GOT ANYBODY WHOM YOU CAN TRUST . . . WHO COULD COME TO BALTIMORE AND TALK IT OVER WITH ME STOP THIS IS NO IMPULSE OF THE MOMENT BUT A THEME THAT HAS BEEN ON MY MIND FOR A FORTNIGHT

SCOTT FITZGERALD

He sent similar wires to Sam Marx, the story editor of MGM, and they were wisely ignored. Only with the death of Thalberg in December of 1936 would employment again be offered Fitzgerald at MGM.

His habit of calling people at all hours produced a curious echo in Charles Jackson, whose *Lost Weekend* was published in 1944. While drunk his hero, Don Birnam, conducts an imaginary class in American literature and discusses both *Gatsby* and *Tender Is the Night,* neither of which would be in any curriculum for at least another five years. Parenthetically, Birnam says of himself:

> He would not bother to tell the students — too personal, unbecoming — that when he had finished *Tender Is the Night* at nine-thirty in the morning, he had telephoned all over the Atlantic seaboard till he finally located Fitzgerald at Tuxedo [La Paix]; and the man had said: "Why don't you write me a letter about it? I think you're a little tight now."

Birnam concluded his praiseful lecture by asserting: "One word more. Fitzgerald never swerves by a hair from the one rule that any writer worth his salt will follow: *Don't write about anything you don't know anything about.*"

It is possible that this scene in a largely autobiographical novel may have been based on Jackson's attempts to contact Fitzgerald in 1934. *The Lost Weekend* was a huge success in 1944, with the critics as well as with the reading public; Jackson's enthusiasm for the eclipsed Fitzgerald was likely one of the reasons The Viking Press embarked on the publication of Malcolm Cowley's *Portable Fitzgerald* the following year, the book that, along with Edmund Wilson's editing of *The Crack-Up* in the same year, began the re-evaluation of Fitzgerald as a neglected figure.

Despite the continuing poor quality of Fitzgerald's commercial fiction, Ober kept up his efforts. By this time he had his own personal financial stake in the stories, for he had advanced his author the money they both hoped to obtain from the magazines. As the months advanced, Fitzgerald's debt to Ober increased steadily. By the end of 1934, a terrible year for him in many ways, Fitzgerald began to think a drastic change was necessary — one that would involve travel.

6

Of course you're a rummy. But you're no more of a rummy than Joyce is and most good writers are. But Scott, good writers always come back. Always. You are twice as good now as you were at the time you think you were so marvelous. . . . You can write twice as well now as you ever could. All you need to do is to write truly and not care about what the fate of it is.

Go on and write.

— Hemingway to Fitzgerald, May 1934

Tell them anything, tell them frankly that you've advanced me the limit but for Gods sake raise me something on this story.

— Fitzgerald to Harold Ober, 1937

As BECAME THE CASE with Faulkner in the early 1940s, Fitzgerald began to think a change of scene might give him some relief from the continual misery produced by daily drinking, an alcoholic despair that was compounded by the undeniable evidence that his writing powers were fading rapidly. For Fitzgerald, however, Hollywood was still two years in the future; his "geographical cure" for his illness in February 1935 was Hendersonville, North Carolina, where he embraced a new life without alcohol. His *Ledger* entry for that month indicates that he "went on wagon for all liquor and alcohol on Tuesday 7th (or on 6th at 8:30 P.M.)." This turn to sobriety was one of short duration; within a few weeks he had begun his daily consumption of the twenty or thirty bottles of beer he felt he required to continue writing. He stayed most of 1935 and 1936 in the South, spending summers at the Grove Park Hotel in Asheville, near the Highland Hospital, where Zelda became a patient in 1936. It was while he was living at the Skyland Hotel in Hendersonville, however, that he wrote what he thought of as his "gloom articles" for *Esquire*, the three short pieces that have come to be known in book form as *The Crack-Up* — perhaps his most important posthumous work, which re-established his reputation in the postwar years.

It may be that Hemingway's compassionate letter of the previous year had something to do with the reappearance of the old Fitzgerald, now suddenly eloquent again about the subject of his own spiritual breakdown. Miraculously, the *Esquire* pieces demonstrated that even after hitting bottom with the Philippe stories, he was still capable of writing with the power and authority of the past. Hemingway had been correct in his assumption that Fitzgerald's talent had not left him. Good writers *did* come back.

In terms of describing his emotional collapse, the "Crack-Up" pieces of 1936 are as remarkable for what they reveal as for what they don't. As if surely aware that his friends and acquaintances would expect to hear something about alcohol as a factor contributing to the problem he described, Fitzgerald simply lied, telling his readers that his own crack-up came about neither *in the head nor in the nerves*. The peculiar distinction he makes here is in order to dissociate himself from the well-known journalist William Seabrook, who had that same year published *Asylum*, the best-selling account of his collapse into alcoholism.

> Seabrook in an unsympathetic book tells, with some pride and a movie ending, of how he became a public charge. What led to his alcoholism or was bound up in it, was a collapse of his nervous system. Though the present writer was not so entangled — having at the time not tasted so much as a glass of beer for six months — it was his nervous reflexes that were giving away — too much anger and too many tears.

Fitzgerald's disdain for Seabrook sprang from several sources, including the primary one that the author of *Asylum* had openly admitted he had become powerless over alcohol. It is quite likely that Fitzgerald embarked on writing the "Crack-Up" pieces not only because of the sudden interest in mental breakdown created by Seabrook's book but also because of the basic issue of the connection between alcohol and writing that Seabrook raised. At the age of forty-eight, Seabrook, a well-known traveler and writer about exotic places and peoples, had himself committed to Bloomingdale Hospital in Westchester County, New York, when he lost control of his drinking. In giving the reader the gist of his talks with various doctors at the hospital, Seabrook reveals that his alcoholism was the result of his fear about his writing:

> I was afraid I wasn't good enough. Always had been afraid, but maybe in youth believed age would remedy it. Now I was middle-aged and afraid I'd never be good enough.... I had plenty of time to face myself now and survive, I had to take stock of whatever I was and get the courage to face it without trying to drown the image in drink again. I had to stop running away from myself, I had to stop hiding from myself, I had to stop drowning myself in gin.... I had been afraid to do my best for fear my best would not be good enough.

Seabrook spent seven months at Bloomingdale, convinced that he could be cured of his "drunkenness" if he was forcibly deprived of alcohol, even if only for that short time. The cure he envisioned would one day enable him to resume his "social" drinking: "I'd probably live generally sober, no matter how worried or depressed I became over work which wouldn't come right." The idea that he might have to give up alcohol for good disturbed him:

> To go out and never be able to touch a cocktail, glass of wine, or highball again would be a poor sort of cure, if it could be termed a cure at all. I said that I still hoped to be really "cured," cured so well that I would be able not to take a highball with my friends, but even on appropriate occasions to take several and cut up high jinks.

Although the staff at Bloomingdale remained doubtful that such a cure would last, Seabrook left the hospital to ascertain if it would. It is easy to see how strongly Fitzgerald might have identified with Seabrook's plight, since Fitzgerald too had been having grave doubts about the validity of his writing, Hemingway's praise notwithstanding. The curious accusation that Seabrook had become a public charge was without foundation — Fitzgerald was impatient with a cure that not only sounded improbable but was one only a wealthy man, or a man with wealthy friends, could afford.

Seabrook's tragedy lay in becoming convinced that he could drink again once he had made peace with himself over the quality of his writing. If indeed his alcoholism sprang from this, then once he had faced up to it squarely, he could presumably drink with impunity. This was in 1935; alcoholism was not yet recognized as a disease, and some of the doctors at the hospital appeared to agree with Seabrook's version of his cure. His book concludes on a quizzical note: "I seem to be cured of drunkenness, which is as may be."

It wasn't. Within three years of his discharge from Bloomingdale, Seabrook was again drinking a quart or more a day and his writing had come to a stop. In the pages of his autobiography *No Hiding Place,* published in 1942, Seabrook describes his growing torment and depression. He continued to think about his days in Bloomingdale: "They had stopped me from drinking, but as for what made Willie drink, they knew they'd never touched it." Brooding over the cause of one's drinking is common among alcoholics who cannot face the fact they can never again drink safely. They appear to believe that if they can just determine *the cause once and for all,* they can return to the style of drinking they enjoyed previously. It was under these circumstances that Seabrook continued to drink. At one point, the woman who became his third wife, in a drastic attempt to turn things around, recommended that Seabrook immerse his elbows in boiling water and hold them there. He did just that, suffering terrible third-degree burns, but this cure worked no better than the one at Bloomingdale; Seabrook committed suicide with an overdose of sleeping pills in 1945 at the age of fifty-nine.

Asylum probably stirred up Fitzgerald's deepest feelings, for he wrote a superb account of what can now be seen as alcoholic depression, the depression that results in the ever-growing sense that life has lost its meaning — or, as he put it, "In a real dark night of the soul it is always three o'clock in the morning." *The Crack-Up* is magnificent proof that Fitzgerald, as Hemingway had insisted, was not finished as a writer and that given an occasion worthy of his talent, he could still write as well as he ever did.

His friends were not happy with the series in *Esquire,* most of them certain that it could only have a negative effect on his career, which was clearly sinking by the moment. They considered that appearing in print with such a tale of personal woe constituted a form of exhibitionism. In a letter to Perkins, Hemingway accused Fitzgerald of complete shamelessness. As for Perkins, he detested the essays and refused to publish them even after Fitzgerald's death. But Edmund Wilson and John Dos Passos disliked them equally and for much the same reasons; it may be that all four were fully aware that at the heart of Fitzgerald's confessions was the element of alcohol (though not touched on), which had caused such bitter quarrels. As to its effect on his writing, they had only to read his new stories in *Esquire,* month after month, to see what had happened. But despite the lie at the center, the "Crack-Up" series remains a remarkable piece of self-probing carried out by a form of literary sleight of hand in which Fitzgerald demonstrates that he is suffering from deep depression but either cannot or will not reveal its real source.

7

Hell I can't write about this and it is rotten to speak against Scott after all he had to go through. . . . It was a terrible thing for him to love youth so much that he jumped straight from youth to senility without going through manhood. The minute he felt youth going he was frightened again and thought there was nothing between youth and age. But it is so damned easy to criticize our friends and I shouldn't write this. I wish we could help him.

— Hemingway to Maxwell Perkins, February 1936

When you get to the point where you don't care whether you live or die — as I did — it's hard to believe in yourself again — you have slain part of yourself.

— Fitzgerald, notes for *The Last Tycoon*

MORE AND MORE FREQUENTLY now Fitzgerald would lose control of his drinking: his dozen or more beers a day would suddenly give way to straight gin, and he would enter prolonged periods of drinking that could be brought to a halt only when he hired nurses to help him withdraw from alcohol by doling out gin in hourly amounts. The process took several days and cut deeply into his work schedule. Despite some enforced periods of sobriety, the quality of his work didn't improve.

The self-therapy of the "Crack-Up" pieces threw light on his emotional situation, but his continued drinking did nothing to change his steadily worsening finances. His expenses were high; at this time he was paying — or not paying, he was always in arrears — Zelda's hospital bills at the Highland Hospital as well as his daughter Scottie's tuition fees at her various schools. His income for 1935 and 1936 fell far short of these expenses, and his debt to his agent climbed steadily month after month. Ober resorted to sending Fitzgerald statements with his letters concerning their business affairs. These bills were the amounts advanced by Ober upon the receipt of stories of which he was able to sell only a few; most of them failed to find a market anywhere. By the summer of 1937 Ober had nine unsold stories in his files and had placed nothing of Fitzgerald's in nearly a year. In June the Ober statement indicated that Fitzgerald owed his agent nearly $13,000, and his debt in unearned advances at Scribners amounted to almost $9,000. His 1935 collection of stories, *Taps at Reveille,* had sold under 3,000 copies, decreasing his debt at Scribners by only a little over a thousand dollars.

Fitzgerald's weakened sense of story structure was the main reason for the rejections at this time. With the exception of *Esquire,* where Arnold Gingrich continued to print virtually everything Fitzgerald submitted, the doors of the high-paying commercial magazines were now closed to him. But even if he wrote a story a month for *Esquire,* the resulting income would be less than a third of his living expenses. Hollywood was the only answer to his problem, but it took many months to obtain a contract at MGM.

The death of his mother in September 1936 saved him from going under. His share of her estate ($20,000) was enough to ease the burden a bit but offered only a short respite from the problem that wouldn't go away — what does a professional writer do when almost no one wants his material? Another worry was the continuing criticism over the publication of his "Crack-Up" pieces.

When Hemingway referred to him on the opening page of "The Snows of Kilimanjaro" as "poor Scott Fitzgerald," a writer who had wrecked himself by associating with the wealthy, Fitzgerald was both deeply hurt and outraged. Hemingway later told Maxwell Perkins that Fitzgerald "seems to take a pride in his defeat" and that he had made the reference to provoke Fitzgerald into abandoning the self-pitying tone he detected in the "Crack-Up" essays published just a few months earlier. Hemingway was right about Fitzgerald's self-pity, but it was not something new; it was present as far back as the 1931 story "Babylon Revisited," perhaps his most frequently reprinted piece in college anthologies. It is the story of a "reformed drunk," Charlie Wales, who may lose his young child to his dead wife's family because of heavy drinking, which had played a part in his wife's death. The tale is marred by self-pity — Fitzgerald could easily see himself in just this position with Zelda's family and Scottie. The story concludes with the famous "dying fall" lines:

> They couldn't make him pay forever. But he wanted his child, and nothing was much good now, beside that fact. He wasn't young any more, with a lot of nice thoughts and dreams to have by himself. He was absolutely sure Helen wouldn't have wanted him to be so alone.

Fitzgerald is not Wales, but it is clear why this story has become so popular, echoing as it does the biographical facts about a writer whose life has become just as fascinating as his work, and perhaps even more so.

Fitzgerald's sense of outrage about the slight was visible in the letter he wrote to Hemingway, advising him to "lay off me in print" and saying that his *Esquire* pieces did not "mean I want friends praying aloud over my corpse." He was aware, however, that Hemingway meant him no deliberate malice: "No doubt you meant it kindly but it cost me a night's sleep. And when you incorporate it . . . in a book would you mind cutting my name?" Hemingway obliged him by substituting "Julian" for Fitzgerald, but sent him a letter (now lost) that contained a tortured defense of using Fitzgerald's name in the story. Fitzgerald had lost none of his shrewdness in evaluating people's motivations, telling Perkins:

> He wrote me back a crazy letter, telling me about what a great Writer he was and how much he loved his children, but yielding the point — "If I should outlive him —" which he doubted. . . . Somehow I love that man, no matter what he says or does. . . .

> No one could ever hurt him in his first books but he has com-
> pletely lost his head and the duller he gets about it, the more he
> is like a punch-drunk pug fighting himself in the movies.

Fitzgerald's insight here is remarkable for its anticipatory acute-
ness in describing the beginnings of his friend's deterioration, the
first steps in his descent into madness.

Hemingway's words hurt him, but he was far more disturbed
by the remarks made by his Princeton classmate John Peale
Bishop in an essay that appeared in *The Virginia Quarterly Review*. Bishop attacked Fitzgerald on the grounds that he had
"sold out to the rich" by hobnobbing with them in the late
1920s, which had led to his loss of power as a writer.

An event occurring only two weeks after his letter to Perkins
demonstrated that he still regarded Hemingway as perhaps his
closest friend. Determined to obtain a "searching" interview
with the "high priest" of the Jazz Age, Michael Mok of the *New
York Post* tracked Fitzgerald down at the Grove Park Inn in
Asheville on his fortieth birthday in 1936. Mok found his subject in a state of extreme agitation resulting from his current
withdrawal from alcohol, as well as suffering from the pain of
a fractured shoulder. He told Mok about the despair he'd depicted in his *Esquire* pieces, and the reporter took down every
word. His article ran on the front page of the paper, accompanied by a photo of Fitzgerald in his bathrobe. The story itself
contained the grim details of Fitzgerald's frequent trembling
trips to his sideboard to replenish his doled-out ration of gin.
The portrait that greeted his friends and the entire New York
literary establishment was that of a writer who had no compunction about showing his complete hopelessness to the daily
press, who had *really* "cracked up," just as William Seabrook
had.

The impact of seeing the article was so devastating that Fitzgerald took an overdose of a drug that one of his nurses must
have mistakenly left in his room: morphine, rather than paraldehyde. Luckily, he vomited it up and, desperate for help against

Mok and his story, fired off a telegram to Hemingway that began: "If you ever wanted to help me your chance is now." The answer from Montana was affirmative, but by the time it arrived Fitzgerald realized that any outcry would serve only to draw further attention to his condition. He thanked Hemingway for his offer, concluding with "Best always."

The Mok episode may have constituted a spiritual bottom for Fitzgerald; he began making attempts to stop drinking altogether — an agonizingly difficult task to accomplish unaided at his age. He was only intermittently successful and was not able to maintain sobriety for extended periods until shortly before he began working for MGM in July 1937. The stories he wrote while sober don't differ in quality from those written while drinking.

With an apparently permanently hospitalized Zelda, with whom he could not make a formal break, as well as the drinking episodes that kept him in bed for days on end, plus desperate efforts to write stories that would sell, Fitzgerald had little time for romance. Nevertheless, two years earlier, at the Oak Park Inn in Asheville, he had a brief affair with Beatrice Dance, a young married woman from Texas. We know something of this adventure from his letters to Beatrice; hers have not survived. He appears to have had strong feelings for her, but the events of their affair — as reported by Laura Guthrie, a would-be writer who knew Fitzgerald that summer of 1935 — turned into a bedroom farce featuring Beatrice's jealous husband and her mentally disturbed sister, and were complicated by Fitzgerald's need to preserve his maintenance supply of gin, alternating with beer. Once her husband became aware of their intimacy, Fitzgerald thought best to terminate it, and Beatrice returned home. Not until he met Sheilah Graham in Hollywood did Fitzgerald maintain a stable relationship with a woman, one that could replace in part some of the love he'd had for Zelda.

In every way, Hollywood was his last chance — a chance to sober up and attempt to start writing at his best again and a chance to extricate himself from the huge debts piled up in the past few years. When he left to work at MGM, he stopped making entries in his *Ledger,* as if bidding farewell to his life as a successful magazine writer.

8

> Scott died inside himself at around the age of thirty to thirty-five and his creative powers died somewhat later. This last book [*The Last Tycoon*] was written long after his creative power was dead, and he was just beginning to find out what things were about.
> — Hemingway to Maxwell Perkins, November 1941

> Shoot yourself, you son of a bitch. I didn't raise myself from the gutter to waste my life on a drunk like you.
> — Sheilah Graham, 1938

IN *Some Time in the Sun* I have written about Fitzgerald's three and a half years as a Hollywood scriptwriter. But there are a few things to add to that account, especially what he accomplished using the wonderful material he found in California — film making itself — in his unfinished novel, *The Last Tycoon.* Discovering a whole new world to write about was miraculous for a writer who believed, with some justice, that he had exhausted his literary capital. He may have disliked Hollywood as a place to live, but his $1,000-a-week salary (later $1,250) enabled him to live once again in a measure of affluence. Actually, he had not liked Baltimore, Montgomery or Asheville any more than Hollywood.

When he joined MGM, it was clear that he couldn't drink and expect to hold down the job; the studio executives were aware of his problem and would cancel his contract if they discovered that he was drinking with his old abandon. He therefore gave up — for the moment, at least — all alcohol and became known around the studio for the number of Cokes he drank each day, lining up the bottles along the walls of his office. He maintained his abstinence for months at a time, held to it by his regular daily attendance at the studio. But as soon as the job pressure was released, he would try a few drinks, as when, for example, his MGM contract was not renewed at the end of 1938. These few almost invariably led to around-the-clock binges that might go on for a week or more at a time. Such episodes were now more expensive than ever, involving twenty-four-hour nursing care at home and intravenous feeding of glucose to sustain his life functions. After forty, Fitzgerald could no longer eat when in extreme withdrawal from alcohol; the tube feeding was the only answer to the problem.

As I've indicated, chronic insomnia is common among alcoholics. Fitzgerald's was worse than most, although perhaps not as severe as Hemingway's. In California he found it impossible to sleep without dosing himself nightly with chloral hydrate, which might give him three or four hours. If he repeated part of the dose during the night, he needed Benzedrine tablets to get him going the following day. In addition to his Cokes, he drank huge amounts of coffee while working. His heavy smoking continued, as did his exotic eating habits, which were guaranteed to damage his overall health. In effect, Fitzgerald was a sick man after 1938.

But he was not giving up the struggle to regain his diminished reputation as a writer of books. In the late summer of 1939, after he had given up real hope of obtaining another writing job at one of the studios, he began to formulate the plan for a novel about the man, now dead for three years, who had fired him from MGM in 1931: the *wunderkind* Irving Thalberg. Although he may have considered writing about Thalberg as far back as 1936, economic necessity pressed him to begin assembling material. His only income came from the stories for *Esquire* featuring Pat Hobby, but $250 per story was insufficient to keep him afloat. He tried the major magazines with new stories, but they had all the faults of the ones that the editors had been rejecting. If one reads the stories that Professor Bruccoli has collected in his huge volume of unpublished Fitzgerald, *The Price Was High*, it is easy to see why *The Saturday Evening Post* turned down the later ones with regularity. When Bruccoli writes that "the talent that had provided more than 100 *Post* stories was now bankrupt," he is telling us the raw truth: Fitzgerald had been dying as a creative writer since about 1933. It was exactly the kind of decline suffered by William Faulkner after about 1942, when the same magazine editors began turning down *his* new stories. With the short story market closed to Fitzgerald, writing a novel that could be serialized in a national magazine like *Collier's* or the *Post* and ultimately published in book form by Scribners was the only real possibility in late 1939 when he began *The Last Tycoon*.

Even a casual reading of the book reveals its varying quality — how much of this variation was due to Fitzgerald's off-and-on drinking? In her three books about him, Sheilah Graham has related many details about Fitzgerald's habits in California, asserting that he drank for only nine of the forty-two months he spent there. Because he was under contract at MGM and Fox, as well as at a few other studios, for nearly twenty-four mainly nondrinking months, her figure may well approximate the truth. She does not venture to guess, however, how much he drank when she was away from Hollywood in connection with her columnist's job, or when Fitzgerald himself was out of town. Given the opportunity to drink while Sheilah was absent, Fitzgerald did just that on at least one occasion, as his former secretary, Lucy Kroll Ring, reveals in a recent memoir. Until now, most accounts of Fitzgerald's life, including my own, mistakenly assumed he drank nothing in his last year. Lucy Ring corrects that assumption.

In her book, *Against the Current*, Ring relates the events of a night in the autumn of 1940 when Sheilah Graham was out of town. Fitzgerald took Lucy and her brother Morton to a restaurant on Sunset Boulevard, where he unexpectedly ordered a bottle of wine. Perfectly aware of what just a few drinks could do to her employer, she was filled with dread but nervously drank a glass to be polite; Morton was a minor and did not drink. Fitzgerald finished off the bottle and began a long, rambling lecture about Hemingway. After dinner he took his young guests back to his apartment, where he broke out the gin and proceeded to drink enough of it to appear "glazed." Miraculously, he was able to stop drinking that night; fear of Sheilah's reaction to any resumption of his drinking appears to explain his ability to curtail it then. Sheilah's pressure on him to stay dry had replaced the job pressure at the studios. Although he knew that she would leave him for good if he resumed drinking, he still took chances. The addictive power of alcohol continued to exert its pull despite the utter helplessness to which it now reduced him.

For a writer believed "creatively dead" to start a new novel was an act of great courage. He no longer had the financial backing of Harold Ober; after nearly twenty years' service as his banker, Ober finally refused the function and Fitzgerald became his own agent. But Fitzgerald had at least two major assets in the undertaking: he had known Thalberg well enough in 1927 and 1931 to write about him with authority, and, in addition, his two years of working within the studio system had supplied him with a subject entirely new in American fiction. Perhaps even more important, Thalberg's life could become a symbol of the American success story. Here was a subject that, with luck, he could transform into another *Gatsby*, the book in which he raised a success story to mythical proportions. He started *The Last Tycoon* with two goals in mind: to write a widely popular book as well as one that would rival his earlier triumphs, a difficult if not impossible task for him in his present condition.

Fitzgerald began in July 1939 by preparing an impressive array of notes and detailed outlines. After agreeing to submit a 15,000-word sample of the novel to Kenneth Littauer of *Collier's*, Fitzgerald became nervously impatient and sent him only 6,000 words. Since the total purchase price was going to be $25,000 — a lot of money at the time — Littauer said no and Fitzgerald broke off negotiations with the magazine. This was foolish, for *Collier's* had a genuine interest in the story; if Fitzgerald had delivered his remaining 9,000 words, the chances are strong that they would have taken it. With the help of Perkins in New York, Fitzgerald then attempted to sell the sample to *The Saturday Evening Post,* which also reacted negatively. It may be asked, if he was willing to use Perkins as a negotiator, why didn't he seek a contract for the book from Scribners? The answer is that he was still in debt to them for nearly $6,000, and only the publicity engendered by a huge magazine success could justify an advance large enough to accommodate their debit balance.

In a furious rage with himself and everyone else, he began several weeks of steady drinking, but came back to the book early in 1940, working on it when not engaged on one of his seventeen Pat Hobby stories about a Hollywood hack writer. The immediate cash reward of writing screenplays could not be ignored, and he accepted all the offers made, breaking off work on *The Last Tycoon* each time he did so. For $300 a week he spent four months adapting "Babylon Revisited" as a screenplay for Lester Cowan, converting his relatively quiet story into a film with chases and murder. Nunnally Johnson thought highly of Fitzgerald, and after they had become good friends Johnson hired him, at a thousand a week, to adapt Emlyn Williams's *Young at Heart* for Twentieth Century–Fox. Neither the "Babylon" script (retitled *Cosmopolitan*) nor the Fox was filmed as written by Fitzgerald. He had spent nearly six months on them, and it was not until the beginning of September 1940 that he again resumed full-time work on the book. This stopping and starting could account for some of the novel's unevenness, but there may have been a more important reason.

Although Fitzgerald believed he might have been placed on a Hollywood blacklist because of his drinking, it may well be that he was seldom hired after 1939 because of the quality of his screenplays after that time. Nunnally Johnson, who had no animus against Fitzgerald, wrote me:

> I read some of the work he did alone and unaided by a collaborator and it was downright bad. Worst of all, it was shamelessly

imitative. Realizing that he could not cut the mustard on his own, he echoed some pretty shoddy stuff.

In another letter, Johnson specified how Fitzgerald's scriptwriting impressed fellow professionals:

> I am sure that Scott would have torn up [the script for *Cosmopolitan*] a few years earlier. But now there were other circumstances to be considered. Whether it was a fair sample of his work at the time I don't know. I can only say that several of the writers who read other scripts or parts of other scripts felt he was clearly running out of gas, and all reported it in sorrow, for they were friends of Scott's and it hurt them to find him failing.

His talent was now decidedly erratic; it is not surprising that the uncertainties and weaknesses of the scripts should also appear in the unfinished novel. The introduction of Hollywood as a subject in his work did much to restore Fitzgerald's ability to write material that was at least publishable, but he had not regained the sustained power he'd possessed in the mid-1920s in "The Rich Boy" and *Gatsby*. That aspect of his talent had disappeared forever when he damaged his wings, as Hemingway says, those wings which had borne him so far aloft, a flight that he evoked in *The Last Tycoon* when he wrote what is perhaps the novel's most celebrated passage: "He had flown up very high to see, on strong wings, when he was young. And while he was up there he had looked at all the kingdoms, with the kind of eyes that can stare straight into the sun."

9

> He got something of the old magic into it [*The Last Tycoon*]. But in the things between men and women, the old magic was gone and Scott never really understood life well enough to write a novel that did not need the magic to make it come alive.
> — Hemingway to Maxwell Perkins, November 1941

VARIOUS ATTEMPTS have been made to demonstrate that the friendship between Fitzgerald and Hemingway perished with rancor on both sides. The most frequently cited items of their supposed quarrel are the "poor Scott" episode when "The Snows of Kilimanjaro" was first published, as well as Hemingway's critique of *Tender Is the Night* and his remarks about the posthumously published *Tycoon*. In his letter to Perkins, Hemingway was clearly mistaken when he said that the outline published in the book was simply a tool with which to obtain an advance, telling him, "But you know Scott would never have finished it with that gigantic . . . outline of how it was to be." While it is true that there is a seeming disparity between the manuscript material and the outlines, it is equally clear that Fitzgerald followed his last outline closely. Hemingway was perceptive in pointing out the unfinished book's greatest strength: "I thought the part about Stahr was all very good. You can recognize Irving Thalberg, his charm and skill and grasp of business, and the advance of death over him." But Hemingway also indicated to Perkins one of the real weaknesses of the book, that the women in it were all "pretty preposterous. Scott had gotten so far away from any knowledge of people that they are very strange." Interestingly enough, this was similar to Fitzgerald's own view of his lost ability to perceive, as he told Zelda:

> I feel people so less intently than I did once that this [writing *The Last Tycoon*] is harder. It means welding together hundreds of

stray impressions and incidents to form the fabric of entire personalities.

Assembling the bits and pieces of Stahr's working day in order to create a believable character was a triumph for Fitzgerald, for Stahr is not the Thalberg of Hollywood reality. Often seen as "an executive with taste and courage" and "endowed with supreme intelligence and taste," the real Thalberg was not quite all these things. His intelligence admitted of no doubt, but his taste was not far from that of his ostensible enemy, Louis B. Mayer, the president of MGM. When Thalberg once said to a screenwriter, "When I say a gag won't play, it won't play. I, more than any single person in Hollywood, have my finger on the pulse of America. I *know* what people will do and what they won't do," he was asserting his ability to please crowds. Like Mayer, he shared a sincere devotion to the profit motive and seldom had his attention diverted from the demands of popular taste. It was Thalberg who played a large part in the destruction of the film careers of Eric von Stroheim, Buster Keaton and the Marx Brothers. Fitzgerald was able to catch this cold side of Thalberg, who was once characterized by one of his chief lieutenants, Eddie Mannix, as a man who could "piss ice water."

The real Thalberg wasn't that different from Mayer: profit for MGM was their common goal. Their only real quarrel was in determining how much of a piece each would retain when the pie was cut. The rivalry between Stahr and Brady (Mayer) gave Fitzgerald considerable trouble: he could glamorize Stahr as Thalberg but he was forced to *invent* his archenemy, Brady, thus producing a plot whose major characters use blackmail and murder to achieve their corporate ends. Here Fitzgerald resorted to the demands of the popular-magazine market, where melodrama of this sort is the staff of life; it is the same kind of fictive solution that he used in the script for *Cosmopolitan*. When Hemingway attacked the book as projected in the published outline, he was probably thinking of this life-and-death struggle of two great tycoons — a plot device common enough in magazine serials of the day. Here one can see Fitzgerald's loss of genuine creative power, resorting to stock solutions peopled with stock characters.

Virtually all the minor characters are also one-dimensional, but it is the women who fare worst of all. Kathleen Moore, the heroine of the story, although based largely on Sheilah Graham, remains a vapid blank, surprisingly so in view of the liveliness of the model. It may be that Fitzgerald could "do" Thalberg so well because his impressions of the producer had been formed back in 1927 and 1931 when he was *all* perception, the faculty he'd now lost in portraying Sheilah as Kathleen. The vexing problems of the female narrator, Cecelia, have often been discussed. All the evidence indicates that Fitzgerald, despite strong misgivings, was in a sense "stuck" with her, deciding to have her be the recipient of confidences that would justify her knowledge of events to which she was not a party — "They *told* me . . ." As for what was to be the concluding episode of the book, the plane crash in the mountains and the subsequent looting of the bodies of the passengers, it too smacks of magazine melodrama; there is no genuine tragic struggle in *The Last Tycoon*.

Suppose he'd lived to finish it — isn't it likely that it would have been a book far superior to the sections he left at his death? All the evidence indicates otherwise. His economic plight at the end of 1940 was such that he had to finish the book as fast as he could. With the short story market gone and screenwriting out for the foreseeable future, his only viable property was *Tycoon* as a book for Perkins. On December 13 he wrote his editor: "The novel progresses — in fact progresses fast. I'm not going to stop now till I finish a first draft which will be sometime after the 15th of January." The goal of finishing the book by late February or early March was a realistic one. It is likely that we would have read what was in those outlines.

In *Some Time in the Sun* I attempted to correct the then standard picture of Fitzgerald in Hollywood as a trembling wreck of a man, miserably paid for his labors and deeply depressed over his "failure." In so doing I pointed out that this portrait came about because of the work of Arthur Mizener in his pioneering biography, as well as the writings of Budd Schulberg in his novel *The Disenchanted* and in his book about writers he'd known, *The Four Seasons of Success*. My view of Fitzgerald's last years is that of a man undefeated, a writer who took his screenplay jobs seriously, who was rapidly working his way out of debt and who was in love with a woman for the first time since he'd met Zelda. Most important of all, he was busy at work on his first new novel in nearly a decade, and he was at least trying to remain sober.

A third source for the myth of the crushed and beaten Fitzgerald was Lillian Hellman. In *An Unfinished Woman* she told a tale about Hemingway and Fitzgerald concerning which she was the sole witness — nobody else has ever confirmed a word of it. It deals with what proved to be the final meeting between the two men, at the home of Fredric March in Hollywood in July of 1937, when Hemingway had come to Los Angeles to raise money for the Loyalist forces, then opposing the revolt against the Spanish government. The event at the Marches', on the night of the thirteenth, was a screening of Joris Ivens's film *The Spanish Earth,* for which Hemingway had written the commentary. Hellman records nothing about any conversation between Hemingway and Fitzgerald.

After the screening many of the guests, including Hemingway, went on to Dorothy Parker's house to finish out the evening. According to Hellman, she asked Fitzgerald to take her there; he obliged by driving down Sunset Boulevard at "between 10 and 12 miles per hour," with "trembling hands" on the wheel. On their arrival, Fitzgerald was reluctant to enter because of his "fear" of Hemingway: "I'm afraid of Ernest, I guess, scared of being sober when . . ." But her entreaties succeeded, and Hellman supplies us with a highly dramatic scene in which Hemingway smashed a wine glass in the fireplace just as she and Fitzgerald entered the living room. Fitzgerald was so rattled that he left to talk with a half-drunk Dashiell Hammett, who was in the kitchen with Parker. At this point Hellman's story trails off, and she states she had no idea how long Fitzgerald stayed on in the house or whether he made contact with Hemingway.

If Fitzgerald had no qualms about meeting Hemingway at the March house, why would his fear suddenly surface at Parker's? If he was really afraid to see Hemingway, why did he attend the screening in the first place? Several days after the event, Fitzgerald sent Hemingway a telegram: "The picture was beyond praise and so was your attitude," which doesn't sound as though he avoided Hemingway that night. Since it is a matter of record that Fitzgerald and Hemingway had had a genial chat in New York the previous month, and since Fitzgerald had been sober for several weeks prior to his starting work at MGM on July 7, it is unlikely that he would have demonstrated any of the characteristics Hellman ascribed to him the night of July 13. Hellman was unaware that the two writers had enjoyed a convivial lunch with Robert Benchley only the day before the *Spanish Earth* screening. In a letter to his wife, Benchley describes the meeting of his old friends from the Paris days of the twenties as "warm and good-humored."

What was Hellman's motivation in concocting the tale? Perhaps only a desire to make up a good story and a wish to say something nice about Fitzgerald at Hemingway's expense, as when she makes a rapid transition in the next few pages of her book to describe an encounter between Hammett and Hemingway in New York in 1939. This time both men are drinking heavily, and Hammett goads Hemingway: "Why don't you go back to bullying Fitzgerald? Too bad he doesn't know how good he is. The best." Again, Hellman was the only surviving witness to this episode, and knowing Hammett's literary/political taste, it is probably as unlikely as the story about the *Spanish Earth* party. Hellman's animosity toward Hemingway in these anecdotes is unmistakable. She had told Fitzgerald not to be afraid of Hemingway, following her advice with "He [Hemingway] could never like a good writer, certainly not a better one." (What about Pound? Joyce?) Ultimately, her views have their roots in Mizener and Schulberg.

*

Once reporting for work each day at a studio stopped being a factor in maintaining his sobriety, it was probably Fitzgerald's affair with Sheilah Graham that exerted the greatest pressure on him to continue abstaining. Graham had become aware of AA, then in its infancy, in 1939 but Fitzgerald was decidedly negative: "I was never a joiner." His rationale was that "AA can only help weak people because their ego is strengthened by the group. The group offers them the strength they lack on their own." Here Fitzgerald equates giving up alcohol with a confession of weakness — a confession he was not about to make, possibly because he may have felt it threatened his manhood. Like Faulkner in this respect, Fitzgerald refused to see that he had become powerless over alcohol, even with the evidence of all the pain and agony of repeated disasters staring him in the face. He was perfectly aware, as was Faulkner, that the cost would be high if he continued drinking but was quick to flare up in anger if the subject was broached, as when he told off Ober in a 1939 letter: "Anyhow I have 'lived dangerously' and I may quite possibly have to pay for it, but there are plenty of other people to tell me that and it doesn't seem as if it should be you."

If it wasn't going to be Sheilah or Ober, who had been both agent and banker for nearly twenty years, who then *could* have told him? Zelda had tried with no more success than the rest.

On Saturday the twenty-first of December 1940, Fitzgerald and Graham were in her apartment expecting a visit from Fitzgerald's doctor, who had agreed to bring over Scott's latest cardiogram. He'd recently suffered two heart attacks, which had slowed up his progress on *The Last Tycoon* and curbed many of his physical activities. After lunch she listened to a recording of the *Eroica* while he jotted down the names of football players in the current *Princeton Alumni Weekly*. Without warning, he was struck with his third and final attack. He sprang to his feet, clutched the mantelpiece and fell to the floor. Sheilah's attempts to revive him were in vain: Scott Fitzgerald was dead at forty-four.

*

The funeral was attended mainly by family friends. One writer who attended was John Sanford: "The next time you saw him, he was dead, laid out in an open coffin at some out-of-the-way funeral parlor. A dim place it was, and quiet except for the carpet's asper underfoot. In death, his face was snow again."

Edited by Edmund Wilson, the incomplete *Last Tycoon* was published in late 1941, just before Pearl Harbor. It did little to advance his reputation, but the publication of *The Crack-Up* and *The Portable Fitzgerald,* both in 1945, started the immense tide of biographies and critical studies about his work that now seem excessive. But the best of his writing remains extraordinary. And despite attempts to paint Hemingway as his constant denigrator, Hemingway's eloquent tribute captures some of the quality that makes Fitzgerald's best work so compelling:

> His talent was as natural as the pattern that was made by the dust on a butterfly's wings. At one time he understood it no more than the butterfly did and he did not know when it was brushed or marred. Later he became conscious of his damaged wings and of their construction and he learned to think and could not fly any more because the love of flight was gone and he could only remember when it had been effortless.

In this poetic evocation Hemingway omits any mention of alcoholism as the primary cause of his friend's decline. This omission is not surprising for a man with the same problem.

Hemingway

✺

"I'M NO RUMMY"

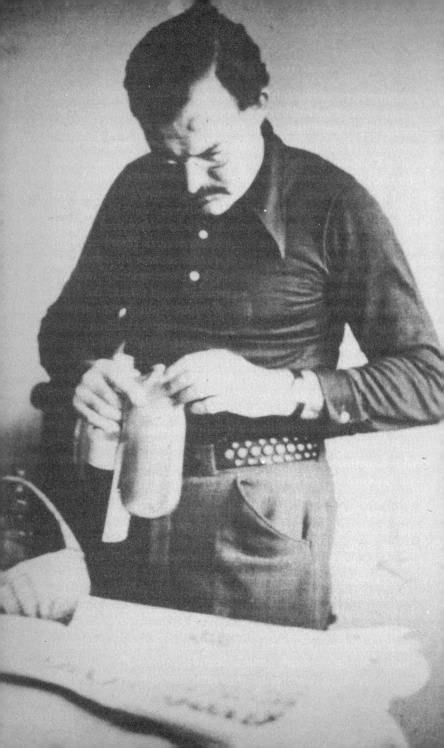

1

Have spent my life straightening out rummies and all
my life drinking, but since writing is my true love I
never get the two things mixed up.
— Hemingway to A. E. Hotchner, September 1949

AT NO TIME did Hemingway regard himself as an alcoholic. As
he saw it, he'd mastered the art of drinking in his mid-teens; the
huge amounts he consumed daily in later life simply reflected an
immense tolerance for alcohol. He regarded that immense thirst
for spirits not as a sign of addiction but as yet another aspect of
his large appetite for the pleasures of life. He was unaware that
an early, huge tolerance for alcohol is often a sign of the presence
of the disease. In Hemingway's view, writers like James Joyce,
Faulkner and his own friend Fitzgerald were clearly "rummies"
first and last; he once told Charles Poore that "rummies are rummies and can't help themselves and shouldn't drink. But if you
learned to drink before you were fourteen and drank ever since
and love to drink and can still write well at 53 do you rate as
an alcoholic?" But at fifty-three Hemingway wrote nowhere
nearly as well as he once had, and he certainly did rate as an
alcoholic.

He was still in his early twenties when he discovered that he
could easily outdrink nearly everyone he encountered; at the
same time he became competitive about the amounts he con-

Hemingway in Barcelona, December 1937

sumed, demonstrating to Morley Callaghan in Toronto that he could lower seven beers to the younger man's three. From the very beginning he found that drinking sharpened life for him like nothing else, perhaps even made it meaningful; life without it was flat and dull. He began to judge people's character when they were under the influence of alcohol; in 1923 he observed: "I like to see every man drunk. A man does not exist until he is drunk. . . . I love getting drunk. Right from the start it is the best feeling."

The biographers of Hemingway took him at his word. Carlos Baker and A. E. Hotchner avoided the term "alcoholic" with regard to their subject. Scott Donaldson, in his fascinating compilation of facts about Hemingway, *By Force of Will,* devotes only two pages to the drinking and identifies him as a "heavy drinker." Not so with the two most recent accounts. Jeffrey Meyers and Kenneth Lynn have no compunction about labeling Hemingway as an alcoholic; both writers choose, however, to view his disease as a product of the depression that darkened his last years. But clearly Hemingway's alcoholism began far earlier than is generally thought, and there is little doubt that drinking did get mixed up with his writing. It played a major role in the deterioration of his great talent, just as surely as it did in the diminished vigor of those other two "rummies," Faulkner and Fitzgerald. The creative decline in Hemingway's work occurs at roughly the same age as it did for both Faulkner and Fitzgerald, despite their varying initial tolerances.

Hemingway's fiction should never be taken as verbatim transcriptions of the incidents of his life. His stories and novels often differ significantly from the events they are loosely based on. But he frequently made good use of the actual, as in an early Nick Adams story, "The Three-Day Blow," in which two teenage boys get drunk together. Here Hemingway succeeds brilliantly in depicting the new excitement of feeling high. When Nick leaves Bill to bring water from the kitchen, "he passed a mirror in the dining room and looked in it. His face looked strange. He winked at it and went on. It wasn't his face but it didn't make any difference."

Nick is attempting to recover from the sense of loss over breaking up with his girlfriend, Marjorie. As he continues to drink, his feelings about the affair undergo a transformation. Toward the end of the story, Hemingway writes that Nick was "still quite drunk but his head was clear." The Scotch and Irish whiskey he consumed have wiped away the pain and left him thinking that "the Marge business was no longer so tragic. It was not even very important." The story reveals much about Hemingway's early perception of alcohol: it could dispel pain with no ill effects on the drinker. You could drink the entire evening and, while becoming "drunk," magically remain unaffected by the alcohol. If it was that good for pain, wouldn't it follow that it would be effective for a great many other things? In time Hemingway would often refer to alcohol as the "giant killer," the ever-helpful ally against fears, the fears that he had derided as a child by repeatedly exclaiming "'*fraid of nothing!*" to those around him.

Hemingway carried his knowledge of the joys of alcohol along with him to the Italian hospital in Milan where he spent several months recovering from the wounds he had suffered after being struck by shell fragments from a trench mortar in the spring of 1918. The nursing staff was appalled by the number of empty bottles discovered in his clothes closet but found they were dealing with a young man who liked his liquor and brooked no opposition to acquiring as much of it as he could. His first great love, Agnes Von Kurowsky, noted his intake and chided him gently for it in a letter:

> Be nice now and don't get rash when you hear I'm not coming to Milan. . . . By this I mean don't lap up all the fluids at the galleria. But I don't really believe it is necessary for me to give that little advice. You're learning fast and soon will be caught up with me in years of experience.

Hemingway was as unable to catch up with Agnes in curbing his consumption of alcohol as he was in decreasing the seven years that separated them. When Agnes cast Hemingway aside, her decision produced a shattering emotional upheaval in him that he attempted to assuage with alcohol; by his lights it appeared to work as well for forgetting Agnes as it had for Nick's Marjorie. His marriage in 1921 to Hadley Richardson softened the hurt inflicted by Agnes.

Along with her wit, charm and beauty, Hadley displayed a lively interest in drinking, and her young husband found their shared taste for alcohol exhilarating. Still, his drinking gave Hadley some concern during the very first week of their marriage. After meeting a bootlegger and buying a supply of potables, Hemingway got drunk enough to appropriate someone's motorboat on Lake Walloon and then ran it back and forth for hours before returning to his bride, who was not amused by his absence.

She forgave him, and the following year saw the couple living in Paris as Hemingway abandoned a promising career in journalism to pursue a course in serious writing in the company of Gertrude Stein and Ezra Pound. Hemingway was only twenty-three, but his overpowering charm and warmth, together with his brown-eyed good looks, made him an immediately popular figure in the Montparnasse quarter, so much so that he was a celebrity there by 1925. He later thought of this early period as perhaps the happiest in his life, the time of innocence and apprenticeship.

2

Jesus I wish you were over here so we could get drunk like I am now and have been so often lately. . . . Don [Stewart] wrote he drank you dead. . . . He's claiming to be a drinker now. . . . Drinker? Shit.
— Hemingway to John Dos Passos, April 1925

Since I finished the book have been doing good deal drinking again. Can drink hells any amount of whiskey without getting drunk because my head is so tired.
— Hemingway to Ernest Walsh, September 1925

HEMINGWAY'S "'fraid of nothing!" philosophy extended to alcohol, and he had at least two main reasons for believing he could drink as much as he pleased without suffering any consequences to either his work or his health. In these Paris years he drank moderately after completing his day's output and did not then require a morning drink to rouse him creatively for his daily stint. He adhered strictly to his resolution not to drink while actually engaged in writing, a decision that he felt distinguished him from many of his contemporaries, particularly his new friend Scott Fitzgerald, who quickly became a terrible object lesson to Hemingway. He could not fail to see what Fitzgerald's drinking was doing to him creatively, especially after he began to rely on alcohol while attempting to complete the writing of his ill-fated "boy who kills his mother" novel. Fitzgerald began to drink *before* writing as well as after and was soon drinking nearly all the time. Hemingway concluded correctly that his friend's creative impotence was due to his getting the booze mixed up with the writing process itself. But Hemingway believed that as long as he could keep his own writing separate from his drinking, he had nothing to worry about. Hemingway's use of Fitzgerald as an object lesson was, of course, similar to Fitzgerald's view of Ring Lardner in their Great Neck days.

As for Hemingway's health, he had the joyful evidence of his senses. Since he engaged regularly in strenuous physical exercise — boxing and tennis in Paris — he felt that his superb metabolism could easily burn up all the excess alcohol in his system as fast as he consumed it. He once wrote Maxwell Perkins:

> You can certainly get drunk on Port and it is bad afterwards too. Those famous 3 or 4 bottle men were living all the time in the open air — hunting, shooting, always on a horse. In that life as in skiing or fishing you can drink any amount.

The single but telling factor that he omits here is youth. Hemingway's sheer physicality spared him much of the withdrawal agonies suffered continually by Faulkner and Fitzgerald, who spent far less of their time in outdoor pursuits. Hemingway's condition permitted him to drink heavily every day well into his late forties before the alcohol began to produce any discernible damage to his body; he never had to endure the endless round of hospitals and drying-out establishments that became a regular part of life for the other two. Only in his last year or so was Hemingway forced to accept hospitalization. But it is important to note that while his body stood up far longer to these effects, his creativity began to suffer at very nearly the same age that his two great rivals began their decline.

Fiercely proud of his continuing ability to outdrink anyone, Hemingway had observed the drinking behavior of Duff Twysden and Pat Guthrie — whom he brilliantly re-created as Brett Ashley and Mike Campbell in the pages of *The Sun Also Rises** — noting that they appeared to think they drank so heavily because of inward pressures. The prime fact that they drank this way was due to their addiction to alcohol, but this was a piece of knowledge unknown to Hemingway and most others in

---

*He once referred to the book in later years: "I wrote, in six weeks, one book about a few drunks."

the 1920s or for the next forty years. Hemingway himself saw alcoholic drinking as a response to inner pressures, and it was for this reason that he soon took up his stance as an expert on "rummies." In a 1949 letter to Hotchner, Hemingway observed: "Drinking is fun; not a release from something. When it's a release from something, except the straight mechanical pressure we are all subjected to always, then I think you get to be a rummy."

In addition to overlooking his own all too powerful inward pressures, he failed to notice that whether you were drinking to release something or just drank for the fun of it made no difference in the long run; continued drinking resulted in alcoholism no matter what the drinker's motive might have been. Not realizing that alcohol is addictive, he did not know that the addict requires a constantly larger supply of the addictive substance in order to feel at peace. Finally, he remained ignorant of the fact that alcoholism breeds its own kind of pressure, that of alcoholic depression.

Their shared alcoholism was only one of the bonds that held together the genuine friendship of Scott Fitzgerald and Hemingway. It's obvious that Fitzgerald envied Hemingway's ability to write exceptionally while consuming each day great amounts of alcohol. Conversely, Hemingway noticed that Fitzgerald was paralyzed by a relatively small quantity. When Hemingway asked himself why this should be so, he explained it by those "inward forces" at work, mostly in the form of Zelda, whom Hemingway regarded as the primary source of all Scott's troubles. As Hemingway saw it, it was all a question of attitude — if you had the right attitude toward alcohol, you could drink all you wanted with impunity. If you didn't, you became like Fitzgerald, who, as the twenties advanced, became hopelessly bogged down in the novel he'd begun in 1926 and who started writing an endless series of commercial stories for *The Saturday Evening Post* in order to support himself in the style we've read so much about.

In those Paris years the day's drinking for Hemingway did not begin until his self-imposed quota of words had been achieved; keeping alcohol and writing apart seemed easy enough, and Hemingway appeared to have a special talent for drinking, despite occasional signs that all was not as benign as it might appear. In 1928 he suffered the first of his long series of self-inflicted accidents — the one involving his pulling the wrong chain in the hall toilet of his apartment, thereby bringing down the entire heavy glass skylight. The wound left a scar on his forehead that he carried for the rest of his life. Although there is no certainty what part, if any, alcohol played in this or the other freakish accidents to which he remained prone, he seems to have been drinking before virtually all of them.

Hemingway endured much inner turmoil in 1927 when he decided to leave Hadley for Pauline Pfeiffer. It was a decision that he obviously regretted over the years, as can be seen at the end of *A Moveable Feast* where he says of Hadley, "I wish I had died before I ever loved anyone but her." On the page following he tells us that "it wasn't until we were out of the mountains in late spring, back in Paris before the other thing started again." Pauline was that other thing, the woman he remained married to for over a decade and for whom he devised the name P.O.M. (Poor Old Mama) in *Green Hills of Africa*.

His writing flowered miraculously in the late twenties with a power comparable only to that of Faulkner at the same time. Besides *The Sun Also Rises* and *A Farewell to Arms,* Hemingway published a series of short stories that continue to command our admiration as do those of no other American writer of this period: "Big Two-Hearted River," "Cat in the Rain," "The Undefeated," "Hills Like White Elephants," and "In Another Country." The opening paragraph of the last of these may be taken as the kind of "magic" that he strove for in these non-commercial stories:

> In the fall the war was always there, but we did not go to it any more. It was cold in the fall in Milan and the dark came very early. Then the electric lights came on, and it was pleasant along

the streets looking in the windows. There was much game hanging outside the shops, and the snow powdered in the fur of the foxes and the wind blew their tails. The deer hung stiff and heavy and empty, and small birds blew in the wind and the wind turned their feathers. It was a cold fall and the wind came down from the mountains.

Hemingway described his magic in 1935 as the

kind of writing that can be done. How far prose can be carried if any one is serious enough and has luck. There is a fourth and a fifth dimension that can be gotten. . . . It is a prose that has never been written. But it can be written, without tricks and without cheating. With nothing that will go bad afterwards.

His "fourth and fifth dimension" simply indicates his great desire to achieve a lasting resonance, which he did by writing in these Paris years with an unmatched precision of detail combined with a stylistic beauty that made him the most influential writer in America, to which he returned pretty much for good in 1929. His apprenticeship was complete; he was the American "drinking writer" par excellence, the champion.

3

I am tempted never to publish another damned thing.
The swine aren't worth writing for. I swear to christ
they're not.
— Hemingway to Maxwell Perkins, June 13, 1933

No matter what time I go to sleep wake and hear the
clock strike either one or two then lie wide awake
and hear three, four and five. But since I have stopped
giving a good goddamn about anything in the past
. . . I just lie there and keep perfectly still and rest
through it and you seem to get almost as much repose
as though you slept.
— Hemingway to Scott Fitzgerald,
    December 21, 1935

IT'S BEEN NO SECRET since Hemingway's death that he was a
deeply troubled man, with a history of depression that dated
back to adolescence. Despite his disavowals, Hemingway endured many of those "inward pressures" that he so shrewdly
detected in others. Increasingly after about 1930, he started using alcohol for purposes other than merely "changing his ideas"
at the end of the day's work. He drank in the evenings partly to
fight the insomnia that plagued him more and more frequently,
as well as to quiet his anxieties about the reception of his new
work. He began to refer to alcohol as the "giant killer," unaware
that while large doses will induce sleep, it is often a sleep of short
duration that leaves the drinker wide awake at just those hours
that Hemingway mentioned to Fitzgerald.

As Hemingway's drinking increased, it served to exacerbate
his depressions, which worsened in the 1930s in his new home
in Key West. Although alcohol can provide momentary relief
from problems, the cumulative effect of heavy drinking inexorably produces new problems that require still more alcohol to

keep them at bay; in a sensibility like Hemingway's, the effect was like pouring gasoline on a smoldering fire. He became unpredictable in his rages. Two similar events, a week apart, would often produce entirely different reactions. His temper became easily roused; the storms against his lovers and friends were terrible to witness. His scorn for those he believed to be his literary enemies was unequaled in its ferocity. These attacks alternated with self-pitying accounts of his troubles.*

But these fits of irrational distemper were spaced out sufficiently to keep his deeper concerns hidden from those around him. Many of his old friends who visited him — John Dos Passos and Waldo Pierce among them — saw only the ebullient "Hem" of the Paris years, a man who remained unflaggingly enthusiastic about books and people, big-game hunting, deep-sea fishing and bullfighting. He had always been a tireless reader, but in Key West, without the distraction of literary people, he read enormously, with eight to ten books going at once, making him perhaps the best-read American novelist of this century. The owner of a library containing over nine thousand volumes, Hemingway read widely in a variety of fields and did not have to rely on translations to form his judgments about new French or Spanish writers. He subscribed to dozens of periodicals from New York, Paris, London and Madrid; the supply of printed matter reaching Key West — and later, Havana — was torrential.

---

*Over the decades a number of explanations have been offered for the origins of Hemingway's tortured psyche, ranging from Malcolm Cowley and Philip Young's "war wound trauma" thesis to Kenneth Lynn's recent one that views Hemingway as suffering a lifelong sexual hurt because his mother dressed his sister Marceline and him as girls one week and as boys the next during their first two years. According to Lynn, this is the reason why Hemingway was so sensitive about his masculinity and why his characters act the way they do; the "hurt" idea becomes the key to explain the nature of his art. Lynn's explanation is demeaning to both the man and his art. The Meyers and Lynn biographies suffer from a distinctly uncharitable view of their subject; they don't like Hemingway, and the feeling is visible on nearly every page.

Lorine Thompson, the wife of his friend Charles, said of Hemingway, "He wanted to know everything. Didn't make any difference what it was." He read military history, treatises on bullfighting, the latest Drieu La Rochelle and Céline novels from Paris, volumes on exploration and hunting lore, as well as all the novels and essays of Virginia Woolf. Like Faulkner, he was an avid reader of crime fiction; he possessed over fifty Simenon novels. His taste in modern literature was remarkably astute, and many of his judgments seem quite accurate fifty and sixty years later. Much of his reading was done late at night after his day of writing in the morning and deep-sea fishing in the afternoon, the kind of fishing that produced bone-aching weariness that nonetheless often left him wide awake at three and four in the morning. It was a rigorous style of living that few could match.

Despite the increased drinking and the insomnia, the quality of his work held up wonderfully well, just as did Faulkner's at this time. In the early 1930s Hemingway wrote a number of his best stories, which dealt with despair, suicide, near madness and a kind of existential dread — stories like "A Way You'll Never Be," "The Gambler, the Nun and the Radio" and, above all, "A Clean Well-Lighted Place," the one in which the old waiter asks a question that Hemingway may have asked himself:

> What did he fear? It was not fear or dread. It was a nothing and a man was nothing too. . . . He would lie in the bed and finally, with daylight, he would go to sleep. After all, he said to himself, it is probably only insomnia. Many must have it.

The story had few admirers in 1933 — James Joyce was an exception — and it was the critical community's refusal to see his best work for what it was that roused Hemingway's ire. This was particularly the case of the only full-scale book he published in the early thirties, his bullfighting treatise *Death in the Afternoon,* which he labored on for two years and which finally sold just about as well as Fitzgerald's *Tender Is the Night.* But there were good reasons for his critics to worry about the book: it is marred by a kind of special pleading addressed to his readers in which Hemingway begs them to accept the aesthetic value of the regular disembowelment of horses in the Spanish bullring. Aware that his readers would not accept too much of the *corrida* mystique, Hemingway attempted to liven up his text with one excellent story and lots of literary gossip, but the one indisputably first-rate portion of the book is its final chapter, a moving evocation of the Spanish landscape. Unlike Hemingway's previous work, there is a self-conscious quality to much of the book, as if he were anticipating what people might say about him:

> Why isn't there more dialogue? What we want in a book by this citizen is people talking; that is all he knows how to do and now he doesn't do it. The fellow is no philosopher, no savant, an incompetent zoologist, he drinks too much and cannot punctuate readily and now he has stopped writing dialogue.

His advance concern was well taken: the critics were savage and the reading public remained indifferent, a severe blow to a writer who had achieved a worldwide triumph with *A Farewell to Arms*.

4

[Hemingway's] . . . intimate feelings about Fitzgerald
seem to have been more kindly and respectful than
what has gotten into print then or since.
— Andrew Turnbull, 1967

[The critics] don't like [*Winner Take Nothing*]. But
Papa will make them like it.
— Hemingway to Maxwell Perkins, June 1933

ALCOHOLICS frequently display a strong interest in the severity
of the disease in their friends and acquaintances. It is not surprising then that Hemingway maintained his curiosity about
Fitzgerald's health in his letters to Perkins, especially about Fitzgerald's drinking and the effect on his work. Hemingway continued to believe that Fitzgerald's drinking was caused by his
destructive involvement with Zelda and her problems. (Hemingway had once written Perkins: "I think 90% of all [his] trouble
. . . comes from her," and Fitzgerald might be the "best writer
we've ever had . . . if he hadn't been married to some one that
would make him waste *Everything*.") Part of Hemingway's interest was motivated by genuine fondness for his friend, but
surely another portion arose from his fascination with what was
happening to a fellow writer insofar as it might be applicable to
himself, the Hemingway who couldn't sleep and who had discovered the special joys of the double frozen daiquiri, a drink
for which he built up an immense tolerance. Sometimes Hemingway put the question directly to Fitzgerald: "I hear that
you're not drinking and haven't been for months. Then that
you're on it. That your insides are on the bum etc. etc. Let me
know how you are and what you're doing, will you?"

Fitzgerald's decision in 1936 to publish the account of his
"crack-up" in the pages of *Esquire* angered Hemingway, who
thought that the airing in print of private feelings about oneself

was unseemly. He may also have been uneasily aware that his own depressions were far worse than Fitzgerald's, for 1935 and 1936 seem to mark a watershed in the transformation that came over Hemingway, what some have seen as a profound personality change. The new Hemingway was a man increasingly defensive about his daily consumption of alcohol, a man who became savagely angry over the critical reception of his latest work. He was fast becoming the "Papa" of the later years, the international celebrity photographed regularly at the docks in Key West after catching a record-breaking marlin, or on safaris, or at the front lines in the Madrid of the Spanish Civil War. His reputation as a dockside brawler began to grow rapidly.

In 1936 a young Russian critic, Ivan Kashkin, wrote an appreciation of Hemingway's work in the pages of *International Literature,* a Moscow journal published in English. Its subject wrote a long letter of thanks to Kashkin, which Hemingway concluded with a lengthy postscript that raised the point of his constant use of alcohol in so many of his novels and stories:

> Don't you drink? I notice you speak slightingly of the bottle. I have drunk since I was fifteen and few things have given me more pleasure. When you work hard all day with your head and know you must work again the next day what else can change your ideas and make them run on a different plane like whisky? When you are cold and wet what else can warm you? Before an attack who can say anything that gives you the momentary well being that rum does? I would as soon not eat at night as not to have red wine and water.

Alcohol can be all the things that Hemingway claims for it, but it seems likely that Kashkin had touched on a tender point — hence the note of special pleading that is clearly visible here.

In 1933 Hemingway was subjected to two kinds of attack, which he often tended to see as a single entity. A personal one came from Gertrude Stein, who, in her *Autobiography of Alice B. Toklas,* accused him of cowardice because of his critical onslaught against Sherwood Anderson. She did so by invoking characters from one of her victim's favorite novels, the raftsmen in *Huckleberry Finn,* who can rant and bluster but can't fight. She also implied that there was more to Hemingway than met the eye: "But what a story that of the real Hem, and one he should tell but alas he never will. After all, as he himself murmured, there is the career, the career."

Stein's attack was a double-barreled one for it struck at his most vulnerable areas: his physical courage and his literary abilities. In objective fact Hemingway *was* a brave man, but now he was ridiculed for being "yellow" in the pages of a best-selling book. Stein had also insisted that although Hemingway was known as a major innovator in American writing, he was only a poor imitator of her style and technique, which he hadn't mastered correctly. His prose was, moreover, "90% Rotarian." The aspersions about his originality he could deal with easily enough — anyone with intelligence could see the difference between them — but those concerning his manhood presented difficulties, since that was somehow bound up with his writing. Both Hemingway and Stein grew up in a culture that considered a strong interest in literature and the arts as something weak and unmanly, even effeminate. In her hints about "the real Hem" Stein was undoubtedly alluding to her former pupil's remarkable literary talent, which contained an uncommonly large share of what were then deemed feminine characteristics. It was a sensibility that could depict many delicate nuances of feeling with uncanny grace; the presence of such qualities in a male was suspect to her. The subject was one that Stein and Hemingway had discussed at length in the old happy days in Paris. Stein was a lesbian and had repeatedly defended her sexual identity to Hemingway while at the same time denouncing male homosexuality as something truly noxious. Hemingway chose to take her hints about his true nature ("the real Hem") as a direct impugning of his manhood — that is, he was really a homosexual.

Stein's attack had a lasting effect. It was from about this time that Hemingway began to escalate his all-out machismo, which would grow to become a monstrous parody of itself and resulted in a Hemingway who, by his own account, could outwrite, out-drink, outfight, outfish, outhunt and outfuck anyone on this planet. He began having his brawls and dockside fights with people such as the publisher Joseph Knapp and the poet Wallace Stevens, culminating in his famous wrestling match with Max Eastman in Max Perkins's office. Alcohol became a cause and effect of that machismo, making it easier for him to take chances and strike poses that the relatively sober Hemingway would have resisted in the 1920s. He had come a long way from sparring with Ezra Pound while discussing the art of poetry to these bloody confrontations on the docks and in the bars of Key West.

In due course he seemed to be saying, "If you attack my work, you attack me." The proposition was a fully reversible one; he linked Stein's attack with the barrage reviewers leveled against him in late 1933 when he published his collection of stories *Winner Take Nothing*. Hemingway's reply to the critical establishment was summarized in a letter to Max Perkins, in which he clearly united the two kinds of attacks:

> You see what they can't get over is (1) that I *am* a man (2) that I can beat the shit out of any of them (3) that I can write. The last hurts them the worst. But they don't like any of it. But Papa will make them like it.

The critics were mostly wrong about *Winner Take Nothing,* and Hemingway was fully justified in his outrage, but that rage became habitual against reviewers who did not praise him sufficiently. The situation repeated itself in 1935 when his safari book, *Green Hills of Africa,* took a drubbing from nearly all the reviewers. He wrote to John Dos Passos about his feelings:

> If nobody can tell when a book is good why the hell write them? If anybody would take on my dependents — aw well what the hell. You can be goddamned sure nobody would. I would like to take the tommy gun and open up at 21 or in the N.R. [*New Republic*] offices or any place you name and give shitdom a few martyrs and include myself.

Fitzgerald had not cared for the safari book and had dared to tell its author, but Hemingway was far more temperate in his letter to him:

> Was delighted from the letter to see you don't know any more about when a book is a good book or what makes a book bad than ever. . . . You know you are like a brilliant mathematician who loves mathematics truly and always gets the wrong answers. . . . Of course you're like a hell of a lot of other things too but what the hell. Also you are like nobody but yourself and in spite of the fact that you think when you meet an old friend that you have to get stinking drunk and do every possible thing to humiliate yourself and your friend your friends are still fond of you. I'm damned fond of you.

By offering Fitzgerald this jocular form of disagreement, Hemingway demonstrated his restraint, a trait that he was rapidly losing in dealing with people and situations he felt were hostile to him. Besides expressing his continuing affection for Fitzgerald, it is apparent that Hemingway uneasily regarded his friend's alcoholism as perhaps something *within his control,* that Fitzgerald had deliberately become drunk at their most recent meeting in New York in early 1933 when Hemingway and Edmund Wilson were forced to deal with an abusive Fitzgerald who reviled them before passing out on the floor of the restaurant. Recalling that disaster only served to reinforce Hemingway's belief that he wasn't like that, for *he* knew how to control his drinking. He wouldn't have attributed his growing combativeness and megalomania to liquor, but it is significant that his writing at this time contains ever-increasing references to alcohol. In *Green Hills of Africa,* Kandinsky, the Austrian, tells Hemingway that he can't understand his interest in drinking: "That has always seemed silly to me. I understand it as a weakness." Hemingway's reply was not far from the one he offered Kashkin: "It is a way of ending a day. It has great benefits. Don't you ever want to change your ideas?"

Hemingway remained confident that alcohol presented no

real problem for him. His work was seemingly unimpaired, and in the summer of 1936, when he was thirty-seven, he published two of his best stories, "The Short Happy Life of Francis Macomber" and "The Snows of Kilimanjaro," but they would be the last he would complete for a long time. He was soon off to the wars again, the Madrid of the Spanish Civil War in early 1937, accompanied by the new woman in his life, Martha Gellhorn, who could write and was several years younger than any of his previous loves. She even dared to talk back to him and had no compunction about telling him when he'd had too much to drink.

5

> . . . trouble was all my life when things were really bad I could take a drink and right away they were much better.
> — Hemingway to Archibald MacLeish,
>   December 1943

> . . . will have to take Marty to the movies as a present for being drunk Saturday night. . . . Started out on absinthe, drank a bottle of good red wine with dinner, shifted to vodka in town . . . and then battened it down with whiskys and sodas until 3 a.m. Feel good today. But not like working.
> — Hemingway to Maxwell Perkins, February 1940

THE DANGER-LOVING photographer Robert Capa took a number of pictures of Hemingway when he was a North American Newspaper Alliance correspondent in Spain. One of these, snapped in Barcelona in May of 1937, shows Hemingway painstakingly decanting liquor into a hot-water bottle. He was making sure there would be no dry spells on his visits to the front lines or between shell bursts. The hot-water bottle was eventually supplanted by a military canteen, and Hemingway began to acquire the reputation of a man always ready to offer you a drink and almost never known to refuse one. The Capa picture can be taken as emblematic.

After his second visit to Spain that fall, he began to suffer the first telling effect of his increased drinking when he was felled by a sudden liver attack in Paris en route home; the assault required the specific drugs recommended for combating incipient cirrhosis. The French doctor forced Hemingway to stop all alcohol for a period that seems to have been short, a few weeks at best. He appears not to have had any strong withdrawal symptoms, or if he did, he kept them to himself. This first indication of a physical decline was accompanied by a creative one of major proportions.

Hemingway regarded himself primarily as a novelist — he later liked to think of himself as defending the title — but by 1936 seven years had passed since he'd written a new one. In that time much of his energy had been channeled into the nonfiction books he'd published about the Spanish bullring and his African safari of 1933. Both were marred by formlessness; passages of considerable beauty were followed by numbing accounts of many things that only their author found absorbing. By and large, the prose of the two books ranges from superb to boringly long-winded. But Hemingway prided himself on his abilities as a writer of fiction, and it is in the pages of the novel he published in late 1937 that we can see what had happened to his style.

To Have and Have Not is the only one of his novels to be set almost entirely in America; the book reflects the time of the Great Depression and in particular the place where Hemingway had made his home since 1929. Key West was an economic disaster area in the 1930s, a place where the prevailing wage scale was actually lower than that paid out by Washington in the form of relief. The local taxes could not be collected, and the schools

were often closed. Many Key Westers made their living by vio-
lating the Volstead Act and bringing in liquor to the Keys from
Cuba; after the repeal of Prohibition in 1933 some turned to
smuggling alien Chinese from Cuba to the Florida coast.

Hemingway had created a man he called Harry Morgan and
wrote two excellent stories about him in 1934 and 1936. Morgan is a "conch" who makes a precarious living by performing
the illegal acts described above in addition to allowing his boat
to be chartered by wealthy Americans from the mainland; he is
the man Humphrey Bogart portrayed in the 1944 film version
of the book. After considerable indecision, Hemingway produced his new novel by using the two Morgan stories as the
foundation for a book that would have "social significance," one
that would contrast the wealthy "haves," who sleep uneasily on
their yachts in the harbor, with the poor but noble conches, who
live from moment to moment fighting the threat of starvation.

Structurally weak, *To Have and Have Not* is a sentimental
story that very much smacks of the social realism that was so
trendy at the time. But perhaps the saddest thing about the book
is the clear sign of the deterioration of Hemingway's prose: there
is a marked difference between the superb opening chapters (the
earlier magazine material) and the remaining two thirds of the
novel. The satiric later chapters tell us banal things about the
evils of American capitalism versus the innate nobility of "the
people." This final social-message section was written in a
matching banal style, as evidenced by a passage concerning the
night thoughts of a wealthy grain broker:

> It would be enough for him to think about how much it would
> be better if he had not been quite so smart five years ago, and in
> a little while, at his age, the wish to change what can no longer
> be undone, will open up the gap that will let worry in. Only
> suckers worry.

At thirty-eight Hemingway has lost his extraordinary capacity
to render experience in a language that remains fresh, that can
be "written, without tricks and without cheating. With nothing

that will go bad afterwards." From this point on it does go bad; Hemingway's once exceptional command of language can be seen only fitfully. Although he had twenty-four years of life ahead, he published only three books in that time, each either flawed in design or weakened by a prose that increasingly tended to be on the edge of self-parody.

After his third and last visit to the Spanish front, Hemingway came home — first to Key West and Pauline and then to Havana with Martha Gellhorn — to write the book that occupied him for seventeen months and made him a world figure. No serious work of fiction in this century made as strong an initial impression on the reading public as *For Whom the Bell Tolls*. It was the book that everyone read and almost everyone liked, highbrows and lowbrows alike. In America alone it sold 800,000 copies in its first two years, a figure surpassed only by *Gone with the Wind*. In order to write it, Hemingway placed himself "back in training" by cutting back on the constant round of drinking he had practiced in Spain. He still adhered to his policy of not drinking before or during the time when he wrote, but the daily amounts he consumed had increased. He boasted to Charles Scribner that he "had not drawn an even semisober breath" once he'd returned the corrected galleys to Perkins.

Both Hemingway and Fitzgerald were uncannily aware of the strengths and weaknesses of each other's work. When Hemingway sent an advance copy of his book to Hollywood, Fitzgerald thanked him in a perceptive letter praising specific sections of the novel: "The massacre was magnificent and also the fight on the mountain and the actual dynamiting scene." But he was far more truthful with Zelda when he told her that it "is not as good as the *Farewell to Arms*. It doesn't seem to have the tensity or the freshness nor has it the inspired poetic moments." In his letter to Hemingway, Fitzgerald was referring to Pilar's extraordinary narration of the mass killing of the Fascists in her village as well as to the superb account of El Sordo's defensive action on the hilltop. He had correctly identified these scenes as the high points of a novel that suffers from a variety of ills, not the least of which is its language. Many of the characters speak in a kind of English never spoken on this planet. Hemingway had two chief goals in creating this language, the first being an attempt to suggest the feeling of Spanish in English and the second an effort to circumvent the then current statutes concerning the use of four-letter words. Rendering the speech patterns of one language through another probably cannot be done; Hemingway's clear failure here results in a kind of quaintness that approaches the grotesque, as when Pilar berates the gypsy Rafael: "You lazy drunken obscene unsayable son of an unnameable unmarried gypsy obscenity." Much of this dialogue now seems coy and labored; it is dismaying to encounter an endless series of variations on "I obscenity in the milk of thy mother." Coy also are the once famous sex scenes between Maria and Jordan in which "the earth moves," scenes that cried out to become targets of satire.

But what little dissension there was concerning *For Whom the Bell Tolls* arose not so much on literary grounds but rather about the book's politics. Many left-wingers felt that Hemingway had sold out the cause of the Spanish Republic and them by portraying characters loyal to its government yet capable of the massacre that Pilar so powerfully describes. On the whole the attacks were insignificant, and the book was the most highly praised American novel of the century. After a decade in which he had produced four books that drew extremely mixed receptions, he finally emerged as the foremost novelist of his generation, a writer who was admired by both the leading critics and the reading public — a situation rare in American writing.

Alcoholism is characterized as a disease of denial, and this may explain in part Hemingway's concern about being regarded as a "rummy." Despite his smashing victory over his detractors, he displayed an increasingly combative attitude toward anyone who attacked his work but also those who hinted that alcohol might be a factor in his alleged decline. Because of his status as Scribners' number one author, Hemingway was able to block their publication of Edmund Wilson's essay on his work, "Hemingway: Gauge of Morale." The long study did not appear in book form until the following year, and then under the imprint of Houghton Mifflin, after Hemingway had sought in vain to obtain an injunction against it. Wilson was the first American critic to review Hemingway's early work, and his opening pages demonstrated just how good it had been, but then he came down hard on the nonfiction books and *To Have and Have Not,* pointing out that the author of these works had become "a public personality . . . a legend . . . [who had become] arrogant, belligerent and boastful." Wilson accused this later Hemingway of engaging in "what seems to be a deliberate self-drugging." In a passage concerning Hemingway's play *The Fifth Column,* Wilson returned to this theme, linking the hero of that work with his creator:

> The drugging process has been carried further still: the hero, who has become finally indistinguishable from the false or publicity Hemingway, has here dosed himself not only with whiskey, but with a seductive and desirous woman.

It is easy to see why Hemingway felt that Wilson was coming awfully close to making a direct connection between alcohol and the falling off in quality of his later works, especially when he feared "that Hemingway will never sober up."

Wilson's attack hurt Hemingway in an extraordinarily vulnerable area: his ever-growing dependence on alcohol, which was accompanied by his fierce determination to defend its use. While he was completing *For Whom the Bell Tolls,* alcohol had been very much in his mind, as when Jordan delivers an astonishing encomium to the power of absinthe:

> One cup of it took the place of the evening papers, of all the old evenings in cafés, of all chestnut trees that would be in bloom now in this month, of the great slow horses of the outer boulevards, of book shops, of kiosques, and of galleries, of the Parc Mountsouris, of the Stade Buffalo, and of the Butte Chaumont . . . and of being able to read and relax in the evening;

of all the things he had enjoyed and forgotten and that came back to him when he tasted that opaque, bitter, tongue-numbing, brain-warming, stomach-warming, idea-changing liquid alchemy.

Here Hemingway, virtually indistinguishable from Jordan in many of the book's pages, views alcohol as the handmaiden of memory. Since memory was an indispensable ingredient in his writing, it is not surprising that he began to drink more compulsively than ever, especially those double frozen daiquiris at the Floridita bar in Havana; he set the house record for the number of these consumed in a single drinking session.

6

I never had so damned much time to think in my life, especially nights on the water and here when I can't sleep from haveing lost the habit.
— Hemingway to Hadley Mowrer,
November 25, 1943

Maybe I need to hear a lot of things from you to straighten me out . . . but there are a lot of things that don't taste good any more that used to taste all right.
— Hemingway to Archibald MacLeish,
c. May 5, 1943

ALCOHOLISM WAS only one of Hemingway's problems. He differs from the other writers discussed in this book in that he is the only one who also suffered from the effects of the clinical depression that led to his suicide in 1961. This depression, undoubtedly familial in origin, was unusually severe and frequently fatal for the Hemingways. The evidence suggests that although Hemingway is not known to have had a genetic vulnerability to alcohol, he surely inherited one for depression, the kind that caused his father's suicide in 1928. Two of Hemingway's sisters and his only brother took their own lives. The continuing strength of this factor is demonstrated by the instability of Hemingway's children: two of his three sons required hospitalization for emotional problems and received shock treatment as part of their therapy; their illness was similar to their father's.

Apparently, Hemingway believed he could keep the personal demons of his depression at bay with alcohol. (His Anselmo, in *For Whom the Bell Tolls,* says of whiskey: "*That* is what kills the worm that haunts us.") He did not know that alcoholism breeds its own kind of depression that can be relieved only by still more alcohol, exacerbating the problem. The result is a life held together by liquor; sobriety becomes an intolerable burden. It has been observed that "alcoholism has a life of its own," and clearly Hemingway's physical addiction grew steadily while he continued to manifest two of the chief signs of the disease: extreme denial and a huge tolerance.

His enormous worldwide fame, especially after the sale of *For Whom the Bell Tolls* to Paramount, introduced Hemingway to a variety of people from the film and mass-magazine world, people who would become regular visitors to his *finca* in Havana. He was now a major commercial "property." His prophecy to Fitzgerald in Paris that one day the wheel would turn full circle had been fulfilled; Papa *had* made them like it very much. He began to ask people his famous question "How do you like it now, gentlemen?" on any and all occasions, perhaps with that wheel still in mind. But in 1941 he wasn't writing anything that could be sold, preferring to take an extended trip to war-torn China to celebrate his marriage to Martha Gellhorn. When they returned to Cuba, he embraced a regular life there that Martha deemed boringly hedonistic and nonproductive — a life of sailing, deep-sea fishing, endless talk and lots of frozen daiquiris. She jokingly called him "the pig" and "the beast" because of his slovenly ways but he refused to change. By the end of 1943 he appeared to be neither the writer nor the man of action she had known in Spain in 1937. Martha finally left Cuba in order to be in England for the anticipated 1944 invasions, and it may have been her departure and the loneliness it caused that goaded him into taking on an assignment to cover the fighting fronts in Europe for *Collier's*, first the RAF's role in the invasion and later the breakthrough into Germany in early 1945.

Correspondents usually find little difficulty in obtaining all they can drink at military command posts, and Hemingway was no exception. In England and then in France the drinks never stopped, so much so that he began having restorative morning drinks, usually champagne. In nearly all the accounts of his military exploits with the American forces in France and Germany he appears to have been completely sober on few occasions, returning to his old Spanish custom of wearing canteens filled with gin and vermouth for instant martinis. His role as correspondent rekindled his love for all things military. In his talk, his letters and later in his fiction, he began to use military terms whenever possible, believing them to be the clearest way of expressing himself.

When he returned home to his *finca* in April 1945, he was plagued by the aftereffects of two brain concussions experienced in his year overseas. He suffered blinding headaches, and his insomnia was back in full force along with sharply impaired vision. The state of his health made him resolve to achieve a "90% reduction in his drinking." Part of his desire arose from wishing to please Mary Welsh, with whom he was now in love but who had worried about his drinking in London and Paris. The Hemingway she married in March of 1946 did not appear to have changed his drinking pattern.

Hemingway alone of the writers examined here innocently believed that it was perfectly safe to continue drinking. Unlike these others, his constitution was strong enough to stave off the morning shakes and D.T.'s suffered by Faulkner and Fitzgerald. There were many mornings when Hemingway awoke with what he called his "mastodon hangovers," but they did not plunge him into cycles of nonstop drinking, the common cure for hangovers of many alcoholics. He adhered to his severe regimen of "boiling it out" by constant exercise. Nevertheless, his decline as a writer is clear, and a great share in it must surely be attributed to alcohol, which is notorious for dissolving a writer's capacity to make the finer distinctions that the creation of a work of art requires. In the later Hemingway, there is often a heavy-handed approach to people and situations that contrasts sharply with the infinite grace and delicate tension of the earlier work. He became a writer of novels about people we don't care much about and whose activities bore us, often related in a prose that would have embarrassed the man who had written *The Sun Also Rises*.

His "90% solution" appears to have been a vain hope, although he surely had to endure some reduction of his drinking in order to reactivate his writing, which had been in virtual suspension for nearly six years. But alcoholics discover that they have immense difficulty in containing their drinking by the imposition of an arbitrary regimen; despite all their resolve to cut back, they rapidly return to the amount they find comfortable, their maintenance level, which is always increasing.

When he told interviewers in the late 1940s that he had gone beyond arithmetic into calculus in his new writing, Hemingway was probably referring to the extremely long novel that he began early in 1946 and on which he continued to work for most of that year. After abandoning it for a decade, he returned to it for extensive revisions and additions, completing his work on a manuscript of 1,200 pages at the end of 1958. This was *The Garden of Eden*, the book that caused something of a publishing scandal for Scribners (more properly Macmillan, which now owns the firm) because of the extraordinary "editing," which reduced Hemingway's manuscript by approximately 70 percent. This evisceration resulted in the complete disappearance of the young couple based to some degree on Scott and Zelda Fitzgerald, Nick and Barbara Sheldon, whose sexual games are contrasted with those of the two major figures, Catharine and David Bourne. Gone also is Andy (based on John Dos Passos), who serves to bring the various characters together. But far more importantly, as Barbara Probst Solomon has pointed out in her *New Republic* article "Where's Papa?," the underlying structure based on the idea of metamorphosis is now completely lost, and what the reader of the published version is faced with is the frenzied activity of two young people exchanging their sexual identities for no apparent reason. But in Hemingway's original text both Catharine and David refer specifically to the influence on them of Rodin's sculpture that bears the name of Ovid's great work. It is Catharine's shock at seeing the statue in the Prado in Madrid that sets the book's machinery in motion.

A reading of the complete manuscript at the JFK Library in Boston confirms that Solomon is correct when she claims that the unedited version supplies a far richer reading experience than the published text and demonstrates that Hemingway was still capable, at forty-seven, of describing locales with unmatched power. But there is a curiously lifeless quality to the characters in this work, who think mostly about their physical appearance. Hemingway seems trapped in a morass of the pathological or bizarre; one can read for hours as the characters endlessly discuss the quality of their suntans or the configurations of their hair styles. The whole world outside is in total suspension. There are lengthy descriptions of what the characters think they'd like to drink, how these drinks are prepared and savored. The effect can be oddly hypnotic, for there is enough of Hemingway's great talent to make us want to know what comes next. Suddenly, from out of all the chatter, someone will speak out with some of the power of the younger Hemingway. His ability to evoke landscapes remained as strong as ever.

Working against the combined effects of his depression and alcoholism, it is astonishing that Hemingway would attempt to write a novel as daringly different as *The Garden of Eden*. It is a tribute to his courage as a writer that he would make the effort in such unfamiliar territory for him, and saddening that he failed. As to why he stopped work on the book in early 1947, we know that he told Robert Cantwell in 1950 that he had completed a 165,000-word novel that was "too hot to handle." If this seems a doubtful reason, one must recall that Mary Mc-Carthy stopped writing *The Group* after its opening chapters because she was assured that no publisher in New York would issue such a work. This was in the mid-1950s, and she did not resume writing it until the early sixties, when there was a more relaxed attitude in publishing toward the treatment of sex in books. Another reason may have been that Hemingway just wasn't sure what to do with his two couples and their obsessions. His "provisional ending" leaves much in the dark.

Undaunted (as he might have said), Hemingway began another long book, which he often referred to as his "sea novel." It was to be an attempt to weld a series of episodes based on his own life in Cuba as well as his summers in Bimini back in the 1930s when he had been the father of three growing boys. Most of the material from the working manuscript was posthumously published in 1970 as *Islands in the Stream,* a work in search of a coherent center and in which Hemingway is indistinguishable from his hero Thomas Hudson, who is nevertheless identified as a painter.

Even with all the Scribners editing that sought to eliminate the duller sections, we are left with a three-part work that often seems tedious despite some occasionally brilliant scenes, as when in the Bimini narrative Hudson saves his middle boy from the jaws of a shark. The second and longest episode takes place all in one afternoon at the Hotel Floridita bar in Havana, where Hudson meets a wide assortment of friends and drinks uncountable frozen daiquiris, by now his favorite drink and to which he pays tribute:

> He had drunk double frozen daiquiris, the great ones that Constante made, that had no taste of alcohol and felt, as you drank them, the way downhill glacier skiing feels running through powder snow and, after the sixth and eighth, felt like downhill glacier skiing feels when you are running unroped.

The third and last part of this just barely held together collection of narratives is a "sea chase" adventure yarn about Hudson's pursuit with his friends of some fleeing Germans who have survived the wreck of their submarine.

Despite some occasionally superb pages, *Islands in the Stream* nevertheless remains mysteriously out of focus. The exchange of sexual identities was still preoccupying him, as can be seen in a dream sequence in which Hudson is about to make love to his wife:

> Then it was all the way it should be and she said, "Should I be you or you be me?"
>
> "You have first choice."
>
> "I'll be you."
>
> "I can't be you. But I can try."
>
> "It's fun. You try it. Don't try to save yourself at all. Try to love everything and take everything too."
>
> "All right."
>
> "Are you doing it?"
>
> "Yes," she said. "It's wonderful."

Alcohol is ever present in this novel; nearly all the characters consume vast streams of it. In the Havana section, Hudson berates a drunk called Revello at the bar:

> You're never sober either. . . . You start to drink in that little bar by the house and by the time you come here for the first one of the day you're potted. . . . What time of day did you take your first drink this morning and how many have you had before this first one? Don't you cast the first stone at any rummies. It's not rummies, he thought. I don't mind him being a rummy. It's just that he is such a damned bore.

Although Hudson questions Revello's morning drink, he sees nothing out of the ordinary in the Scotch he himself has had for breakfast. Evidently, Hemingway wished as much as ever to put distance between himself and the world of "rummies," a theme that became stronger in his letters and is a familiar trait among alcoholics: complete fascination with what others drink, accompanied by complete blindness to one's own intake.

The sea novel was also put aside for reasons we can only surmise, but he was probably aware that too much of the material remained impenetrable. Since Thomas Hudson and his creator are much the same, it is not surprising that Hemingway does not tell us why Hudson is such a troubled man: Hemingway just doesn't know. It was not until 1949 that he began to write the first book he cared to publish since 1940, a novel that started off as a short story about duck shooting in Italy.

It is noteworthy that the quality of the writing in the book he offered the public in 1950 was distinctly lower than in *The Garden of Eden* and *Islands in the Stream,* as is nearly everything else about it. The eagerly awaited *Across the River and into the Trees* is almost universally regarded as his weakest attempt at fiction, a novel about still another man who can be recognized as having no aesthetic distance from its author. Colonel Cantwell is Hemingway with all the seething wrath he felt about many things that year. His heroine Renata is as vacuous in the book as was perhaps her prototype, Adriana Ivanich, the young woman he'd met in Venice and with whom he fell in love. One of the few pleasing aspects of the book is the portrayal of the landscapes.

The characters in *The Sun Also Rises* were heavy drinkers, especially Brett and Jake, but they appear abstemious compared with Cantwell, to whom Hemingway has attributed his own vast capacity. He tells us about each and every drink the colonel consumes, starting with his arrival in Venice in the late afternoon.

Cantwell begins with a gin and Campari before moving on to the bar at the Gritti Palace Hotel, where he drinks three very dry double martinis. When he leaves the bar for his room, his waiter gratuitously serves him a gin and Campari, which the Colonel regards as "an unwanted drink," but he finishes it nevertheless, as he tells himself that "it is bad for him." It's then time to meet Renata at Harry's New York Bar, where he lowers three Montgomerys, explaining to her that they are extra-dry martinis made with a ratio of fifteen parts gin to one of vermouth. Now the couple return to the Gritti Palace to order their dinner and the wines to drink with it. They begin with a bottle of Capri Bianco, proceed to two bottles of Valpolicella, followed by a bottle of champagne, Roederer *brut* '42. They like the Roederer well enough to order another bottle but have to settle for Perrier-Jouet, which brings their meal to a close.

When they leave the hotel for their lovemaking in the gondola, they take along another bottle of the Valpolicella. At the end of his evening, the Colonel has a nightcap from still another bottle of Valpolicella, which the waiter has thoughtfully left in his room. Over a period of six or seven hours Cantwell has consumed between twenty-four and twenty-eight ounces of alcohol in the gin drinks and a dozen or so in the various wines. It all adds up to more than a quart, which would render most of us insensible. Although the Colonel is described as terminally ill with a cardiac condition, he is nevertheless capable of performing the sexual act in the gondola with Renata at least twice and arising the next morning "at first light" with no aftereffects.

There is something of "cloud cuckoo land" in the ritualistic manner the characters muse over the name-brand drinks they order, but Hemingway was seemingly oblivious to reality here because this was the way *he* then drank in order to maintain himself comfortably in daily existence; *as he saw it, he was clearly portraying the reality he knew.* It is this departure from the everyday world that indicates what is so wrong about *Across the River.* Since Hemingway has plainly lost his ability to create living characters, the Colonel and his young lady really have nothing to communicate to each other except to bandy inane remarks about the quality of the food and drink they are served:

"Is the steak good?" the Colonel asked.
"It's wonderful. How are your scaloppine?"
"Very tender and the sauce is not at all sweet."
"Do you like the vegetables?"
"The cauliflower is almost crisp; like celery."
"We should have some celery. But I don't think there is any or the *Gran Maestro* would have brought it."
"Don't we have fun with food?"

Only fourteen years separates the Hemingway of "In Another Country," who once spoke of the fourth and fifth dimensions of prose, from the writer who filled his pages with this mindless chatter.

7

> Wine I never thought they could take away from you. But they can.
> — Hemingway to Archibald MacLeish, June 28, 1957

> When I read Faulkner I can tell exactly when he gets tired and does it on corn just as I used to be able to tell when Scott would hit it beginning with Tender Is The Night.
> — Hemingway to Harvey Breit, June 29, 1952

WHEN HEMINGWAY ARRIVED in New York late in 1949 to deliver the manuscript of *Across the River* to Scribners, Lillian Ross met the Hemingways at the airport and scrupulously recorded nearly every word he spoke in her presence for the next two days. The result was her celebrated essay for *The New Yorker*, "Portrait of Hemingway." Ross took note that Hemingway was not willing to enter a cab into the city until he had lowered three double bourbons at the airport bar. Once he reached the Sherry-Netherland Hotel, he ordered champagne for all and was still drinking it when Ross left for dinner. The next morning Hemingway called her over for a longish talk during which he continued to work on the room's supply of champagne, switching over to Tavel (a rosé wine) when lunch was served in the room. The following day included a visit to the Metropolitan Museum of Art, during the course of which Hemingway drank regularly from a silver pocket flask that contained what he needed to get him through the morning until lunch. At fifty Hemingway had unquestionably become that which he had always scorned: a rummy, or a man who cannot go without a maintenance drink for more than an hour or so without extreme discomfort. As his son Patrick remarked, the moment his father was deprived of alcohol he became badly depressed; he now required at least a quart per day.

Conforming to the adage that you cannot underestimate the taste of the American public, *Across the River and into the Trees* sold extremely well despite a critical reception that was mostly hostile. His next book, coming just two years later, was *The Old Man and the Sea,* which succeeded in winning him the Nobel Prize. Telling people that the novella is a trite, sentimental tale often produces an effect similar to informing children that there is no Santa Claus and that they will get no Christmas presents. It is a self-conscious work brimming over with Christ and crucifixion symbols; it is fatally marred by its whimsical, folksy talk about the Indians of Cleveland and the Great DiMaggio. Hemingway had set down a far superior tale about indomitability in "The Undefeated" in 1927, a story written without sentimentality but with the care of a writer in perfect control of his material. What should be hard and taut about *The Old Man and the Sea* is instead soft and self-indulgent.

Nevertheless, the little book took the world by storm and has become a fixture in the curriculum of American schools because it is short and contains "symbols" that the teacher can unveil for the student; it is currently the American student's major contact with Hemingway. The fantastic triumph of the book included its being hailed by people of taste such as Bernard Berenson and Cyril Connolly, who compared it to Flaubert's "A Simple Heart." This sudden swing in opinion about his work made his oft-repeated question "How do you like it now, gentlemen?" take on new meaning.

Like nearly all of Faulkner's later work, *The Old Man and the Sea* is based directly on observations from the distant past: Hemingway had written an embryonic version of his tale about Santiago and his giant marlin for the pages of *Esquire* in 1936.

"Invention from knowledge," as he liked to call his method of writing, was his uncanny ability to create situations, places and people entirely from what he had seen. But that talent was now in abeyance, and the occasionally self-parodic image of Papa Hemingway was in full command. By the time *Across the River* and *The Old Man and the Sea* had appeared, Hemingway had lost the "magic," the thing he justly praised in the best of Fitzgerald and Faulkner. By the early 1950s his writing had become as marred as Faulkner's was at this time. In the midst of a book in which he had invested a great deal of emotional capital, he indulged in literary vendettas against people like Sinclair Lewis, whom he pilloried in *Across the River*. There was now a kind of boozy sentimentality running through his work, visible on many of the pages of *The Old Man and the Sea*. It is fair to say that with a single magnificent exception to come, everything he published after 1940 partakes of this increasingly prosaic quality.

There was one area in which he did not lose his touch: his ability to render landscapes, the look and feel of places, is very nearly as powerful in the Bimini passages of *Islands in the Stream* and in the opening pages of the published version of *Garden of Eden* as in the final chapter of *Death in the Afternoon*. Why should this be so? Since landscapes are intrinsically "passive," Hemingway could still employ the tools he had mastered in Paris in the twenties; the earth doesn't talk back to you. But creating characters and breathing life into them on paper requires being sharply in touch with the people around you, a talent that the pontifical, "dozen daiquiris in a single afternoon" Hemingway had lost. His sensibilities had become progressively dulled, though not in the way he had anticipated back in 1938:

> In going where you have to go, and doing what you have to do, and seeing what you have to see, you dull and blunt the instrument you write with. But I would rather have it bent and dulled and know I had to put it on the grindstone again and hammer it into shape and put a whetstone to it, and know that I had something to write about.

By 1953 no whetstone on earth seemed likely to resharpen that instrument.

Starting in the late 1940s his physical health began to decline sharply, partly owing to the aftereffects of the brain concussions he had received in Europe but perhaps much more damagingly to the vast amounts of food and drink he had consumed. Besides defective vision and a constant ringing in his ears, his weight soared to 256 pounds, leaving him at least 50 pounds overweight; this problem was compounded by blood pressure readings of 225/125,* a combination that even he called lethal.

For the next decade he forced himself to follow dietary regimens in order to control his intake, but only with short-term results. Nine years later, in 1956, his blood pressure was 215/105. By then the medical profession knew the implications of a high cholesterol level: that year his stood at 380, a fearsome one when considered in conjunction with the high blood pressure.

Besides his health worries and concern about his new work, some words of William Faulkner succeeded in stirring up Hemingway's growing irascibility. He had a strong interest in Faulkner as a writer noted for both his brilliant prose and his legendary drinking. He had been reading the work of the man he liked to call "old corn drinking mellifluous" ever since *Soldier's Pay* in 1926 and had all the major books in his library, with the curious exception of *The Sound and the Fury*. In 1944 he told Jean-Paul Sartre in Paris that Faulkner was "a better writer than I am," a judgment that was carried back home to Malcolm Cowley and that ultimately had much to do with his decision to edit *The Portable Faulkner* in 1946. While Cowley was assembling the book, Hemingway wrote him:

> [Faulkner] has the most talent of anybody and he just needs a sort of conscience that isn't there. . . . He will write absolutely perfectly straight and then go on and on and not be able to end it. I wish the christ I owned him like you'd own a horse and train him like a horse and race him like a horse — only in writing.

---

*Moderate drinkers often experience lowered blood pressure, but it is not uncommon for alcoholics to display vastly elevated levels. Normal readings for a man Hemingway's age range from 130 to 140 over 80 to 90.

Cowley had told Hemingway about Faulkner's unhappiness in having to continue working in Hollywood; Hemingway commiserated, concluding his letter with "How beautifully he can write and as simple and as complicated as autumn or as spring. I'll try and write him and cheer him up."

If blame must be attached to the quarrel between them, it falls on Faulkner. Desperate for money, he had agreed in the summer of 1947 to give a series of informal talks to the students at the University of Mississippi and while there made a series of ratings concerning the "courage" of his writing contemporaries. He ranked Thomas Wolfe first, who failed but tried so much, and Hemingway last of all, because he just stuck to what he knew best and refused to experiment. The Associated Press picked up the story, and Hemingway, whose prose style, while simple enough on the surface, was revolutionary in its impact on nearly all the best writing of his time, saw his stature as a writer and as a man being demeaned. Since his physical courage had only once before been challenged, and then by Gertrude Stein, Hemingway was irate enough to foolishly ask his wartime friend Colonel Buck Lanham to write what amounted to a testimonial in a letter to Faulkner about Hemingway's bravery under fire in the Hürtgen Forest.

Faulkner had meant no real harm, later telling Harvey Breit, his friend on the *New York Times Book Review,* that "[Hemingway] . . . did it fine, but he didn't try for the impossible." Abashed at the consequences of his act, Faulkner wrote apologies to both Lanham and Hemingway, to which Hemingway responded with a long "apologies accepted" letter in which he praised Faulkner's work:

> You are a better writer than Fielding or any of those guys and you should just know it and keep on writing. You have things written that come back to me better than any of them and I am not dopy, really.

Hemingway in Madrid, about 1956

"I am your Bro.," he concluded, "if you want one that writes. . . . Have much regard for you."

Hemingway was actually answering Faulkner's second and far more deeply felt apology, which he sent on the twenty-fourth of June:

> But what I wish most is I'd never said it at all, or that I could forget having done so, which perhaps I could and would if it had not been about a first rate man. . . . The bloke I'm still eating shit to is Faulkner.

But Faulkner never engaged in literary correspondence, and nothing came of Hemingway's offer. Their 1947 problem might have remained settled had it not been for two events that further angered Hemingway. The first was the decline of Faulkner's writing after 1948. Hemingway wrote Harvey Breit of his distaste for the prose in "The Jail," a section of *Requiem for a Nun* that had appeared in *Partisan Review:* "an abortion of all grammar. . . . It must be nice to have received the Nobel Prize and then to write any sort of shit and be treated respectfully." He informed Malcolm Cowley that Nelson Algren was probably the best writer under fifty and that he "has everything that the fading Faulkner ever had except the talent for magic."

But it was Faulkner's remarks about *The Old Man and the Sea* that stirred Hemingway's wrath, creating in him a permanent grudge. Friendly with both men, Breit came up with the interesting notion of having Faulkner review the new Hemingway book for the *Times*. Faulkner either didn't want to review it or simply couldn't but eventually came up with a somewhat incoherent statement about the quality of Hemingway's work. He told Breit that Hemingway was wrong about writers banding together for protection like wolves and that when they did so, they "resemble the wolves who are wolves only in pack, and, singly, are just another dog." It is possible to interpret this statement in a variety of ways, but the person concerned chose to take it as still another gibe at his work and, in a letter, told Breit that Faulkner's loss of talent was clearly due to his drinking, a theme that Hemingway returned to with regularity. After comparing Faulkner's later work with Fitzgerald's, Hemingway claimed that he knew exactly when Faulkner "gets tired and does it on corn." He also spoke of Faulkner's "lack of discipline and of character and the boozy courage of corn whiskey." Breit was surprised to find that Hemingway had discovered a reason for Faulkner's alcoholism:

> You see what happens with Bill Faulkner is that as long as I am alive he has to drink to feel good about having the Nobel Prize. . . . Now he comes out with this wolves and the dog stuff and the condescension of how he rated what remains.

Hemingway's information about Faulkner's hospitalizations for drinking came from Breit and Cowley; his intense interest in the subject and his understanding of the situation display a combination of shrewdness accompanied by behavior common among alcoholics. They often imagine a hierarchy in which one drinker fixates on another who appears to be in far worse shape. It is a device the alcoholic can use to distance himself from his disease: "You see how badly so-and-so's writing is going? Thank God I don't have that problem!" This pecking order existed for Fitzgerald and Ring Lardner and then for Hemingway and Fitzgerald. Now Hemingway had chosen Faulkner to fill the role for him.

He spent little time writing after the worldwide triumph of *The Old Man and the Sea*. The *finca* became a way station for visitors from Hollywood, New York magazine editors, Spanish bullfighters, Adriana Ivanich and her brother, plus hundreds of the curious who wanted to meet the man who had given them so much pleasure. In these years Hemingway became the talkative Papa of the legends, constantly spouting a stream of aphorisms about life and letters. Or at least this is the accepted view that visitors have left us. In sharp distinction to it, however, is the torrent of letters on literary subjects that he addressed to Malcolm Cowley and Harvey Breit. These letters show that although he might have been unable to complete his long fictions to his satisfaction, Hemingway had not lost any of his critical powers, nor his savage wit. Many of the letters offer an extremely vivid account of what was wrong with much in contemporary American writing. He told Cowley that he had "taken away the magic" from *Tender Is the Night* when he chose to reprint the book in its author's "final version," a carefully worked out judgment that many now accept. He liked the work of Eudora Welty but found that of Carson McCullers to be "phoney." His admiration for Nelson Algren's work was unusual for its warmth and perception; his taste remained impeccable.

As uneasily hostile to biographers as Faulkner, Hemingway was deeply troubled by what he considered Arthur Mizener's "grave robbing" in his *Far Side of Paradise*, as well as by Budd Schulberg's novelization of his old friend's life, *The Disenchanted*. He expressed his disgust to Breit:

> Poor Scott. I wonder if Mizener will be able to get some sort of nourishing broth out of the bones this year. It is nice to think of them crouched over their pots: Budd Schulberg boiling out the head; Mizener dicing up the remainder; each tasting the other's brew. Both must be waiting for another corpse to be delivered now.

The huge flow of money from *The Old Man* enabled Hemingway to finance an African safari in 1953, which was concluded in January of 1954 when he made headlines throughout the world by surviving two plane crashes in two days. The second was far more damaging to him than the first. His injuries included a ruptured liver, spleen and kidney, two cracked vertebrae, paralysis of the sphincter muscle and various third-degree burns. But worst was the skull fracture incurred while butting his way out of the broken door of the plane after the crash. This was the most serious of all his concussions, and its aftereffects continued for years. The break in his skull was clearly discernible; a man in a bar the Hemingways had gone to in order to recuperate from the shock told the victim: "Nothing to it, old boy. Let's pour some gin in it," and did so. His magnificent constitution had carried him through what would have killed nearly anyone else, but the psychological anguish from an escape this close to death was strong. His compulsive eating and drinking began to soar again.

Hemingway quarreled bitterly with his sons, finding their goals and achievements no more to his liking than the women they married. When he excluded all three from his will and left everything to Mary Hemingway, he may have been punishing Pauline Hemingway's two sons, Greg and Patrick, who inherited their mother's considerable fortune upon her death in 1951; why Jack Hemingway was accorded the same treatment is conjectural. Neither Jack nor his brothers had much affection for Mary, viewing her more as a scolding nursemaid than as a real wife. Her alcoholism may also have had an effect on the situation. The three boys were strongly affected by their contact with a man of ungovernable temper and wild mood swings; Greg and Patrick had their share of emotional problems that undoubtedly stemmed from the relationship. Jack's description of a long afternoon's drinking at the *finca* in 1955 with his father is perhaps the most memorable passage in his autobiography.

Amazingly enough, it was Jack's first extended time alone with his father since he had become an adult. At eleven in the morning father and son mounted the outside stairs to the roof of the tower that housed Hemingway's work room. Both were armed with high-powered shotguns brought along for the express purpose of drastically reducing the number of buzzards that preyed around the premises of the *finca*. Pretending that they were shooting down enemy planes, Jack and his father blazed away until Hemingway shouted down to a servant to bring them up a pitcher of martinis. The pitcher was quickly consumed as the shooters continued the carnage, with carcasses plummeting down all around them. By the time they had finished the third pitcher, both men were quite drunk and convulsed with laughter.

When Hemingway finally growled "cease fire," the two came down to the deserted living room, where Hemingway decided it was time to view his print of *Casablanca*. Mary, infuriated with the shooting, slammed the door to her room while a servant set up the projector. As the film unreeled before them, both men began discussing its star, Ingrid Bergman. Hemingway asked his son, "Isn't the Swede beautiful? I mean truly, really beautiful . . . beautiful." Jack responded, "Yeah, Papa, beautiful. She's really, truly, truly beautiful." They then started weeping uncontrollably over Bergman's face as *Casablanca* wound on to its conclusion. Jack thought that the experience of viewing the film alone with his father was "totally maudlin and wonderfully close and human all at once." He cherished this single afternoon as the closest one he'd ever shared with his father, concluding his account by wondering if Hemingway "had already foreseen the onset of his ruin. The signs were there for others to see, but I must confess I hadn't the wit to see it for myself. Either that, or I didn't want to."

One of the others who saw was Bernard Berenson. Although five thousand miles separated the *finca* from I Tatti, Berenson picked up a whiff of what was befalling Hemingway from the boozily friendly letters he received from Havana. When it appeared that Hemingway was soon to be a guest, the eighty-nine-year-old Berenson expressed some apprehension in his diary:

> Hemingway's visit is impending, and I look forward with a certain dread to seeing and knowing him in the flesh. Hitherto we have only corresponded. His letters seemed written when he was not quite sober, rambling and affectionate. I fear he may turn out too animal, too overwhelmingly masculine, too Bohemian. He may expect me to drink and guzzle with him.

Berenson's fears were well founded but Hemingway became too ill in Venice to pay his visit.

The accounts of the medical care accorded Hemingway in Cuba are confused and contradictory. His principal physician, Dr. Herrera Sotolongo, has been quoted as once telling his patient, "If you keep on drinking this way you won't even be able to write your name." At other times he can't seem to make up his mind about his distinguished American friend, cutting back on his liquor supply only when he became stricken with alcohol-induced hepatitis. The doctor indicated that Hemingway "began his day with highballs or two Tom Collinses in the swimming pool, or has whiskey and soda, or plain whiskey on the rocks. Later he would have wine with his meals." The hepatitis victim displayed a lively curiosity about all the diseases of the liver, so much so that he purchased a medical treatise on that organ and annotated some twenty passages in the work. Remarkably enough, none of Hemingway's Cuban doctors ever dared to confront Hemingway directly with a diagnosis of alcoholism. They cannot have been that ignorant of the presence of the signs of the disease; if they had told him the truth, it is likely that he would have gone elsewhere for treatment.

But hepatitis was only one of the results of living a life that included awaking as early as four-thirty in the morning to begin the day with a drink and holding a drink in one hand and a pencil in the other. The man who scorned rummies had become the man who, in 1956,

> drank heavily every night, Scotch or red wine, and he was invariably in bad shape when finally induced to go to his room . . . , [in the day] preferring to sit for hours in a rooted position . . . sipping his drinks and talking, first coherently, then as the alcohol dissolved all continuity, his talk becoming repetitive, his speech slurred and disheveled.

If Aaron Hotchner's reportage is accurate, Hemingway would awake after a night's drinking, telling his assembled listeners in Madrid in 1956, "Went five rounds with the Demon Rum last night and knocked him on his ass in one fifty-five of the sixth." He would then begin his restorative drinking of either tequila or vodka until it was time for lunch.

He was now rarely sober but his self-deception continued as before. C. L. Sulzberger of the *New York Times* saw Hemingway at the beginning of 1957 in Paris; his account is more foreboding than Hotchner's:

> Hemingway didn't drink much, but as soon as he had a few glasses of wine, his speech became even more pronouncedly

slurred. If he didn't have such a magnificent constitution, I think he would have died long ago from too much alcohol. I only hope he lives long enough to finish his book.

It is not clear which doctor or doctors in Havana shared Sulzberger's grim outlook, but shortly after Hemingway's arrival home from Europe in early 1957, he was forced to make drastic reductions in his consumption of alcohol. His blood pressure stood at 210/105 and his cholesterol level was still 380, again a lethal combination for a man of fifty-seven. Getting Hemingway down from his usual one to two quarts a day was extremely difficult; any serious reduction would be torture for him. There were few tranquilizers available in 1957, and a patient who wanted to withdraw from alcohol outside a hospital usually had to go cold turkey. At first he was cut down to five ounces per day, but by March 6 he told Harvey Breit that he went "off all alcohol as of last night. Must work hard at being a good boy and not get nervous. Is hell on writing because there's nothing to take you off the plane you were on when knock off work." One month later he brought his New York friend up to date: "Haven't had a drink for five weeks . . . not inspiring." He once again stressed his need for drink: "[Booze] makes it possible to put up with fools, leave your work alone and not think of it after you knock off . . . and be able to sleep at night."

As the weeks passed, he became obsessive about the deprivation, telling Aaron Hotchner on May 28: "No liquor since March 5th . . . as much fun as driving a racing motor without lubrication . . . we'll skip it. Actually that's what I do." But the doctors either hadn't cut him down as much as he'd claimed or else decided to relieve his agony. On the sixth of June he wrote Archibald MacLeish: "And have had nothing to drink since [March 5] except wine, light, at meals and a very little white wine when other people were having drinks." He also told him that if there was no improvement in his condition he "will have to cut out wine entirely." In the full dread of having nothing whatever to drink, he provided another reason for his despair over the loss of alcohol after forty years: "nothing to cushion contact with people that you cannot take without a drink and it is pretty rough."

By July, when his cholesterol dropped to 204, he had endured four months of having only wine with his meals. He had achieved this relative abstinence by will power, a force that produces no significant long-term results in keeping alcoholics sober. Brief deprivations usually result in increased drinking when the alcoholic resumes his "normal" pattern; Hemingway proved to be no exception to this tendency and was drinking more than ever in the two-year period left him before he entered the Mayo Clinic in November of 1960. But the months of drastically reduced consumption may have been one of the reasons for the unexpected reflowering of his talent, which was pretty much absent for more than a decade.

8

> Today is another killer . . . am not in good shape. . . .
> Have drunk no hard liquor. Even good wine seems
> bad for me although it makes me more cheerful and
> get awfully nervous without it.
> — Hemingway to Mary Hemingway,
> August 15, 1960

THERE IS A TRAGIC IRONY in Hemingway's perception that alcoholism could destroy talent, especially that of Faulkner. Hemingway became infuriated with certain aspects of Faulkner's sudden, unexpected fame after 1948. In a period of four or five years, the Southerner was transformed from a difficult writer whose books were nearly out of print into a literary colossus who seemingly could do no wrong. Although Hemingway had been lavish in his praise for Faulkner when he was at his best in the 1930s ("If I had Faulkner's talent Christ Jesus God how I could have written"), he spoke out savagely against the later books, believing them to be terribly weak offerings from a man of such immense gifts. He was probably correct in blaming the mediocrity of these works on their author's alcoholism; his criticism, however, struck a decidedly moralistic note toward a writer he regarded as the king of the literary rummies. His rage against Faulkner exploded in the letters he wrote to friends about his rival's sharp decline:

> . . . that is why I get sore at Faulkner when he just gets tired or writes with a hangover and just slops. He has that wonderful talent and his not taking care of it to me is like a machine gunner letting his weapon foul up. . . . He has the fucking worthlessness of the South and all its truly splendid qualities.

In a 1948 letter to Malcolm Cowley, Hemingway warmed to his growing obsession with Faulkner's drinking and creative failure:

> He has no moral fibre at all; just poses and obstinacies and you know there is something wrong with all rummies. He is almost as much of a prick as Poe. But thank God for Poe and thank God for Faulkner.

As late as 1952 he was still capable of admitting that he might have been overly critical of Faulkner's "rummy ways," telling Harvey Breit:

> Am sure I was hard on Faulkner personally from ignorance. . . . I should not believe second hand reports. His work I know because that is my trade and I'm confident to hold an opinion. Naturally a writer when he reads another writer sees the signs when he is tiring and when to take him out of the game if he were a pitcher.

Presumably, Hemingway's anger against Faulkner was not entirely based on rivalry. He was convinced that Faulkner had destroyed his genius with drink while he, on the other hand, endowed with less talent but "never a rummy," was still writing at his best level. The truth was that by 1955 Hemingway had become just as much an alcoholic as Faulkner and that his new work was clearly inferior to his early books and unpublishable by his own high standards. Nevertheless, Faulkner was currently garnering supreme praises from the prize givers and taste makers in New York, Paris and London, while he had been relegated to second place, a role he despised.

Many of his letters written in the mid-1950s, even ones to perfect strangers, reflect this rage against Faulkner and the world's uncritical admiration for his work. Answering a query about it from a Mr. Ryder, Hemingway recommended that he read *Sanctuary* and *Pylon,* but went on to say:

> Also a short story called The Bear is worth reading. His last book A Fable isn't pure shit. It is impure diluted shit and there isn't a shit tester at Ichang where they ship the night soil from Chunking to but would fault it.

Sometimes his anger took on a sour, malignant tone, as when he told Harvey Breit that Faulkner

> seems a strange sort of phoney cunt. But he could write when he was sober and I am sure he will have the Southern good sense to kill himself. Christ that cult of: the worse I write and worse I sell out — the greater I succeed.

Some of this has a decidedly giddy ring; it was probably written in his multiple-double-daiquiri period. He thought a "prayer" might help his rival:

> Hail Faulkner full of shit corn are with thee. Blessed art thou among phonies and blessed is the fruit of thy womb Fable Holy Faulkner mother of shit never come near us now nor in the hour of our (actual) death amen.
> Perhaps this will cast a spell over him.

Late in 1957, and continuing through 1958, Hemingway wrote the chapters that make up *A Moveable Feast,* the only one of his

posthumously published books that compares favorably with the work he produced before 1940. Much of the published version of the book reads like Hemingway's early fiction: there is a shocking immediacy and freshness to the language, which produces dazzlingly clear portraits of the men and women he had known in Paris in the twenties. Despite the book's favorable descriptions of Ezra Pound, Evan Shipman and Sylvia Beach, much has been made of its allegedly bestial treatment of Ford Madox Ford, Gertrude Stein and most of all Scott Fitzgerald. Hemingway's intense dislike for Ford resembled Henry James's: both writers found Ford to be a pretentious liar given to making up literary anecdotes about nonexistent happenings. As for Stein, Hemingway might have claimed that she had taken the offensive against him twenty-five years earlier in *The Autobiography of Alice B. Toklas*. But it is his treatment of Fitzgerald that has created a picture of Hemingway as a hateful man taking this opportunity to punish his enemies.

Thinking about what Faulkner was doing with his talent may have caused Hemingway to recall what Fitzgerald had done with his in the late twenties and thirties. The extraordinary description of Fitzgerald in *A Moveable Feast* is probably the most convincing one ever written of the person Hemingway once considered his closest friend. There are many who dislike it because of Hemingway's insistence on dealing candidly with Fitzgerald's alcoholism, a subject that no one who knew much about him could have avoided. Some critics believe that Hemingway invented the story of Fitzgerald's concern about the size of his sexual organ. The truth is that Fitzgerald had been telling all sorts of people this story for years, including women he had met for the first time. So while there are warts in his portrait of Fitzgerald, it is pretty certain they were there in the original.

Despite the rancor with which Hemingway began to regard nearly everyone, his fondness for the Fitzgerald he had known in Paris continued to prevail. Important elements of that affection have been screened from us because of the editing that was

Hemingway, about 1960

performed on the manuscript of *A Moveable Feast* by Harry Brague of Scribners and Mary Hemingway. In his original manuscript, Hemingway wrote several openings for his Fitzgerald chapters, revising them again and again, as was his habit, but none of this material found its way into the published book. Why not? It is likely that Brague and Mary felt that many readers might find the Scott Fitzgerald in the two long chapters a pitiful figure and that Hemingway's kinder prefatory remarks about him would be at variance with what he had written in the pages that followed.

Calling these remarks at one time "Foreword to Scott," Hemingway had written:

> There was much more to write about poor Scott and his complicated tragedies and his complicated devotions and I wrote these and left them out. Other people have written about him, and the ones who wrote about him, and did not know him, I tried to help on the parts about him that I knew, telling them of his great generosities and his kindnesses.

These are not the words of a man filled with hatred for a friend who was dead for nearly twenty years but are a tribute to a friendship so highly regarded Hemingway kept a picture of Scott, Zelda and himself under the glass top of the large bureau in his bedroom at Finca Vigía.

In 1959, in the spring of his sixtieth year, Hemingway returned to Spain to follow the fortunes of two bullfighters, Ordoñez and Dominguín, and write about them for *Life* magazine. While in Europe that summer he resumed his customary consumption of huge amounts of alcohol; the entire trip became a frenzied period of nonstop drinking and carousing. It was during this year that he began to manifest the increasingly erratic behavior that left him deranged and a patient at the Mayo Clinic the following year. It appears that although Mary Hemingway and Aaron Hotchner were perfectly aware that he was suffering from alcoholism, little attention was paid to Hemingway's drinking at the clinic, where he was placed on a ration of one liter of wine per day.

Many of the facts about Hemingway's mental health are not known; neither the Mayo Clinic nor the various doctors who attended him there are willing to discuss the details of his case. But some facts are available: like Faulkner, Hemingway received a dozen or so electroconvulsive shocks in the late fall of 1960 and again in the early spring of 1961 on his second visit to the clinic. The second hospitalization had been preceded by his second suicide attempt in Hailey, Idaho, his new home in America following the takeover in Cuba by Castro. When he entered the clinic, his blood pressure had again risen to the extremely dangerous level of 225/125, and drugs were required to bring it down to a normal reading. But this time his weight began to drop rapidly until he reached 155 pounds, a state that left him with the appearance of a man at least twenty years older than he was. The ravaged Hemingway of the spring of 1961 is virtually unrecognizable.

In his last months at the clinic, he may have changed his mind about his "nonrummy" status, for two of the books he read there concerned the disease he had so long denied: *The Liver and Its Diseases* and *Sedatives and the Alcoholic,* a volume published by Alcoholics Anonymous. But his alcoholism was only one part of the terrible afflictions facing him. He suffered from both liver and kidney dysfunction; his frightening loss of weight he at one time ascribed to cancer. But worst of all was the certain knowledge that he had lost his ability to write; the struggle to place one sentence after another was now beyond his strength. These pressures, and perhaps more that we shall never know, led him to make his own private peace by pulling both triggers of his shotgun on July 2, 1961, three weeks short of his sixty-second birthday.

O'Neill

∞

1

I will be an artist or nothing.
— O'Neill to Beatrice Ashe, February 11, 1914

Only a drink makes me feel alive at all.
— O'Neill to Agnes O'Neill, February 16, 1920

EUGENE O'NEILL decided to stop drinking at the relatively early age of thirty-seven. This was the same time in life when Faulkner, Fitzgerald and Hemingway began to exhibit their declines. O'Neill knew, as the three novelists did not, that he had no choice. His sole reason for giving up alcohol was his powerful desire to continue writing plays, an enterprise he knew was surely doomed if he continued to drink. Unlike the other three, whose creativity diminished ever more sharply as they continued to drink, O'Neill's dramatic talent flowered in his later years when he began to write a series of plays about the subject that concerned him most deeply: the power of addiction and its killing effects on human character. There is little doubt that O'Neill is best remembered today not so much as the author of *The Emperor Jones* and *Strange Interlude* but rather as the man who wrote *The Iceman Cometh, A Touch of the Poet* and *Long Day's Journey into Night,* all of which were achieved after more than a decade of sobriety.

O'Neill probably inherited his alcoholism: both his parents

O'Neill in New York City, 1946

possessed alcoholic histories. O'Neill's father, James — the nationally famous actor who toured the United States for decades in his production of *Monte Cristo,* based on Dumas's novel — appears to have been a "controlled" alcoholic. He drank a great deal daily but was able to hold himself together well enough to pursue a highly successful career. (Neither of his two sons ever managed in their lives to exert their father's control over drink.) James O'Neill married Ella Quinlan, whose father had been a teetotaler until he reached the age of forty. He then began to drink champagne, destroying his health in the process. Ella may have inherited her father's addictive nature; she became a morphine addict after the birth of her third child, Eugene, who was tempted to believe that his birth was the reason for her turning to the drug. (Ella's second child, also a boy, died in infancy.) The O'Neills' first son, James junior, or Jamie, was ten years older than Eugene, who idolized him and followed his lead as a drinker as soon as he could. Whiskey always flowed freely at the O'Neill home; the playwright's childhood rang to the sound of toasts being offered and gladly accepted.

As a child O'Neill adored his mother while hating the father who shipped him off to boarding school in Riverdale, New York, at the age of seven. Many years later, in an attempt to understand his childhood and the forces that had shaped him, O'Neill drew a diagram of the psychic elements that had exacted their toll. O'Neill's handwriting was always tiny, even smaller than Faulkner's, but in his diagram he succeeded in making his print so diminutive that it nearly defies being read with a magnifying glass; these words were written for his eyes alone. He noted his disenchantment with his mother, who, when under the influence of the morphine, wandered around the family home in New London like a "haunted creature." In a comment added to a section of the diagram dealing with his early nightmares, he appended these words:

AT EARLY CHILDHOOD FATHER WOULD GIVE CHILD WHISKEY & WATER TO SOOTHE CHILD'S NIGHTMARES CAUSED BY TERROR OF

DARK. THIS WHISKEY IS CONNECTED WITH PROTECTION OF
MOTHER — DRINK OF HERO FATHER

In later years O'Neill was convinced that these "few drops" he was given as a child had much to do with his addiction to alcohol.

When Eugene attended Princeton for the single academic year of 1906–07, he achieved an even worse scholastic record than did Scott Fitzgerald, who followed O'Neill there eight years later. Besides incessantly reading books of his own choice, O'Neill liked to shock the more gently reared boys at the school with his drinking prowess, especially his consumption of hard liquor. At the time, social drinking was largely confined to beer and wine, while the harder stuff was regarded as the proper comfort for people these students thought of as bums. When the shock of his whiskey drinking had worn off, O'Neill determined to show his friends the effects of absinthe, widely regarded in those days as the ultimate in its power to intoxicate. After persuading Louis Holladay, a Greenwich Village friend, to bring a bottle of the infamous fluid to the Princeton campus, O'Neill consumed enough of it to throw him into a frenzy of violence in which he destroyed virtually all the furniture in his room. He had been searching for his revolver; when he found it he "pointed it [at Holladay] and pulled the trigger. By good fortune it was not loaded." Two of his classmates recalled that "O'Neill had gone beserk [sic]. . . . It took three to pin him to the floor where he shortly collapsed and was put to bed." The presence of the absinthe was kept secret, and the school authorities never suspected the truth behind what had happened that afternoon.

In keeping with his drinking prowess, O'Neill wrote a poem that expressed his desire to meet girls who liked to drink as much as he did:

> Cheeks that have known no rouge
> Lips that have known no booze,
> What care I for thee?
> Come with me on a souse,

> A long and everlasting carouse
> And I'll adore thee.

He did little work at Princeton, flunked all of his courses and never returned to the campus for his second year. He was only eighteen and was ready for the world of sailors, whores and drinkers, the world that Maxim Gorky had evoked in *The Lower Depths,* which O'Neill came to admire.

It was not until 1915 that O'Neill embarked seriously on his writing career that changed the course of the American theater. In the seven years after he left Princeton, O'Neill experienced much, including a fruitless gold-mining venture in Honduras, an impressive number of sea voyages on which he served as an able-bodied seaman and a successful six-month battle with tuberculosis in a Connecticut hospital. At twenty-two he entered into a marriage that would never have taken place had the bride not been pregnant. O'Neill wed Kathleen Jenkins in 1910 in order to give her baby his name; the young couple never lived together. The boy's father never saw his son until he was twelve, for Kathleen obtained custody of the child at the time of their divorce in 1912, an action that O'Neill did not oppose. Eugene O'Neill, Jr., was born with a double risk of familial alcoholism: Kathleen's mother had left her husband because of his drinking.

O'Neill's drinking in the years between 1910 and 1917, when he met his second wife, Agnes Boulton, was characterized by a single-minded ferocity that is probably rare even among alcoholics. By his early twenties, O'Neill was a daily customer at such well-known hangouts in New York as Jimmy the Priest's and The Hell Hole, where the patrons came to get drunk and remained that way until they passed out or were carried out. These are the dives that O'Neill re-created as Harry Hope's Last Chance Saloon in *The Iceman Cometh.* Here he drank the cheapest whiskey day in and day out for weeks on end until he would finally collapse and shakily regain sobriety over a painful recovery period. He went through dozens of blackouts, once awakening from one as a train he was on approached New Orleans; he could not recall boarding it. He frequently awoke to the humiliation of having been beaten up in fights whose origins he could never remember. The frenzied quality of O'Neill's drinking at this time sets him apart from the other writers discussed here. Still a young man, O'Neill was in an advanced stage of alcoholism that the three novelists would not reach for at least another decade. Yet during these years of continual drinking O'Neill had a firm conviction that liquor sharpened reality or, more simply, that alcoholic reality was the only reality that mattered. At the same time he began to realize that drinking was a threat to his creativity.

In his nightly sessions at The Hell Hole O'Neill became well known for his uncharacteristic loquaciousness after only a few drinks; when sober, O'Neill was painfully shy and slow-spoken. Liquor galvanized him into an impassioned flow of words about his ambitions and hopes as a writer for the stage. Women found him extremely attractive and he began, and as quickly ended, a series of affairs. When he wasn't drinking with his friends, he was avidly reading the plays of all the ages, especially those of his contemporaries: Shaw, Yeats, Synge, Gerhart Hauptmann and, above all, Strindberg, who remained his greatest influence. Money was always tight, but there was no real need for O'Neill to hold down a job: his father doled out an allowance to Jamie and Eugene despite his certain knowledge that a great deal of it was spent on booze. On one occasion in 1912 the drinking nearly cost O'Neill his life when he deliberately took an overdose of veronal, then a widely used opiate. He had been using the drug to fight off the effects of his hangovers. He was awakened from his lethal slumber by a friend who arrived just in time.

The bodily tremor that plagued O'Neill through most of his life began to manifest itself during these early years in New York. Many of O'Neill's friends assumed that the noticeable shaking of his hands was the result of the huge quantities of liquor he drank. One of them, Frederick Hettman, recalled that in 1910

Gene didn't eat much. He was interested in drinking. When he was short of money he tried to get through the day with just beer, but if he were in funds or someone was treating, his favorite was a big glass of gin with just a drop of vermouth and soda — that had a bigger kick than anything else.

His hangovers were deadly. In the early morning, after drinking through much of the night, he would turn up at the bar of the Garden Hotel on Twenty-sixth Street, where his parents stayed while in the city. Usually penniless, he was always extended credit for the morning drink he so desperately needed. But with his hands shaking so badly, it wasn't easy to get the first one down:

> O'Neill would prop himself against the bar and order his shot. The bartender knew him, and would place the glass in front of him, toss a towel across the bar, as though absent-mindedly forgetting it, and move away. Arranging the towel around his neck, O'Neill would grasp the glass of whiskey and an end of the towel in one hand and clutch the other end of the towel with his other hand. Using the towel as a pulley, he would laboriously hoist the glass to his lips. His hands trembled so violently that even with this aid he could scarcely pour the whiskey down his throat, and often spilled part of it.

But those with sharper eyes noticed that O'Neill's tremor appeared to come and go in a way that perhaps suggested other factors than just alcohol as the cause. Ella O'Neill suffered from a similar tremor, and her son eventually believed that he had inherited it from her. He also felt that his shaking had been steadily worsened by his constant drinking. Alcohol certainly played some part in its development. It is significant that when O'Neill spent four months in a New London boarding house in 1914, the owner's daughter, Jessica, noticed that "his coffee cup used to shake in his hand when he first came to stay with us . . . but after about four months, the trembling got better." This was at a time in O'Neill's life when he was just beginning to write and had briefly cut back on his enormous intake of alcohol.

2

Alcohol enabled him to do what he wanted to do — *not* what was expected of him, or was the conventional thing to do.
— Agnes Boulton, 1958

You are wife of all of me and mother of the best of me.
— O'Neill to Agnes Boulton, November 30, 1919

O'NEILL'S CAREER as a playwright was given its strongest push when his *Bound East for Cardiff* was performed by the Provincetown Players in 1916, first on Cape Cod and later in New York. The Players owed much of its fame, both then and now, to having produced many of the early O'Neill plays. Their enthusiasm for his work was the first step in discovering a wider audience for his distinctly noncommercial theater. O'Neill's initial encounter with the group came about when his Greenwich Village friend Terry Carlin invited him to travel up to Cape Cod for the spring and summer of that year. Carlin, a self-confessed anarchist, was thirty-three years older than O'Neill, who created a very moving portrait of his old friend as the embittered Larry Slade in *The Iceman Cometh*. In the play Slade identifies himself as an alcoholic "foolosopher" who talks too much. His prototype is often thought of as the man who first acquainted O'Neill with the plays of Ibsen and, more important, gave him the idea that the outcasts of society were fitting subjects for drama. Their common alcoholism sealed their friendship; the two men loved to talk and drink without ceasing through the long nights. In later years, both O'Neill's second and third wives, Agnes Boulton and Carlotta Monterey, refused Carlin entry into their homes because of his boorish manners and drunkenness. But O'Neill's devotion to the friend of his youth never wavered; when Carlin died a pauper's death in Boston in 1934, O'Neill paid for the cremation.

Most of the aspiring writers in Provincetown at that time were heavy drinkers. Some of the women there prided themselves on their ability to outdrink the men: Edna St. Vincent Millay and Djuna Barnes were noted for their immense capacity. One exception was the enigmatic Louise Bryant, with whom O'Neill had an affair just prior to and after her marriage to the journalist John Reed. She exhibited unconventional sexual conduct but never drank; her father had died of alcoholism, and perhaps for this reason she made every effort to stop O'Neill from drinking. Eventually she did begin to drink, in her thirties, and died her father's death in Paris at the age of forty-nine.

After John and Louise Reed left for Russia, just in time to observe the coming to power of the Bolsheviks, O'Neill met Agnes Boulton, who became his second wife early in 1918. Still in love with Louise, O'Neill was convinced that Agnes bore a striking resemblance to her, an opinion that few shared. She was certainly a beautiful woman; her daughter Oona resembled her strongly. Agnes had been widowed while still in her early twenties, shortly after the birth of a daughter, Barbara. Mainly out of financial need, she embarked on a writing career in New York by turning out longish romantic stories for the leading magazines and some for the less popular ones; at least one story was cited by Edward J. O'Brien in his annual collection, *The Best American Short Stories*. She might have continued with her career but O'Neill, like Fitzgerald, was not happy having another writer under the same roof and eventually discouraged Agnes's literary ambitions.

O'Neill was drinking with his brother, Jamie, the night he first met Agnes in a Greenwich Village bar. She was attracted to him immediately by his intensity of expression about writing and the theater. In the course of walking her home to her hotel, O'Neill appeared equally captivated with Agnes, telling her, "I want to spend every night of my life from now with you. . . . I mean this. *Every night of my life*." He may have said just these words, which are taken from an account of their early life together that Agnes published five years after O'Neill's death. Calling her narrative *Part of a Long Story*, she occasionally wrote in a style that resembled the romantic fiction she created for the magazines. Nevertheless, Agnes is utterly convincing in her portrayal of a young O'Neill whose actions were often understandable only when one knew how much he had been drinking. At their second meeting a few days later at a Village party, O'Neill ignored her completely, as if he had never seen her before. That was the night he climbed on top of the mantel to move the hands of the big clock at the end of the room while shouting an off-key rendition of his favorite song:

> "Turn back the universe,
> And give me yesterday.
> TURN BACK THE ·UNIVERSE . . ."

He later apologized to her, explaining that he had been "blotto" that night or, as he preferred to view it then, immersed in the "true reality" of intoxication.

From the beginning Agnes realized that alcohol played an enormous role in O'Neill's life. She recounts a tortuous attempt on her part to get the two O'Neill brothers out of New York on a train bound for Provincetown. She did not reckon on the difficulty of interrupting the around-the-clock drinking cycle the brothers had entered at the Garden Hotel, the same place where O'Neill used to cadge his morning drink. After purchasing the railroad tickets at Grand Central Station, Agnes returned in time to observe her traveling companions finishing off a bottle, an act that postponed the trip for that day. The following morning O'Neill discovered that his hands were shaking badly: "I'll have to shave. . . . Listen, angel-face, you go down to the bar and get them to mix me a milk shake with a shot of brandy." She obliged him and O'Neill proceeded to shave, but he was soon ordering her to pay another visit to the bar downstairs: "Bring me an eggnog this time — two eggs and a double shot of brandy, dear."

By the time O'Neill had lowered the brandy eggnog, Jamie had awakened and entered their room with a fifth of Old Taylor, which the brothers opened immediately. This act delayed the trip another day. Each day the morning "recovery" drinks served only to get them high enough to order yet another bottle and then talk and drink through the small hours. After a few days O'Neill became unable to keep any food down, and Agnes was dispatched for the brandy eggnogs every two or three hours. It took over a week of steady pleading to get them on board the train. Looking back at the episode after thirty years, Agnes recalled her lack of experience in dealing with an alcoholic: "What I did not know then was that after one drink the cycle must be fulfilled."

In the first year of their marriage, Agnes and O'Neill rented quarters in Provincetown. At the end of 1918 O'Neill's father bought a small house on the dunes for the young couple. Here Agnes continued to write while observing the effect of alcohol on her new husband, who never appeared drunk in any recognizable way: "He never raised his voice, he never staggered or walked into things, never 'passed out.' He never seemed to be what is called *drunk*, nor did I think of it that way." Commenting guardedly on some of his "rather dreadful outbursts of violence, and others of bitter nastiness and malevolence," Agnes appeared to view O'Neill's continual drinking as his chosen manner to escape the pressures of everyday life: "He seemed to have entered another world where he greatly enjoyed himself for quite a while — until physical sickness and despair at last overcame him."

When sober, O'Neill had little to say. He laughed so rarely that his close friend of three decades, George Jean Nathan, remarked, "I have heard Eugene O'Neill laugh aloud once and once only." When he wasn't writing in these early years, he spent a great deal of his time outdoors. Aside from the drinking, O'Neill, like Hemingway, took care of his body. He swam for hours every day after his morning stint of writing. Despite the prodigious quantities of alcohol consumed, his weight rarely exceeded 140 to 150 pounds.

Agnes had no doubt about O'Neill's love for her. Whenever the two were separated, even if only for a day or so, O'Neill would write her impassioned letters bemoaning her absence and informing her of his overwhelming need for her. He quickly became emotionally and physically dependent on Agnes for nearly everything. She learned to get him through his difficult recovery periods after a three- or four-day drunk when he might have to remain in bed for several days; she was both wife and nurse to O'Neill. Convinced of his genius, she had few qualms about the drinking, even when O'Neill would lash out at her with sudden, irrational bursts of jealousy concerning her imagined lovers.

The darker side of his alcoholism became visible after only six months of the marriage. On a late-1918 trip to New York to observe the rehearsals of *Where the Cross Is Made,* Agnes and O'Neill went out to dinner to an Italian restaurant with a number of close friends associated with the burgeoning Provincetown Players. O'Neill drank moderately through the long evening but suddenly she

> saw Gene pouring a large straight drink for himself. I waited a few minutes, then got up and walked down to where he was sitting and squeezed in next to him, whispering in his ear that maybe we ought to go back to the hotel. He got to his feet, gave me a push that sent me backward, leaned toward me, swinging as hard as possible with the back of his hand and hit me across the face. Then he laughed, his mouth distorted with an ironic grin.

O'Neill's male friends ignored Agnes's plight and chose instead to continue listening to the playwright's lecture about Ibsen. Only Stella Ballantine, wife of the actor Teddy Ballantine, dared speak her mind by telling O'Neill just what she thought of a man who struck his wife in public. O'Neill rose in a blind fury and commanded to everyone in the party, *"Get out of here — all of you!"* All of Agnes's endeavors to pierce O'Neill's mood were in vain as he continued to ignore her. Eventually, Stella brought her back to her hotel, where she waited for O'Neill's return. Hearing footsteps in the hallway toward dawn, she opened the door and "saw a sick man standing in front of me." She allowed him entry and O'Neill sat on the edge of the bed:

"He reached out and put his arm around me, holding me tightly and quivering." Such episodes became a regular part of her life; they became the price of living with a literary genius.

3

> I'm a dramatist through and through. . . . What I see everywhere is drama . . . human beings in conflict with other human beings or themselves.
> — O'Neill to Malcolm Mollan, December 3, 1921

> I will never . . . or never have written anything good when I am drinking, or even when the miasma of drink is left.
> — O'Neill to Agnes Boulton, 1918

LIKE FAULKNER, O'Neill enjoyed a huge burst of creative power in the early and mid-1920s that made him America's foremost dramatist by 1925. The plays, uneven in quality from the start, included *Beyond the Horizon, Anna Christie, The Emperor Jones, The Hairy Ape, All God's Chillun Got Wings, Desire Under the Elms* and *The Great God Brown*. O'Neill found American theatergoers receptive to his outspoken views about sex and race, as well as to his theatrical experiments — throbbing drums in *Jones* and the use of masks in *Brown*. O'Neill brought to the stage dramatic subjects that until then were considered taboo: prostitution in *Anna Christie,* a racially mixed marriage in *All God's Chillun,* and the commingling of sexuality and the lust for property in *Desire Under the Elms*. Going against the tide of viewing the playwright as a provider of popular entertainment, O'Neill's often savage attacks on accepted thinking won him the Pulitzer Prize in drama three times in the twenties. At thirty-seven he had become a commanding figure in modern world literature, a writer who earned the praise of nearly all the serious critics of the day as well as that of Broadway audiences.

O'Neill continued in his attempts to keep his love for alcohol apart from his work, a task that became increasingly difficult as he grew older. Like the other writers in this book, O'Neill began to find it ever harder to recover from his extended drinking periods and then resume his work in the mood he'd left it. His once immense tolerance for alcohol was changing sharply as he aged. The "miasma" of drinking that he wrote of to Agnes was undoubtedly the physical and spiritual illness that follows heavy drinking, a deep-seated feeling that might last for days. As early as 1922 he'd felt the need to consult a doctor about the painful depressions he'd begun to suffer after a bout. O'Neill's close friend the stage designer Robert Edmund Jones suggested that O'Neill visit his psychoanalyst, Dr. Smith Ely Jellife, not only about the drinking but also about the increasing hostility he was exhibiting toward Agnes. She had taken him to task over the liquor and had also begun to complain that his sexual attention to her was perfunctory. We don't know what Dr. Jellife recommended, but O'Neill did not alter his drinking behavior at this time.

Although they agreed that alcohol was "the good man's failing," the men of the O'Neill family believed that their drinking was an inherited problem. They, of course, meant inherited in the sense of a cultural fate rather than a genetic characteristic. As can be seen in Long Day's Journey, the alcohol sometimes served to bring the two sons and their father together in the close harmony of familial love, while at others it seemed only to provoke irrational rages that tore them apart. O'Neill became far friendlier with his father toward the end of his life than he had been in his youth. As for Jamie, O'Neill felt a deep affection for his brother, who had failed, perhaps had *tried* to fail, in nearly everything he'd ever attempted. Jamie had done little but drink and consort with whores since his teens. He drank so much that he was in constant dread of D.T.'s; the family's code phrase for their onset was "The Boys from Brooklyn are coming over the bridge!"

Jamie's not unexpected death in 1923 became still another cause of O'Neill's worries about alcohol. His death was the third in the series that had wiped out all of O'Neill's immediate family in three years. James senior had died after suffering the agonizing pain caused by intestinal cancer; his last words to his family were "Life . . . is rotten." Surprisingly, Jamie then took it upon himself to give up his whores and became his mother's constant, cheerful companion. For his mother's sake, he swore off liquor entirely and became a dutiful son, but his exemplary new life was short. Right before Ella's death of a stroke in Los Angeles, Jamie resumed drinking with all the pent-up thirst produced by two years of a sobriety that had been achieved for someone other than himself. His gruesome story about the five-day train journey across the country with his mother's coffin lying up ahead in the baggage car became the scene related by James Tyrone in *A Moon for the Misbegotten*. Jamie brought ten bottles of whiskey aboard the train and drank all of them. He also picked up a plump blond prostitute — "a pig" — with whom to while away the hours on board the train. By the time it reached New York a number of Ella's valuables had disappeared, and Jamie was far too drunk to attend her funeral.

In the last year of his life Jamie was hospitalized repeatedly for alcoholism in what appeared to be a frenzied desire to die as quickly as possible. He would drink anything that made him drunk; as O'Neill wrote his dentist friend (much later his editor and Faulkner's at Random House) Saxe Commins, "Jim was 'nuts complete' when taken [to the sanitorium]" and "almost blind from the booze." O'Neill had little doubt that his brother's utter failure in life and early death at forty-five was due almost entirely to alcohol, and Jamie's death unquestionably had much to do with O'Neill's decision to stop drinking for good three years later.

It would take another sixteen years before O'Neill would feel ready to write about his family and the terrible pain they regularly inflicted on one another — the experiences that produced

Long Day's Journey into Night. Although on the surface things were going extremely well for O'Neill, the despair and anger caused by his drinking intensified steadily. Back in 1920, when the Volstead Act first went into effect, O'Neill had written Agnes that "there's nothing here at all for me now that [Prohibition] is in force." In his teens he'd demonstrated that he too would drink nearly anything if it made him drunk; now in the early 1920s, while still living on Cape Cod, he sometimes drank a locally made brew called Tiger Piss, terrible stuff that had to be consumed in a rapid series of gulps because of its nauseating taste and the fact that it burned going down. In a fit of drunken bravado, to show that he *would* drink just about anything, O'Neill urinated in a half-empty bottle of Tiger Piss and drank it straight back.

The feeling of alcoholic despair often erupted in drunken rages, mainly directed at Agnes. They fought over many things, particularly her desire to broaden the couple's social life, which until then had revolved around O'Neill's preference for seeing only theater people who were actively concerned with the production of his plays. Agnes wanted to entertain on a far grander scale, but O'Neill was opposed on the grounds that drunken parties would be deadly for his work. But this was only a minor problem. By 1923 O'Neill had begun to see Agnes and himself as locked in permanent marital warfare, a state of mind he seems to have picked up from reading and rereading his favorite modern playwright, Strindberg. It is impossible to say how much of O'Neill's difficulties with Agnes arose because of his identification with Strindberg and how much from the genuine obstacles causing discord. Alcohol always played a part in their quarrels, however, especially those involving physical violence; the level of O'Neill's aggression increased the more he drank. On at least two occasions at outdoor parties in Provincetown he dragged a screaming Agnes by her hair over the sand dunes and back to their home. Agnes's women friends were sometimes required to spirit her away from the house when O'Neill was on an extended drunk.

Until the autobiographical *Welded,* written in 1923 and arguably O'Neill's worst drama of those years, he'd never drunk while in the process of completing a play, but that year he drank heavily and once became so enraged with Agnes that he took every picture of her that he could find and cut them into tiny pieces. His wrath is evident in the play, where O'Neill places his marital problems in full view of the audience. Agnes becomes Eleanor, an actress starring in her husband's plays, while O'Neill portrays himself as the embattled artist whose deepest concern is his integrity. The couple make love, fight, break up and then predictably reunite. The O'Neill-like husband tells Eleanor at the play's end that there will always be hate in their relationship. She dutifully accepts his view and he elaborates on it: "And we'll torture and tear, and clutch for each other's souls — fight — fail and hate again (*he raises his voice in aggressive triumph*) *with joy!*" Strindberg may have been the inspiration for this speech, and in the next few years the O'Neills followed his path pretty much the way O'Neill outlines it here.

Just prior to and following Jamie's death, O'Neill made several efforts to quit drinking, all of them unsuccessful. At least one of these attempts failed because some of his friends didn't care for a sober but somber O'Neill who had little to say. Edmund Wilson became friendly with O'Neill in 1925, mainly because of Wilson's marriage to the young actress Mary Blair, who appeared in a number of the major O'Neill plays of the 1920s, including *The Hairy Ape* and *All God's Chillun Got Wings*. In the second of these she shocked some New York theatergoers when, as Ella, she kissed each night the hand of the black actor Paul Robeson. For her courage in enduring the scorn and outrage in the press and in the torrent of hate mail she received, O'Neill rewarded her with the lead in the Broadway production of *Desire Under the Elms*. In his journals of the twenties, Wilson recalled an evening spent in a restaurant with a sober O'Neill. Wilson quickly became bored and persuaded him to drink some wine, "to prime him," a suggestion that he did not resist. The diners returned to Wilson's Washington Square apartment, where Wilson "paid a heavy price" for his effort to warm up O'Neill:

> Once started talking, it seemed O'Neill would never stop. What was striking was that he quite lost connection with anything that was said by me or Mary. He did not answer questions or seem to recognize that we were there at all. He disregarded all our hints. We got up and crossed the room; we made remarks which with anyone else would have brought the session to a close. But his talk was an unbroken monologue. And he drank up everything we had in the house: when a bottle was set before him, he simply poured out drinks for himself, not suggesting that we might care for any.... There being nothing more to drink, [O'Neill] did not leave until four in the morning.

An all-night drinking episode like this would inevitably inaugurate a cycle of several days' and nights' duration similar to the ones suffered by Faulkner and Fitzgerald. By the beginning of 1925 O'Neill had two main concerns about his drinking: his health, which appeared to be severely endangered, and the quality of his work, which *Welded* and *The Fountain* undeniably proved was threatened. His failing marriage appears to have been of lesser import. Perhaps this came about because while O'Neill began trying to cut out alcohol completely from his life, Agnes clearly had no such intention. She liked to drink.

4

You've got to have all your critical and creative fa-
culties about when you're working. I never try to
write a line when I'm not strictly on the wagon. I
don't think anything worth reading was ever written
by anyone who was drunk or even half-drunk when
he wrote it. This is not morality, it's plain physiology.
— O'Neill to Barrett Clark, *c.* 1925

An heir is expected . . . and Mrs. O'Neill and I have
decided that in order to mitigate the chances of he,
or she, devoting "its" entire life to serious drinking,
"it" had better be born outside the U.S.
— O'Neill to Arthur Hobson Quinn, April 3, 1925

THE OSTENSIBLE REASON for O'Neill's eventual decision to
settle in Bermuda and purchase Spithead, his seaside home there,
was his wish to avoid the discomforts of eastern seaboard
weather, a climate in which he had spent most of his life. He
may also have been seeking the previously identified "geographical cure" for his alcoholism.

Several years before he decided to move south, O'Neill had
made many changes in his style of life, most of them caused by
the sharp increase in his income after 1921. In addition to in-
heriting one half of his mother's estate of $150,000, O'Neill's
royalties from his plays began pouring in: in 1922 he made
$42,000 this way, or close to half a million dollars in the cur-
rency of the late 1980s. Now a relatively wealthy man, O'Neill
purchased Brook Farm in Ridgefield, Connecticut, a huge house
with fifteen rooms on thirty acres of property. Here he enter-
tained some of his writing friends from his Village days, including Hart Crane and Malcolm Cowley. At the time of Cowley
and Crane's late-1923 visit to Brook Farm, O'Neill was attempting desperately to stop drinking; no liquor was served before

dinner to the thirsty guests from New York. Later in the evening O'Neill took Crane and Cowley down to the cellar to show them three fifty-gallon casks of homemade hard cider, the product of his industrious chauffeur. With Hart Crane's predictably strong encouragement, one of the casks was broached, a pitcher obtained and

> Gene takes a sip of cider, holds it in his mouth apprehensively, gives his glass a gloomy look, then empties the glass in two nervous swallows. After a while we fill the pitcher again. When I go upstairs to bed, long after midnight, Gene is on his knees drawing another pitcher of cider, and Hart stands over him gesturing with a dead cigar as he declaims some lines composed that afternoon.

The following morning Agnes informed her guests that O'Neill would not be down to join them — he would be "working" that day. But the truth was that O'Neill had not been able to stop downing the cider; he kept on with it and then fled to New York, where he could continue drinking without Agnes's censure. Frantic with worry, Agnes searched out all of O'Neill's familiar hangouts in the city for a week before finding him in a coma in an upstairs bedroom of The Hell Hole. After a week-long jag, it would take the better part of yet another week to get himself in shape to resume writing. It was only a year or so after this experience, and others like it, that O'Neill started seriously considering living in a completely different environment. Bermuda was the answer, a warm place not suffering from the evil side effects of Prohibition — perhaps even a place where he could drink normally.

Many alcoholics believe that they have to hit bottom before they can even begin to think about cutting out alcohol from their lives. The year 1925 was certainly O'Neill's worst: one prolonged drunk succeeded another, producing painful depressions that lasted for days. His attempts at tapering off with beer and wine succeeded only in postponing the time when he would return with full vigor to the stronger stuff he craved. His obsession began to appear in his work: Dion Anthony in *The Great God*

Brown is on a voyage to self-destruction through drinking. As for the general quality of O'Neill's work up through this period, it became more and more erratic — from the excellence of *The Hairy Ape* and *Desire Under the Elms* to the shaky, half-hysterical atmosphere in *The Great God Brown* and *The Fountain*.

When Agnes became pregnant with the "it" who became Oona Chaplin, the O'Neills hired a nurse, Maude Bisch, the wife of a New York psychiatrist, and she became aware that O'Neill was unable to sleep after one of his bouts. She obtained a supply of paraldehyde for him, the evil-smelling drug that makes hangovers vanish, the same remedy that Fitzgerald and Faulkner were given regularly in the 1930s. After Dr. Bisch arrived in Bermuda, he met O'Neill and the two had a series of conversations about O'Neill's drinking. These talks brought O'Neill one step closer to taking the final one of cutting alcohol out of his life for good. Since the two quickly became friendly, it would have been unsuitable for Dr. Bisch to assume the role of therapist, but in the following year O'Neill met the physician who exerted the greatest influence on his determination to quit drinking.

Psychoanalysis in this country was still in its infancy in 1926 when O'Neill became one of the very first American writers of note to seek such treatment. Then, as now, psychoanalysis had relatively little success in dealing with alcoholism, and O'Neill's amazing ability to stop drinking after only six weeks of therapy cannot be attributed solely to it, although that factor cannot be discounted entirely. Extraordinary circumstances surrounded O'Neill's meeting with his therapist, Dr. Gilbert Hamilton, a New York analyst whose pioneering work was later recognized by Kinsey. With the strong financial support of a scientific organization, Dr. Hamilton was attempting to investigate the sex lives and marital problems of two hundred men and women; the subjects, which came to include O'Neill, were all married but only one member of each couple was studied by Dr. Hamilton, who used his version of the free association method in giving his subjects cards with questions printed on them. Sitting in a chair with his subjects facing away from him, Dr. Hamilton allowed them as much time as they wished to answer. He made no attempt to comment or interrupt the subjects, whose response times ran from two to thirty hours. Three years after the completion of the interviews, the results were revealed in a book, *Research in Marriage*; the anonymity of the subjects was maintained by using numbers rather than names. But O'Neill's replies can be easily identified, as he is the only one who specifies that his relationship with his mother was difficult because of "her drug habit."

It was Kenneth Macgowan, perhaps O'Neill's closest associate in the theater, who brought his friend into contact with Dr. Hamilton. Macgowan, himself a participant in the research project, believed that O'Neill might have some chance of arresting his alcoholism if he could establish a relationship of trust with his physician. After noting in his diary that "Kenneth has made a date with Hamilton for me," O'Neill revealed how important he regarded the approaching meeting: "A ray of hope amid general sick despair." One reason for Macgowan's urging O'Neill to try therapy was his belief that Agnes could not be expected to help her husband give up alcohol; Macgowan was convinced that she actually encouraged O'Neill to drink.

Immediately after completing his share of the question-answering, O'Neill began intensive therapy with Dr. Hamilton, for whom he drew up the diagram mentioned earlier in an attempt to set forth the facts concerning his early years and "the familial forces that had shaped him." He described the terrible shock he'd felt on the night of his mother's suicide attempt and his first knowledge of her morphine addiction, which he summarized as "discovery of mother's inadequacy." We have no way of knowing if O'Neill really believed that his unresolved feelings about his parents were the "cause" of his alcoholism. But we do know that he agreed with Dr. Hamilton that he had strong Oedipal guilt fixations, which affected his relationships with women. He later told Macgowan that he didn't need Dr. Hamilton to tell him about these conflicts: all the doctor had to do was read his plays. It would be another fifteen years before O'Neill undertook *Long Day's Journey into Night,* in which he triumphantly summoned up the shades of his "misbegotten family" and probed their common problem: addiction.

We can assume that O'Neill's alcoholism was arrested in 1926 because he wanted it that way: he had long since known, at least intellectually, that if he kept on drinking, his work would inevitably decline. The first signs were already there. *The Great God Brown,* written in 1925, is a messy experimental play in which all the main characters wear masks that they keep changing as rapidly as their moods — the result comes close to farce. O'Neill had a relatively poor ear for dialogue. Here he is at his worst, in a display of fake poetry, when Dion confesses his love for Margaret:

> And I love you! Oh madly! Oh forever and ever, amen! You are my evening star and all my Pleiades! Your eyes are blue pools in which gold dreams glide, your body is a young white birch leaning backward beneath the lips of spring.

In the next act Margaret has become worried about Dion's drinking and barges into his office with a question that appears to be coming from a less than poetic Margaret:

> I finally sent the boys out looking for you and came myself. (*With tired solicitude*) I suppose you haven't eaten a thing, as usual. Won't you come home and let me fry you a chop?

When O'Neill attempts to have his central character philosophize, Brown informs us, "This is Daddy's bedtime secret for today: Man is born broken. He lives by mending. The grace of God is glue!" When the dying Brown's mistress, the earth goddess Cybel, tells him at the end of the play that there is only love and that he should recite the prayer she has taught him, he gratifies her:

> Who art! Who art! (*Suddenly — with ecstasy*) I know! I have found him! I hear him speak! "Blessed are they that weep, for they shall laugh!" Only he that has wept can laugh! The laughter of Heaven sows earth with a rain of tears, and out of earth's

transfigured birth-pain the laughter of Man returns to bless and play again in innumerable dancing gales of flame upon the knees of God!

There is a furious bombast in the play that anticipates some of Faulkner's writing in the books after 1942.

Although O'Neill's work was the single most important thing to him in the world, it is difficult to understand how he could give up alcohol with such apparent ease. After all, he had been a daily drinker for over twenty years; a life without liquor would truly be a new life for him. But drinkers almost never renounce their addiction because it lies in their interest to do so: often they are convinced that alcohol is the cure for their problems when it is frequently the cause. In any event, O'Neill ascribed his giving up alcohol to Dr. Hamilton's therapy. His case is extraordinarily rare in American writing; Raymond Carver is one of the few writers who successfully quit drinking before losing his talent. Another reason O'Neill stopped is that he never believed, as did Faulkner and Fitzgerald, that his writing would benefit in any way by drinking. Unlike Hemingway, O'Neill never felt that he enjoyed an immunity to the long-term effects of alcohol.

5

He'll probably never write a good play again.
— George Bernard Shaw to Lawrence Langner, 1926

One day when he came to tea he had a cold — he
always had a cold — and he looked at me with those
tragic eyes and said, "I need you." He kept saying, "I
need you, I need you" — never "I love you, I think
you are wonderful" — just "I need you, I need you."
... And he did need me, I discovered.
— Carlotta Monterey, 1956

O'NEILL'S NEED for Agnes began to wane after 1926. When
alcoholics give up drinking they often discover much that is new
and disturbing to them in the light of their sobriety, especially
in the area of their closest relationships. What has been warmly
familiar and comforting may appear alien. Many years after
their divorce, Agnes asserted that one of the main reasons she
had married O'Neill was to bring some order into the life of a
fellow bohemian who was so much impaired by alcohol. In their
years together, she had performed the difficult triple functions
of wife, mother and nurse. Now her husband suddenly dis-
owned his bohemianism and placed his sober creativity at the
center of his life. Her third task, as nurse, was superfluous. Once
O'Neill had stopped drinking, Agnes felt she had lost control of
a situation in which she had been dominant for a decade. The
tables were turned, and O'Neill began urging her to curb *her*
drinking while discouraging any aspect of social life that might
involve alcohol; he soon forbade any liquor in their home.

Although there appears to be little doubt that while O'Neill
had loved Agnes as much as he could love any woman, his need
for her was the central fact of the relationship. But that depen-
dency waned daily as he faced an Agnes who evidenced no sign
of giving up alcohol herself, and who told him that he would

most likely not write any more good plays while he remained sober. It is impossible to say how long their marriage might have lasted if O'Neill had not met Carlotta Monterey, the young California actress with whom he fell in love and who became his third wife. Switching over to needing Carlotta more than Agnes was painful for O'Neill, who found himself in love with both women at the same time. However, once he'd left Agnes to live abroad with Carlotta, his love for Agnes turned to unbridled anger. He once wrote her:

> I really can't believe you love me . . . or have ever loved me for years. You could not possibly have done the things you did. You could never have touched a drink, for example. It would have choked you to death — if you really loved me. And now I am really loved I see only too damned clearly by contrast all you failed to give me. I am not blaming you. It was true of me, too.

When Agnes held out in their divorce proceedings for what she asserted was a fair share of O'Neill's income, he blamed her attitude on her drinking:

> There have been so many ugly rumors. . . . But when you've had even a few drinks you are neither fine nor honorable. . . . You might very well do — or not do — something that would burn me up with hatred and keep me from working.

Because Agnes insisted on her terms, O'Neill instructed his lawyer to begin searching the church records in England in order to find out if her first marriage had been legal. Would he have to shoulder the financial support of her daughter, Barbara? Part of his wrath clearly stemmed from the tremendous guilt he felt over abandoning Agnes and the two children, Shane and Oona. It was not until the summer of 1929 that Agnes and O'Neill were finally divorced in a Reno courtroom, with only Agnes present for the proceedings.

At thirty-six Carlotta was noted for her determination in obtaining whatever she wanted. She'd first met O'Neill in 1923, but he had not been that much impressed by either her or her performance as Mildred Douglas in *The Hairy Ape*. But after meeting him again in the summer of 1926 when he was in Maine with his family, Carlotta seemingly decided that what O'Neill needed was an immediate replacement for Agnes. Already married and divorced three times, Carlotta was considered a great beauty — she had been Miss California of 1923. She affected a regal manner and spoke with a pronounced English accent that she picked up while attending drama school. Although her career in the theater had been a relatively minor one, Carlotta appears to have thought that in becoming Mrs. Eugene O'Neill she would be making her own contribution to American dramatic art. When O'Neill realized that the virtually teetotaling Carlotta was willing to take on all of Agnes's household responsibilities, he was attracted to her all the more, especially when he discovered that she had a yearly income of $14,000. This sum was an annuity that had been created for her by one of her former lovers, an elderly Wall Street broker. Carlotta managed to keep the real source of the annuity a secret from O'Neill until the 1940s; he'd believed it came from a relative. There is no doubt that her offer to pay one half of the household expenses had its share in his decision to break with Agnes and begin living with the woman he now believed he loved. The couple left America in 1928 for a three-year period, much of it spent in France.

When *Strange Interlude* became O'Neill's longest-running play, he may have thought that some of its success arose from his newfound sobriety. But in fact he did not regain any real measure of his talent as a dramatist for several years; one does not recover from the effects of long-term alcoholism in any magical, overnight fashion. Nevertheless, *Strange Interlude* was written by a man who labored at a frenzied pace; he completed the play in only two months of "eleven hours a day" work.

Despite its immense length, over three hundred pages in volume form and taking nearly six hours to perform, *Strange Interlude* achieved instant smash-hit status, running on Broadway for 426 performances. It won O'Neill his third Pulitzer Prize and was later filmed by MGM as a vehicle for Clark Gable. Within a year or so it was being produced all over the world. Today the story of Nina Leeds appears to be more of a pretentious nine-act soap opera than a major play by the leading American dramatist. *Interlude* is chock-full of interior monologues that owe much to Joyce's *Ulysses*. A hint of the play's blend of Jung and Freud can be detected in Nina's final speech in which the title is explained: "our lives are merely strange dark interludes in the electrical display of God the father."

Returning to the early stage convention of the aside, O'Neill's unhappy characters frequently address themselves — really the audience — inwardly at considerable length, in some cases as much as a page of text at a time. The play's original director, Phillip Moeller, hit upon the notion of having all the characters on stage at the time adopt a "freeze" position while one of the monologues was in progress, thus placing an unpleasant burden on those actors performing their "frozen" parts. A parody of the play's technique, performed by Groucho Marx in *Animal Crackers,* is actually an astute comment on what was wrong with the play: since the audience knew far more about what was going on than did the characters, there was no real sense of drama. The play's huge success was largely due to its, for the time, daring use of such themes as adultery, abortion, hereditary insanity and what now appears to be, in the case of Charlie Marsden, an example of "closet" homosexuality. The presence of these volatile elements blinded theatergoers to the play's intrinsic faults. It is significant that O'Neill never again repeated his interior monologue experiment.

In all fairness, O'Neill was capable of writing wretchedly at any time of his life. Merely remaining sober was no guarantee that he could write well on all occasions. It could be argued that his two plays dealing with the problem of religious faith, *Dynamo* (1929) and *Days Without End* (1934), while written several years after he stopped drinking, are among his very worst efforts in their dependence on inflated language and absurd dramatic situations.

*

In the months after leaving her in November 1927 for Carlotta, O'Neill's rage against Agnes mounted steadily. In long, discursive and occasionally incoherent letters to his attorney, Harry Weinberger, O'Neill began to accuse Agnes of adultery, blackmail and many other offenses. He belittled his drinking and even blamed her for the problem:

> ... the plain facts in this case to me are that a woman, whom I took when she was nothing but a shabby hanger-on, an unsuccessful cheap fiction writer, with no status of any kind, with a child alleged to be born in wedlock. ... That she ever helped me in my work is a grotesque fiction. She was always intensely jealous of my work as compared to what she could do. At times, even, she did her best to hamper it. ... Another idiotic claim of hers is that she stuck to me in spite of my old drinking. Well, drink never interfered with my working, my drinking has been greatly exaggerated, and she stuck because I was bread and butter and luxuries, because she liked to get drunk herself, and because when I drank she could feel a bit superior, a martyr. There were many times, indeed, when she urged me to drink.

Behind this smokescreen of accusations were O'Neill's guilt feelings as well as fury over Agnes's insistence that she receive enough alimony to support herself and her three children in Bermuda in the style she'd been living in when O'Neill left her. As the months passed with no hope of an early divorce agreement, O'Neill's anger found its outlet in the first of a series of drinking episodes, which demonstrate clearly that giving up alcohol for good requires more than just will power: drinkers nearly always need some kind of shocking experience that will harden their resolve not to drink.

Louis Kalonyme, an old Greenwich Village drinking friend, became for a short time the go-between for Agnes and O'Neill in their protracted negotiations. He visited O'Neill at the home he shared with Carlotta in the south of France. In the course of the evening the two men began to recall the fun they'd had with Terry Carlin and Jamie O'Neill ten years back, and eventually retired to O'Neill's bedroom with a bottle and became thoroughly drunk. Carlotta recognized that her planned marriage to O'Neill was in danger and attempted to frighten him by packing her bags and leaving the house. She returned, however, the very same morning to assume her role as O'Neill's nurse. One night of drinking cost O'Neill two weeks in bed; at age forty he found it much harder to recover from even a short bout such as this.

Far more damaging to their future together was O'Neill's conduct in the course of a sort of prehoneymoon — an extended series of sea voyages to the Far East. It is not uncommon for people who are attempting to escape one addiction to take up another in the process. In O'Neill's case it was gambling, the pleasures of which he discovered when they arrived in Saigon. Carlotta was furious with him for squandering his money at the tables, but he told her that "she was not going to rule his life." Tensions between them worsened in Shanghai, especially after O'Neill met Alfred Batson, another old Village friend, who took him on a tour of the city's gaudier night spots, where O'Neill began to drink. Returning drunkenly to the hotel, he encountered Carlotta waiting up for him in their room. After a bitter quarrel in which he accused her of spying on him, he called her an "old whore" and struck her so hard that she nearly fell. Carlotta then moved out of the hotel, leaving O'Neill to his own devices, which were what she expected: he remained drunk for days until he finally required hospitalization. While drinking, he kept telling Batson that he'd acted like a "son of a bitch" to Agnes, apparently attempting to convince both his friend and himself that his current binge was caused by his guilt over her.

Keeping abreast of O'Neill's condition through intermediaries, Carlotta forgave him for his lapse. He had written her from the hospital that he would "be a *good 'un*" in the future, but she had reason to doubt his ability to remain sober while traveling from one exotic place to another. Nevertheless, they set sail for the Philippines and then proceeded to Singapore, where O'Neill started a new round of drinking that lasted several weeks. When it was time for them to leave Singapore on the

SS *Coblenz,* O'Neill was still going strong. Carlotta disembarked and allowed O'Neill to sail on as scheduled, by himself. She remained in Singapore for only one day, then booked passage on the SS *President Monroe,* a liner she discovered was following the same route as the *Coblenz.* Very shortly, the couple began exchanging a torrent of radiograms, all aimed at a reconciliation when they reached port. He told her

> I AM HALF MAD WITH UTTER LONELINESS WITHOUT FRIENDS PLANS OR HOPES. . . . I LOVE YOU AND I DESERVE [*sic*] THAT THE DOCTOR HAS MY PROMISE AND WILL KEEP IT.

When Carlotta expressed doubt about his love for her, he tried to reassure her about that as well as his future sobriety:

> OF COURSE I WANT YOU AND NEED YOU AS MUCH AS I LOVE YOU AND EXPERIENCE YOU SPEAK OF WILL NEVER BE REPEATED I GIVE YOU BACK YOUR OWN ADVICE FORGET THE PAST AND START BUILDING SOLIDLY FOR THE FUTURE

They were reunited in Port Said, where an exhausted O'Neill came stumbling up the gangplank of the *Monroe* and fell into Carlotta's arms. They sailed on together to Genoa and France, where they were married in September of 1929. The combination of the Shanghai–Singapore experience and his certainty that Carlotta would not sit through another drinking bout appears to have been the "bottom" that O'Neill required in order to stay sober for the next twenty years. He truly needed her, couldn't consider living without her; there is little doubt that he came to love her as his principal bulwark against the world. The feeling was reciprocated: Carlotta could not imagine a life without him.

6

Mistress, I desire you, you are my passion, and my life-drunkenness, and my ecstasy, and the wine of joy to me! Wife, you are my love, and my happiness, and the word behind my word, and the half of my heart! Mother, you are my lost way refound, my end and my beginning.
— O'Neill to Carlotta O'Neill, May 28, 1932

... at least this time I'll have the satisfaction of knowing I failed at something big and thus be a success in my own spiritual eyes. ...

Oh for a language to write drama in! For a speech that is dramatic and isn't just conversation!
— O'Neill to Joseph Wood Krutch, July 27, 1929

O'NEILL's impassioned address to Carlotta was not hyperbole. In the 1930s and 1940s he relied on her for nearly everything. She did become mistress, wife and mother. One of her self-chosen additional tasks was to keep as many of O'Neill's old friends as far away from him as possible. She may have been prompted to the gradual destruction of these friendships by the belief that continued association would lead him back to drinking. Those hostile to Carlotta think this was only part of her design, the less obvious one being that this enabled her to keep O'Neill under her control. The truth appears to be somewhere between the two, for some have seen Carlotta gradually assuming the role of O'Neill's jailer, ruthlessly alienating him not only from his close friends but from his three children as well, with disastrous effects on them. As O'Neill entered his forties, he became ever more of a recluse, interested only in the progress of his work. His failing health, signaled by the worsening of his tremor, made social life a burden. Eating in restaurants became nearly impossible because of his difficulties with the utensils. It is clear, from reading his correspondence, that at least some of his desire for seclusion arose from his own wishes, with Carlotta simply carrying out his orders; sometimes he chose to hide behind her authority.

There were exceptions to Carlotta's exclusionary policy. O'Neill's co-producer Kenneth Macgowan, the theater critic George Jean Nathan and Saxe Commins, who became his editor at Liveright in 1931 and later at Random House, were all sufficiently sober and businesslike to warrant their being invited to Le Plessis, the mansion the O'Neills bought with some of the huge earnings from *Strange Interlude*. In part because of the supremacy of the American dollar at the beginning of the 1930s, O'Neill was able to live in lordly style in France: Le Plessis had thirty-five rooms; the O'Neills' car was a chauffeur-driven Bugati. Nathan recalled an O'Neill "drinking enormous glasses of Coca-Cola and making everyone believe it is straight whiskey. . . . Years ago he was a drinker of parts . . . has sat on [the barrel] with an almost puritanical splendor and tenacity."

The first sure sign that sobriety was beneficial to the renewal of O'Neill's creativity was *Mourning Becomes Electra*, the work most responsible for his being awarded the Nobel Prize in 1936. Only slightly shorter than *Strange Interlude*, *Mourning Becomes Electra* consists of three separate plays, *Homecoming*, *The Hunted* and *The Haunted*, each running about two hours, the whole to be performed in a single evening. Now in his early forties, as if attempting to make up for all the wasted time of the past, O'Neill frequently worked seven days a week on the trilogy, completing six separate drafts over a twenty-month interval between August 1929 and March 1931. This was the longest time he'd ever spent on a single work: in his drinking days he'd turned out some of his best plays as quickly as Faulkner did in his prime. *The Emperor Jones* was written in ten days, *The Hairy Ape* in three weeks and *Desire Under the Elms* in eight weeks. In his effort to create what he hoped would be his greatest work, O'Neill kept experimenting with masks, soliloquies and asides, but eventually abandoned them all in favor of a straightforward dramatic technique. His success was extraordinary.

O'Neill wanted to write a tragedy that would make the darkly fated, mythical acts of the characters in the *Oresteia* of Aeschylus comprehensible to a modern audience. He accomplished this by conceiving what he regarded as a Jungian theory of character, "which would demonstrate that fate from within the family is the modern psychological approximation of the Greek conception from without, from the supernatural." His method was to impose the characters and basic events of the Greek trilogy onto the dark doings of a repressed New England family, the Mannons, in the days following the Civil War. He made a major change in the third play, here abandoning Aeschylus for Euripides by making Electra rather than her brother, Orestes, the prime revenge seeker against their mother. It is Lavinia's destiny as the last of the Mannons to enter the doomed house to spend her final days with the ghosts of those who have perished. O'Neill's devotion to Carlotta may have had its part in shaping his view of the strong-willed Lavinia, his Electra character.

Despite his concern at being unable to supply the plays with a language commensurate with the great themes he was attempting to replicate, O'Neill's trilogy possesses a considerable dramatic power that continues to impress. Unlike *Strange Interlude,* which takes place in a barely evoked America of the 1920s, *Mourning Becomes Electra* is set in a specific milieu that exists independent of the classical sources. The trilogy was an amazing tour de force and received the greatest critical acclaim of any of O'Neill's plays performed in his lifetime. Only the ongoing Depression prevented it from running more than 150 performances. The O'Neills returned to America in May 1931 for rehearsals and began looking for a permanent home in the United States.

7

Now we need an unquestioning faith in all pipe dreams, however irrational, lest we be defeated in spirit and thrown into the sty of final "realistic" opportunism, where God is a murderous blind hog, and there is no dream, and The Iceman Cometh like a thief in the night, and we wearily welcome him because there is no longer a kick in the booze whatever.
— O'Neill to Norman Holmes Pearson,
July 30, 1942

For the love of God, forgive and come back. You are all I have in life. I am sick and will surely die without you.
— O'Neill to Carlotta O'Neill, January 19, 1948

THE O'NEILLS had developed a passion for privacy in France that they satisfied in America by buying a series of homes in isolated communities in the South (1932 through 1936) and later in the Pacific Northwest (1937 through 1944). Casa Genotta was the first of these, a seaside mansion that O'Neill had constructed for them on Sea Island, Georgia. After bearing five summers of intense heat that made working there difficult, the O'Neills relocated to Tao House, about sixty miles north of San Francisco. This was perhaps the lordliest of all O'Neill's homes; it contained twenty-two rooms, and some of the visitors from the East thought of it as a fortress, its main purpose being to keep people out. The O'Neills continued living there until nearly the end of the Second World War, when they returned to the East for good.

During the years 1932 through 1944, O'Neill completed an astonishingly large and varied body of work. This achievement is even more remarkable because a great deal of it was written by a man whose health began to fail badly after about 1934.

Despite his vigorous style of life at Sea Island, which included arising at seven, beginning work at eight and stopping for lunch at one-thirty, followed by long swimming sessions in the Atlantic, his severe bodily tremor slowly worsened. Most of his doctors thought he was suffering from some variety of Parkinson's disease, but some were not so sure.

It was at Sea Island in the spring of 1932 that O'Neill began shaping the work that consumed the bulk of his creative energies for a decade. This was the group of plays he called "A Tale of Possessors Self-Possessed," a grandiose title surely, and also one that indicates one of O'Neill's shortcomings as a dramatist: he had a faulty ear. He originally conceived of this immense work as a cycle of four or five plays, each of them longer than *Strange Interlude*. As the years passed, the five became seven, then nine and eventually eleven plays concerning the destiny of a single American family, the Harfords, from 1775 through 1932. Over the generations the Harfords were driven by the twin passions of greed and materialism. At the end of his life, O'Neill destroyed the entire cycle save *A Touch of the Poet* and another play he had not completed, *More Stately Mansions,* which were inadvertently sent to Yale with other papers. Since the two surviving plays contain superb material, one wonders why O'Neill burned all the others. From the available evidence, it appears he had established a standard of excellence for his dramas that he found hard to attain. He had been working on all eleven, back and forth from one to another, when he discovered he'd not been able to meet his standards for the fifth play, *The Calms of Capricorn*. In 1939 he put the cycle aside to take up an entirely different project; it was not until he was close to death in the 1950s that he decided to destroy his cycle plays for fear that they would be produced in their unfinished form.

The interruption in 1939 resulted in O'Neill's writing the works that have made him the greatest American dramatist, two plays that are considered his best: *Long Day's Journey into Night* and *The Iceman Cometh*. They are concerned with addiction, a subject O'Neill has written about with more power than any other American writer. Amazingly enough, the idea for both plays came to him at the same time: he made entries in his Work Book for them on June 6, 1939, completing *Iceman* in that year and *Long Day's Journey* in the one following.

Fearing failure for *The Iceman Cometh,* in view of its length and disturbing content, he was unwilling to let it be given a New York production until the end of the Second World War. *Iceman* is regarded by many as O'Neill's second-best play — after *Long Day's Journey.* Both deal strikingly and compassionately with alcohol addiction, but *Iceman* encompasses a far broader social canvas. The inhabitants of Harry Hope's "No Chance Saloon . . . Bedrock Bar, The End of the Line Café, The Bottom of the Sea Rathskeller" are all the drunks that O'Neill recalled from his youth, especially those he met in that near-fatal summer of 1912. *The Iceman Cometh* is extraordinarily repetitious in its efforts to reproduce the repetitious speech of alcoholics; when informed that he said something in the play eighteen times, O'Neill replied that he had *meant* to say it that many times and refused to cut a single word.

Back in 1933, when O'Neill wrote *Ah, Wilderness!,* his extremely successful play about growing up in New London — his only lighthearted work — he liked to say that it was about a happy boyhood there that had not been his in actuality. In *Long Day's Journey* he aimed at showing the reality of his youth as he saw it after a quarter of a century. The writing of *Ah, Wilderness!* has been seen as a preparation for the great work that followed seven years later, but it was more likely the chance correspondence that O'Neill conducted with a Works Progress Administration researcher in California that started him thinking again about the unhappy family into which he was born. The researcher, Patrick O'Neill (not a relative), had sent the playwright a monograph he'd written about the career of James O'Neill, Sr., to read for factual accuracy. O'Neill obliged him and struck up an acquaintance by mail with the young researcher. Over the months that followed, O'Neill began to think more and more about the tragic events of his youth, especially those occurring in 1912, the year he attempted suicide in a New York rooming house.

One critic of *Long Day's Journey* believes that O'Neill's intimate knowledge of alcoholism, with its familiar pattern of repetitious behavior, was helpful in shaping his dramatic vision in this autobiographical work in which all the central characters are held captive by their addictions. Mary Tyrone (Ella O'Neill) is depicted as a morphine addict who has only recently been released from a hospital where she was withdrawn from her drug. Her famous actor husband, James (James O'Neill, Sr.), and his two grown sons, James junior and Edmund (Jamie and Eugene O'Neill), are all clearly alcoholic, each one at a different stage of the disease.

As I've indicated throughout, one of the most common indications of alcoholism is denial: *Long Day's Journey* is filled with a carefully modulated series of denials voiced by the members of the Tyrone family that anything is wrong with them. The painful subject of Mary's drug addiction is assiduously avoided until well into the play. Only when her relapse has become so glaringly apparent that it can no longer be ignored do the Tyrone men acknowledge it and then begin their painful, accusatory recitals of hurt and anger against one another. Each of the three is shown to be as much a victim of alcoholism as is Mary with her morphine. Each man seeks someone to blame for all the family's misfortunes; a tide of guilt and self-recrimination sweeps through the living room as they talk through the long night. Not one of them can face the fact that their common problem is their alcoholism. Edmund is young enough to consider his heavy drinking romantic, even quoting to his father the famous "Be drunken, if you would not be martyred slaves to Time" passage from Baudelaire, which I have quoted in the Faulkner chapter.

The Tyrone men use Mary's relapse as their excuse to get thoroughly drunk. As they hurl accusations back and forth, it is apparent that they cannot hear one another: all three are trapped in the solipsistic world of the alcoholic, where the drinker has lost or is rapidly losing contact with the real world around him. O'Neill aptly wrote George Jean Nathan that *Long Day's Journey into Night* was "a deeply tragic play without any violent action." His words to his old friend, written while completing the play, describe more tellingly than can any commentator what happens to the Tyrones:

> At the final curtain, there they still are, trapped within each other by the past, each guilty and at the same time innocent, scorning, loving, pitying each other, understanding and yet not understanding at all, forgiving but still doomed never to be able to forget.

Alone among the alcoholic writers of his generation, O'Neill was able to confront directly in his art the disease that came close to destroying his talent. He was the only American writer to write at his best when dealing primarily with addiction; the others discussed here, particularly Fitzgerald, who regularly lied to himself and others, used alcoholism as a secondary element in their novels but never as the dead center of one. It took O'Neill thirteen years to discover the subject about which he could speak with an authority that none of his contemporaries could match. His ventures into the hitherto closed world of addiction have no equal in our literature, and it is possible to claim they could have been achieved only by a writer who had traversed the long corridor of alcoholism but returned to tell his tale.

The deeply buried feelings exposed by writing *Long Day's Journey* were painful for O'Neill, so much so that when asked by a few friends to read aloud the play's conclusion, his voice broke and he wept. He told his tiny audience that he considered the closing scene to be the finest he'd ever written. Despite his certain knowledge that the play was his best, he decided to withhold it from theatrical production and publication. Accordingly, he had Bennett Cerf place five copies of the manuscript in the Random House safe in New York in 1945, where it lay sealed and unread for nearly a decade. His specific instructions to Cerf were that the package was not to be opened until twenty-five years after his death. When O'Neill died in 1953, Carlotta told Cerf to publish the play despite the interdiction. When Cerf demurred, citing his old friend's wishes, Carlotta, as executor of the estate, found the law to be on her side in the matter. When Cerf then offered to proceed with publication if Carlotta would preface the text with a statement that it was being offered to the public only because of her wishes, she refused and withdrew the play from the firm that owned the publication rights to all his other plays. She submitted *Long Day's Journey into Night* to the Yale University Press, which published it immediately with great success.

One of O'Neill's ostensible reasons for withholding the play was that it might be an embarrassment to his children, particularly to his oldest boy, Eugene junior, his son by his first wife, Kathleen Jenkins. Eugene was the only one of his three children with whom O'Neill established any real intimacy, a relationship sealed by their common love of literature. After a brilliant beginning as a classics major at Yale, Eugene taught there for several years and seemed assured of a successful academic career. Believing that he wasn't advancing himself rapidly enough, he entered the New York radio world of the late thirties and forties, where his richly modulated voice (apparently not unlike that of Orson Welles) was rewarded with various jobs in the industry. A heavy drinker from the beginning, Eugene was an alcoholic by the time he reached his early thirties. After three marriages and many professional setbacks, most of them caused by drinking, Eugene committed suicide in 1950 at the age of forty. He consumed a bottle of whiskey and then opened the veins of his legs and arms in his bath. Apparently changing his mind at the last moment, he attempted to descend the stairway of his home in order to reach the phone but failed. The language of his suicide note recalls that of his father: "Never let it be said of O'Neill that he failed to empty a bottle. Ave atque vale."

Because of the continued animosity between Agnes and O'Neill, he was never at ease with their two children, Shane and

Oona. A great beauty, Oona was courted in her mid-teens by mail from J. D. Salinger, but she married Charles Chaplin when she reached eighteen. Despite her father's prediction that such a marriage was doomed (Chaplin was fifty-four at the time), the union proved to be enduring. Bearing him eight children, Oona lived in apparent happiness with her famous husband until his death in 1977.

Nowhere near as fortunate was her brother, Shane, who, unlike his half-brother, never found a career that engrossed him sufficiently to pursue it with any vigor. He became addicted to alcohol, as had his father before him, while still in his teens. His other addictions included heroin and marijuana; a good part of Shane's life was spent in procuring narcotics or evading the police because of using or buying them. In 1976, at the age of fifty-eight, he jumped to his death from the fourth-floor window of an apartment house in Coney Island. His mother, Agnes, eventually remarried and then resumed the literary career that O'Neill had disapproved of when they were first married. She wrote a novel, *The Road Is Before Us*, which was well received when it was published in 1944. But her main achievement in writing was the memoir of her early life with O'Neill, *Part of a Long Story*, which possesses an immediacy of detail that marks it off from all the other reminiscences of those who knew O'Neill when young.

O'Neill's later years were clouded by the near-total collapse of his health. His tremor became so severe that he found it impossible to write after 1943. Friends purchased a Dictaphone for him, but it was hopeless. He had written first drafts of all his plays with a lead pencil in a minuscule script and discovered that he could not make the changeover to dictation — unlike Henry James, who accomplished the feat in the 1890s after the introduction of the typewriter. The last play he completed, *A Moon for the Misbegotten*, in 1943, was based on the last, drunken days of his brother, Jamie. In his long confession to Josie, Tyrone tells her about taking his mother's coffin aboard the train to

New York and of picking up the "blond pig" to whom he gave some of her valuables. Writing this work had yet again awakened the old familial ghosts.

When he found that he would never write again, O'Neill settled into a deepening depression that held him fast for the next decade. His whole being had been taken up with playwriting for thirty years; with that world now closed to him, there was little to do but wait out the end of the war and hope to get *The Iceman Cometh* performed in New York. Although having his play produced would be welcome, it was no substitute for writing. It can be assumed that O'Neill began to long for death as early as the mid-1940s when he composed the words he wanted inscribed on his tombstone:

> EUGENE O'NEILL
> THERE IS SOMETHING
> TO BE SAID
> FOR BEING DEAD

At the end of the war the O'Neills sold Tao House and returned to live in New York in an upper East Side penthouse apartment. One reason for the move was so O'Neill could be present for the rehearsals of *The Iceman Cometh,* which the Theater Guild produced with a moderate success late in 1946. By that time he had become a virtual recluse, refusing to see many of his old friends and his three children. As he isolated himself more and more from the world around him, he had the full cooperation of Carlotta. But O'Neill appears to have had a will of iron, at least until the very end: he *wanted* to be alone.

In various attempts to lessen the severity of his tremor, O'Neill's doctors prescribed a number of sedatives, as well as chloral hydrate for sleep. In time, Carlotta commenced taking these along with her husband, and they both became drug dependent. It is tragic that O'Neill, after being able to stop drinking, should in later life become just as addicted to other drugs, prescribed by doctors. The medications that O'Neill and Carlotta began to take in the 1940s produce long-term side effects of depression and, in the case of the bromides, which Carlotta was taking, of psychosis. A great deal of Carlotta's erratic behavior toward O'Neill is understandable in light of the drugs.

They also became increasingly irascible with each other as their circle of friends gradually diminished. With few visitors and little to do, time hung heavily in the O'Neill apartment. In early 1948 they quarreled so bitterly that Carlotta packed her things and left, presumably for good. Suffering from acute loneliness, O'Neill invited a New London friend of his youth, "Ice" Casey, to stay with him. Casey was an alcoholic who loved to reminisce about their boozing days; within a week or so both men were hard at it. These were O'Neill's first drinks in nearly twenty years, and their effect on him must have been extreme. After one sodden evening, Casey retired after taking some sleeping pills. O'Neill, who had remained awake, fell and badly fractured his arm. He lay helpless on the floor for hours, attempting to awaken his friend without success. Not until the next morning did the contrite Casey become aware of what had happened. The fracture required O'Neill's being placed in Doctors Hospital. Almost immediately, Carlotta was admitted to the same hospital with an "arthritic condition" that disguised her real intention of spying on O'Neill's visitors. They were reunited within a few weeks, to the pleased surprise of some and the unhappy astonishment of others. The episode was a curious prefiguring of what happened to the O'Neills when they settled down the following year in a seaside cottage in Marblehead, Massachusetts.

The couple's second major separation took place under far more dramatic circumstances. By early 1951, life in Marblehead — characterized by the ceaseless pounding of the ocean — was punctuated by sleep produced by steady dosages of chloral hydrate and Nembutal. On a snowy night that December, O'Neill left the house without his winter coat and cane, which he now needed for walking. He stumbled and fell just in front of the cottage, breaking a leg just below the knee. Years later, Carlotta recalled that she had jeered at him as he lay helpless on the ground: "How the mighty have fallen! Where's your greatness now, little man?" She then closed the door to the house, leaving him to his pain in the near-freezing cold. Luckily for O'Neill, his doctor was, by chance, making his rounds in the neighborhood and arrived in time to notice the huddled figure in the snow. O'Neill was taken to the hospital while Carlotta, suffering from bromide poisoning and deeply disturbed by the event, was placed briefly in a mental institution.

In the next few months, all of them spent in a hospital bed, O'Neill came close to death on several occasions; his weight once dropped below one hundred pounds. At first it appeared that he had determined never to see Carlotta again, more than half convinced that she had desired his death. But in time their strange love-hate relationship resumed: they were surely "welded" as few couples have ever been. Once again they were reconciled, and O'Neill spent the last year and a half of his life in a suite at the Hotel Shelton in Boston with Carlotta.

He died on November 27, 1953, a wasted figure of a man who had endured great and continual torment for more than a decade. His last words were nearly as savage as his father's had been when he died: "He suddenly struggled up to a half-sitting position and, staring wildly around the room, cried, 'I knew it! I knew it! Born in a goddamn hotel room and dying in a hotel room!'"

Like Hemingway, O'Neill fought the killing despair brought on by depression. In his younger days, O'Neill believed that he could exorcise his depression — his demons of despair — by drinking. After 1926 he faced them without alcohol and salvaged his threatened career as a playwright. In the 1930s and early 1940s, with *Mourning Becomes Electra* and his two great plays about addiction, he rose to his greatest height as a writer. Except for Zola in *L'Assommoir,* O'Neill has more to tell us about addiction than perhaps any major writer. Among Americans he stands alone.

Raymond Carver's poem quoted at the beginning of this book indicates that writers who stop drinking to avoid creative decay need not expect the terrible physical agonies experienced by

O'Neill in his last years. The autopsy report indicated that O'Neill's worsening tremor had been caused not by Parkinson's disease, as he had been led to believe, but by a rare form of degeneration of the cells of the cerebellum, a malady which, like his alcoholism, appears to have been familial. O'Neill's great works about addiction were written by a man who vanquished the disease that has destroyed so many of our best writers but who was then forced to undergo the agonizing impairment that deprived him of the one thing he cared about most — the ability to write. O'Neill's courage in continuing to write until he could no longer hold the pencil has had few, if any, parallels in our literature.

Credits

Grateful acknowledgment is made for permission to reprint the following material:

Random House for *Collected Stories of William Faulkner,* copyright 1950 by Random House; *Sanctuary* by William Faulkner, copyright 1931 by William Faulkner; *Pylon* by William Faulkner, copyright 1935 by William Faulkner; *Selected Letters of WF,* edited by Joseph Blotner, copyright © 1977 by Joseph Blotner; *Faulkner: A Biography* by Joseph Blotner, copyright © 1974 & 1984 by Joseph Blotner.

Charles Scribner's Sons, an imprint of Macmillan Publishing Company, for *Letters of F. Scott Fitzgerald,* edited by Andrew Turnbull, copyright © 1963 by Frances Scott Fitzgerald Lanahan; *Dear Scott/Dear Max,* edited by John Kuehl and Jackson Bryer, copyright © 1971 by Charles Scribner's Sons; *Selected Short Stories of F. Scott Fitzgerald,* edited by Malcolm Cowley, copyright 1951 by Charles Scribner's Sons.

Selected Letters of Ernest Hemingway, copyright © 1981 by The Ernest Hemingway Foundation, Inc.; *Short Stories of Ernest Hemingway,* copyright 1938 by Ernest Hemingway, copyright renewed © 1966 by Mary Hemingway; *A Moveable Feast* by Ernest Hemingway, copyright © 1964 by Mary Hemingway; *Green Hills of Africa* by Ernest Hemingway, copyright 1935 by Charles Scribner's Sons, renewed © 1963 by Mary Hemingway; *To Have and Have Not* by Ernest Hemingway, copyright 1937 by Ernest Hemingway, renewed © 1965 by Mary Hemingway; *For Whom the Bell Tolls,* copyright 1940 by Ernest Hemingway, renewed © 1968 by Mary Hemingway; *Islands in the Stream* by Ernest Hemingway, copyright © 1970 by Mary Hemingway.

Yale University Press for *Selected Letters of Eugene O'Neill,* edited by Travis Bogard and Jackson R. Bryer, copyright © 1988 by Yale University Press.

Doubleday and Company for *The Great Illusion* by Herbert Asbury, copyright 1950 by Herbert Asbury.

The poem "Gravy" by Raymond Carver is reprinted by permission of Tess Gallagher for The Estate of Raymond Carver. © 1988 by Raymond Carver. First appeared in *The New Yorker.*

Photo credits: page 24, AP/Wide World Photos; page 92, AP/Wide World Photos; page 98, courtesy of the Henry W. and Albert A. Berg Collection of English and American Literature of the New York Public Library, Astor, Lenox and Tilden Foundations; page 156, Robert Capa/Magnum; page 194, courtesy of El Callejón restaurant, Madrid; page 206, AP/Wide World Photos; page 212, F. Roy Kemp/New York Public Library at Lincoln Center.

Notes and Sources
Bibliography
Index

Notes and Sources

Introduction

PAGE

4   "to write poems": Horace, I, 19.

5   "than in the US": Anthony Powell to Tom Dardis, December 3, 1984.

9   "drugs and drink": Mellow, xix–xx.
     "social suicide": Connolly, 305.
     "get away with anything": Mellow, xx.
     "bits of damaging evidence": Mellow, 317.

11   "different in France": Ford, xix.

12   "disease of the mind": Roueché, 105.

13   "emotionally sick": Ibid., 122.
     "more heterosexual": Vaillant, 49.

14   "psychological stresses": Ibid., 47.
     "will be consumed": Ibid., 44.

15   "physical morbidity": Ibid.
     "variety of individual symptoms": Ibid.

17   "an impregnable silence": Saint-Exupéry, 50–52.
     "diagnosis of alcoholism": Goodwin, *Is Alcoholism Hereditary?*, 40.

18   "begets another": Mendelson and Mellow, "Biological Components," 60.
     hard-drinking parents: Ibid., 63; Goodwin, *Is Alcoholism Hereditary?*, 63.

20   *greater incidence of alcoholism*: Mendelson and Mellow, "Biological Components," 67; Goodwin, *Longitudinal Research in Alcoholism*, 90, 99.
     "non-alcoholic parents": Goodwin, *Is Alcoholism Hereditary?*, 76.

Faulkner

PAGE
25   "whiskey within reach": Coindreau, 29.
     "whiskey won't cure": Blotner, vol. 2, 1450.
     "into the tumbler": Faulkner, *Collected Stories*, 701, 705.
27   "merciful Jesus": Wilde, 143.
31   "off for home . . . today": Anderson, *Selected Letters*, 213.
33   "romantic, even chic": Johnson, 119.
34   Keeley Cure: Blotner, vol. 1, 34.
37   "produced by a crock": Basso, 11.
39   "achieve its purpose": Anderson, *Death in the Woods*, 221.
     "not affected him": Ibid., 222.
     "delicately built": Ibid.
     "a little drunk": Ibid., 230.
41   "terrible form of paralysis": Asbury, 282–86.
42   "taste rather flat": Spratling, 29.
     "every morning": Ibid., 30.
     "not the alcohol": Ibid.
43   "your leave first": Faulkner, *Selected Letters*, 37.
45   "making me his slave": Blotner, vol. 1, 184.
46   "Watts-Dunton banned liquor": Lorenz, 87–88.
     "use your imagination": Bold, 87.
     "trying to conquer it": Faulkner, *The Sound and the Fury*, 93.
47   "Why do I do it!?": Blotner, vol. 2, 1179.
48   "when I'm drunk": Ibid., vol. 1, 687.
49   "about a little girl": Faulkner, *A Faulkner Miscellany*, 158.
     "paper before me": Ibid., 159.
     "smelled like trees": Ibid.
50   "to be exploded off": Haffenden, 414.
52   dedicated craftsman: Harrison Smith interview with Tom Dardis, July 1960.
     "a real son of a bitch": Wasson, 89.
53   Smith couldn't find it: Louise Williams interview with Tom Dardis, August 1978.
54   "would hardly move me": Faulkner to Harrison Smith, nd, the Berg Collection, New York Public Library.
55   "like collecting stamps": Brodsky and Hamblin, vol. 2, 94.
     as if she didn't exist: Tony Buttitta interview with Tom Dardis, July 1986.
56   "ammonia and creosote": Faulkner, *Sanctuary*, 38–39.
57   "drank his own": Anderson, *Letters*, 252.
     "live in New York": Young, 373.
58   with gentlemanly ease: Louise Williams interview with Tom Dar-

dis, August 1978.

59   paying his English ones: Evelyn Harter interview and Edith Haggard interview, March 1984.

60   "shape I was in": Blotner, vol. 1, 755.

61   "buy it too": Faulkner, *Essays,* 178.

63   "is no excuse": Blotner, 1984, 324–25.

       "since you left)": Faulkner to Harrison Smith, [August 1934], Faulkner Collection, University of Virginia Library.

64   "can drink it": Faulkner, *Pylon,* 189–90.

       "amazed at my temperateness": Blotner, 1984, 350–51.

66   "best in America, by God": Faulkner, *Selected Letters,* 113.

68   "never asked him again": Abadie, 92.

72   "lead to paradise": Broughton, 796.

73   "escape something": Brodsky, 388.

74   "Why do I do it?": Ibid., 393.

       "you can find out": Ibid.

76   "never looked back": Faulkner, *Selected Letters,* 188.

       "takes so long": Ibid., 256.

77   "stuff is no good": Ibid.

       "might do it": Ibid., 234.

       "probably two": Ibid., 246.

       "write fast anymore": Ibid., 256.

       "so do I": Ibid., 257.

       "break the pencil": Ibid., 314.

       "write much more": Blotner, vol. 2, 1232.

80   "another drink all day": Cowley, *The Literary Situation,* 207. The second writer is probably Hemingway.

81   "prepared to leave": Brodsky, 389.

83   "believe all of them": Faulkner, *Selected Letters,* 339.

       "few tins of beer": Brodsky and Hamblin, vol. 2, 90.

84   "real disintegration": Ibid.

       "of a man": Ibid., 89.

       "deserve what they get": Ibid., 94.

       "finish the big book": Ibid.

85   "until I get away": Faulkner, *Selected Letters,* 344.

       "that I still can": Ibid., 344.

87   "I wouldn't do it": Blotner, 1984, 621.

       "as soon be dead": Ibid.

89   "now become ashen": Wasson, 197.

       although not their friendship: Joan Williams interview with Tom Dardis, August 1984.

90   "in Zanuckland": Nunnally Johnson to Tom Dardis, November 8, 1974.

91   "I am wrong you see": Faulkner, *Selected Letters,* 391.

       "admitting it at least": Brodsky and Hamblin, 189–90.

"now drive himself": Howe, 283.
93   "does not please me": Blotner, vol. 2, 1506.
"no holding me": Ibid., 1487.

Fitzgerald

99   "bluer skies somewhere": Fitzgerald, *Correspondence*, 494.
"liquor and literature": Fitzgerald, *Dear Scott*, 41.
100 "more than was good for him": Piper, 9.
attempting to play baseball: Bruccoli, *Epic Grandeur*, 20.
101 "wisdom, health and experience": Fitzgerald, *Correspondence*, 5.
102 Louise Brooks recalled them: Brooks interview with Tom Dardis, April 1981.
103 "what she might do": Mellow, 117.
104 "going to end up": Ibid., 117–18.
"physical hangovers": Fitzgerald, *Dear Scott*, 126.
"strongly on the subject": Hemingway, *Selected Letters*, 250.
105 "color of used candle wax": Hemingway, *A Moveable Feast*, 152.
106 "charming person": Ibid., 154.
"into a fool": Ibid., 167.
107 "released at once": Mizener, 84–85.
109 "There was no view": Hemingway, *A Moveable Feast*, 179.
110 "it is as good": Fitzgerald, *Correspondence*, 165.
"to work anyhow": Ibid., 169.
"financial insecurity": Fitzgerald, *Dear Scott*, 102.
"the movie business": Ibid.
111 "couldn't drink but did": Mayfield, 113.
112 "write the novel": Hemingway, *Selected Letters*, 307.
113 "always bloody platitudes": Ibid.
"ruined each other": Fitzgerald, *Correspondence*, 241.
114 "you didn't stop drinking": Ibid., 246–49.
"I didn't": Ibid., 249.
"before I loved her": Ibid.
"allowed her to drink more": Ibid., 242.
"disinclined to work": Ibid. The emphasis in this letter is Fitzgerald's.
115 *"in my head all night"*: Ibid.
"the rights of man": Ibid., 243.
118 "physical consequences of it": Bruccoli, *Epic Grandeur*, 346.
"she was a drunkard": Ibid., 349.
"do what I say": Ibid.
"three or four drinks a day": Ibid., 351.
"for her insanity": Ibid., 351–52.

119 "the cause of it": Ibid., 351.
    "weren't they?": Ibid.
    "not want to disillusion him": Fitzgerald, *Dear Scott,* 177.
120 "thought of it long ago": Fitzgerald, *As Ever,* 233.
121 "finished the quart": Mizener, 255.
    "he was lost": Thurber, *Credos and Curios,* 153.
123 "completed it in 1933": Turnbull, *Scott Fitzgerald,* 243.
    "made a great difference": Fitzgerald, *Letters,* 259.
124 "view of life": Bruccoli, *Composition of* Tender Is the Night, 109.
125 Cowley wasn't quite sure: Cowley, *Dream of the Golden Mountains,* 187–91.
127 "a little too easy": Fitzgerald, *As Ever,* 209.
    "needed stimulant and used it": Fitzgerald, *Correspondence,* 374.
128 both comic and tragic: Moore interview with Tom Dardis, October 1979.
    "on a possible buyer": Fitzgerald, *As Ever,* 198.
129 "that it will come": Ibid., 206.
    "you are never sober": Ibid., 307.
    "ON MY MIND FOR A FORTNIGHT": MGM files, Culver City, California.
130 "a little tight now": Jackson, *The Lost Weekend,* 149.
    "*you don't know anything about*": Ibid., 150.
131 "Go on and write": Hemingway, *Selected Letters,* 408.
    "on this story": Fitzgerald, *As Ever,* 298.
131 "at 8:30 P.M.": Fitzgerald, *Ledger,* 1935.
132 "too many tears": Fitzgerald, *The Crack-Up,* 71.
133 "not be good enough": Seabrook, *Asylum,* 161, 164.
    "wouldn't come right": Ibid., 257.
    "cut up high jinks": Ibid., 260.
134 "is as may be": Ibid., 263.
    "they'd never touched it": Seabrook, *No Hiding Place,* 356.
136 "wish we could help him": Hemingway, *Selected Letters,* 438.
    "slain part of yourself": Bruccoli, *"The Last of the Novelists,"* 1.
138 "to be so alone": Fitzgerald, *Taps at Reveille,* 407.
    "over my corpse": Fitzgerald, *Letters,* 311.
139 "fighting himself in the movies": Ibid., 267.
140 "chance is now": Fitzgerald, *Correspondence,* 454.
141 "what things were about": Hemingway, *Selected Letters,* 527.
    "on a drunk like you": Graham, 19.
143 "was now bankrupt": Fitzgerald, *The Price Was High,* 12.
144 to appear "glazed": Ring, 96–97.
146 "some pretty shoddy stuff": Nunnally Johnson to Tom Dardis, November 8, 1974.
    "to find him failing": Ibid., August 23, 1975.
    "straight into the sun": Fitzgerald, *The Last Tycoon,* 20.

147   "make it come alive": Hemingway, *Selected Letters*, 528.
       "death over him": Ibid., 527.
       "are very strange": Ibid.
148   "entire personalities": Fitzgerald, *Letters*, 129.
       "intelligence and taste": Bruccoli, *"The Last of the Novelists,"* 12.
       "what they won't do": Dardis, 48.
149   "15th of January": Fitzgerald, *Letters*, 290.
       "scared of being sober when . . .": Hellman, 67–68.
150   "so was your attitude": Fitzgerald, *Correspondence*, 475.
151   "The best": Hellman, 71.
       "not a better one": Ibid., 68.
152   "never a joiner": Graham, 13.
       "it should be you": Fitzgerald, *As Ever*, 418.
153   "face was snow again": Sanford, 273.
       "had been effortless": Hemingway, *A Moveable Feast*, 147.

Hemingway

PAGE
157   "the two things mixed up": Hemingway to A. E. Hotchner, September 1949, JFK Library.
       "do you rate as an alcoholic?": *New York Times*, July 16, 1972, 37.
158   "is the best feeling": Baker, 121.
       "didn't make any difference": Hemingway, *Short Stories*, 121.
159   "not even very important": Ibid., 125.
       "years of experience": Griffin, 99.
161   "Drinker? Shit": Hemingway, *Selected Letters*, 157–58.
       "my head is so tired": Ibid., 169.
162   "can drink any amount": Ibid., 302.
162n   "about a few drunks": Ibid., 365.
163   "you get to be a rummy": Hemingway to A. E. Hotchner, September 1949, JFK Library.
165   "came down from the mountains": Hemingway, *Short Stories*, 267.
       "that will go bad afterwards": Hemingway, *Green Hills of Africa*, 26–27.
166   "swear to christ they're not": Hemingway, *Selected Letters*, 394.
       "as though you slept": Ibid., 428.
168   "difference what it was": Brasch, xxiv.
       "Many must have it": Hemingway, *Short Stories*, 382–83.
169   "has stopped writing dialogue": Hemingway, *Death in the Afternoon*, 120.
170   "into print then or since": in *New York Times Book Review*, July 16, 1967, 5.
       "will make them like it": Hemingway, *Selected Letters*, 395.
       "waste *Everything*": Hemingway, *Selected Letters*, 289–90.

"what you're doing, will you?": Ibid., 424.

171   "red wine and water": Ibid., 420.

172   "the career, the career": Stein, 266.

173   "will make them like it": Hemingway, *Selected Letters*, 395.

"and include myself": Ibid., 427.

174   "damned fond of you": Ibid., 424–25.

"change your ideas?": Hemingway, *Green Hills of Africa*, 28.

175   "they were much better": Meyers, 351.

"not like working": Hemingway, *Selected Letters*, 500.

177   "Only suckers worry": Hemingway, *To Have and Have Not*, 238.

178   "actual dynamiting scene": Fitzgerald, *Letters*, 312.

"poetic moments": Ibid., 128.

179   "gypsy obscenity": Hemingway, *For Whom the Bell Tolls*, 30.

180   "belligerent and boastful": Wilson, *The Wound and the Bow*, 226.

"self-drugging": Ibid., 228.

"desirous woman": Ibid., 235.

181   "liquid alchemy": Hemingway, *For Whom the Bell Tolls*, 51.

"lost the habit": Hemingway, *Selected Letters*, 555.

"that used to taste all right": Ibid., 546.

182   "that haunts us": *For Whom the Bell Tolls*, 205.

183   "in his drinking": Baker, 446.

186   "too hot to handle": Hemingway, *Selected Letters*, 410.

"running unroped": Hemingway, *Islands in the Stream*, 215.

187   "It's wonderful": Ibid., 344.

"such a damned bore": Ibid., 259.

189   "fun with food?": Hemingway, *Across the River and into the Trees*, 127.

190   "But they can": JFK Library, June 28, 1957.

"beginning with Tender Is The Night": Hemingway, *Selected Letters*, 772.

192   "something to write about": Hemingway, *Short Stories*, v–vi.

193   "only in writing": Hemingway, *Selected Letters*, 604.

195   "cheer him up": Ibid.

"not dopy, really": Ibid., 624.

196   "is Faulkner": JFK Library.

"treated respectfully": Ibid., October 23, 1951.

"talent for magic": Hemingway, *Selected Letters*, 681.

"just another dog": Ibid., 771.

197   "courage of corn whiskey": Ibid., 772.

"rated what remains": Ibid., 769.

198   "to be delivered now": JFK Library, October 19, 1952.

200   "really beautiful . . . beautiful": Jack Hemingway, 288.

"didn't want to": Ibid.

"guzzle with him": Berenson, 339.

"write your name": Fuentes, 63.

201   "wine with his meals": Ibid., 64.

201   "slurred and disheveled": Hotchner, 173.
       "of the sixth": Ibid.
202   "to finish his book": Sulzberger, 241.
       "when knock off work": March 6, 1957, JFK Library.
       "sleep at night": April 4, 1957, JFK Library.
       "that's what I do": JFK Library.
       "were having drinks": JFK Library.
203   "pretty rough": Ibid.
       "nervous without it": Mary Welsh Hemingway, 489.
204   "could have written": Sotheby Parke Bernet catalogue, "Fine Modern First Editions," part 2, October 25, 1977. Letter dated September 5, 1948.
       "truly splendid qualities": Ibid., November 16, 1948.
       "thank God for Faulkner": Ibid.
       "were a pitcher": July 4, 1952, JFK Library.
205   "but would fault it": July 24, 1956, JFK Library.
       "greater I succeed": February 5, 1955, JFK Library.
       "spell over him": Ibid.
207   telling this story for years: Wilson, *The Thirties*, 303.
208   "and his kindnesses": JFK Library, folder 178/124.

O'Neill

PAGE
213   "or nothing": O'Neill, *Selected Letters*, 36.
       "alive at all": Ibid., 114.
215   "DRINK OF HERO FATHER": Sheaffer, *O'Neill, Son and Playwright*, 505.
       "was not loaded": Hastings and Weeks, 215.
       "put to bed": Ibid.
216   "I'll adore thee": Ibid., 211.
218   "bigger kick than anything else": Sheaffer, *O'Neill, Son and Playwright*, 175.
       "spilled part of it": Gelb, 294.
219   "conventional thing to do": Boulton, 144.
       "the best of me": O'Neill, *Selected Letters*, 97.
220   "*Every night of my life*": Boulton, 20.
221   "TURN BACK THE UNIVERSE": Ibid., 31.
       "shot of brandy": Ibid., 118.
       "double shot of brandy, dear": Ibid., 119.
222   "think of it that way": Ibid., 142.
       "overcame him": Ibid.
       "and once only": Nathan, 21.
223   "an ironic grin": Boulton, 205.
       "*all of you!*": Ibid.

224   "tightly and quivering": Ibid., 207.
        "or themselves": O'Neill, *Selected Letters*, 157–58.
        "miasma of drink is left": Boulton, 101.

225   after a bout: Sheaffer, *O'Neill, Son and Artist*, 82.
        at this time: Ibid.

226   "blind from the booze": O'Neill, *Selected Letters*, August 7, 1923,
        181.

227   Tiger Piss: Sheaffer, *O'Neill, Son and Artist*, 96.

228   "*with joy!*": O'Neill, *Plays*, vol. 2, 488.

229   "until four in the morning": Wilson, *The Twenties*, 111–12.

230   "plain physiology": Gelb, 376.
        "outside the U.S.": O'Neill, *Selected Letters*, 195.

231   "composed that afternoon": Cowley, *A Many-Windowed House*,
        198.

233   "general sick despair": Sheaffer, *O'Neill, Son and Artist*, 188.

234   "lips of spring": O'Neill, *Plays*, vol. 3, 267.
        "fry you a chop?": Ibid., 291.
        "God is glue!": Ibid., 318.

235   "knees of God!": Ibid., 322.

236   "did need me, I discovered": Gelb, 623.

237   "true of me, too": O'Neill, *Selected Letters*, 277.
        "keep me from working": Ibid., 276.

240   "urged me to drink": Ibid., 293.

241   "rule his life": Sheaffer, *O'Neill, Son and Artist*, 314.
        "old whore": Ibid., 315.
        "be a *good 'un*": O'Neill, *Selected Letters*, 320.

242   "AND WILL KEEP IT": Ibid., 320–21.
        "FOR THE FUTURE": Ibid., 322.

243   "and my beginning": Ibid., 397.
        "just conversation!": Ibid., 351.

244   "splendor and tenacity": Nathan, 21.

245   "from the supernatural": Floyd, 383.

246   "in the booze whatever": O'Neill, *Selected Letters*, 532.
        "surely die without you": Ibid., 579.

250   "able to forget": Ibid., June 15, 1940, 507.

251   "atque vale": Sheaffer, *O'Neill, Son and Artist*, 611.

253   "FOR BEING DEAD": Sheaffer, *O'Neill, Son and Artist*, 553.

255   "in a hotel room!": Ibid., 670.

Bibliography

Works on Alcoholism

Goodwin, Donald W. *Alcoholism: The Facts.* New York: Oxford University Press, 1981.

———. "The Alcoholism of F. Scott Fitzgerald." *Journal of the American Medical Association* 212, no. 1 (April 6, 1970): 86–90.

———. *Is Alcoholism Hereditary?* New York: Oxford University Press, 1976.

———, ed. *Longitudinal Research in Alcoholism.* Boston: Kluwer-Nijhoff Publishing, 1984.

Jellinek, E. M. *The Disease Concept of Alcoholism.* New Haven: Hillhouse Press, 1960.

Mendelson, Jack, and Nancy Mellow. "Biological Components of Alcoholism." *New England Journal of Medicine* 30, no. 17.

———. *The Diagnosis and Treatment of Alcoholism.* New York: McGraw-Hill, 1979.

Milam, James R., and Katherine Ketcham. *Under the Influence: A Guide to the Myths and Realities of Alcoholism.* Seattle: Madrona Publishers, 1981.

Roueché, Berton. *The Neutral Spirit.* Boston: Little, Brown, 1960.

Smart, Reginald G., et al., eds. *Research Advances in Alcohol and Drug Problems.* Volume 3. New York and London: Plenum Press, 1983.

Tabakoff, Boris, Patricia B. Sutker, and Carrie L. Randall, eds. *Medical and Social Aspects of Alcohol Abuse.* New York and London: Plenum Press, 1983.

Vaillant, George E. *The Natural History of Alcoholism.* Cambridge: Harvard University Press, 1983.

General Works

Abadie, Ann J., ed. *William Faulkner: A Life on Paper.* Jackson: University Press of Mississippi, 1980.

Anderson, Sherwood. *Death in the Woods.* New York: Liveright, 1933.

———. *Letters of Sherwood Anderson.* Edited by Howard Mumford Jones and Walter Rideout. Boston: Little, Brown, 1953.

———. *Selected Letters.* Edited by Charles E. Modlin. Knoxville: University of Tennessee Press, 1984.

Asbury, Herbert. *The Great Illusion: An Informal History of Prohibition.* Garden City, N.Y.: Doubleday, 1950.

Baker, Carlos. *Ernest Hemingway: A Life Story.* New York: Charles Scribner's Sons, 1969.

Basso, Hamilton. "William Faulkner: Man and Writer." *Saturday Review* 45 (July 28, 1962), 7.

Berenson, Bernard. *Sunset and Twilight.* New York: Harcourt, Brace and World, 1963.

Bloom, Steven. *Empty Bottles, Empty Dreams: O'Neill's Alcoholic Drama.* Dissertation Abstract International (Oct: 43 [4]), 1983. Microfilm.

Blotner, Joseph. *Faulkner: A Biography.* 2 volumes. New York: Random House, 1974.

———. *Faulkner: A Biography.* 1-volume edition. New York: Random House, 1984.

Bold, Alan, ed. *Drink to Me Only.* London: Robin Clark Limited, 1982.

Boulton, Agnes. *Part of a Long Story: Eugene O'Neill as a Young Man in Love.* Garden City, N.Y.: Doubleday, 1958.

Brasch, James D. *Hemingway's Library.* New York: Garland, 1981.

Brenner, Jerry. "Are We Going to Hemingway's Feast?" *American Literature* 54, no. 4 (December 1982): 528–44.

———. *Concealments in Hemingway's Works.* Columbus: Ohio State University Press, 1983.

Brodsky, Louis Daniel. "Reflections on Faulkner: An Interview with Albert I. Bezzerides." *Southern Review* 21, no. 2 (Spring 1985).

Brodsky, Louis Daniel, and Robert W. Hamblin, eds. *A Comprehensive Guide to the Brodsky Collection. Volume 2, The Letters.* Jackson: University Press of Mississippi, 1984.

Broughton, Panthea Reid. "An Interview with Meta Carpenter Wilde." *Southern Review* 28, no. 4 (October 1982): 776.

Bruccoli, Matthew J. *The Composition of* Tender Is the Night. Pittsburgh: University of Pittsburgh Press, 1963.

———. *"The Last of the Novelists": F. Scott Fitzgerald and* The Last Tycoon. Carbondale: Southern Illinois University Press, 1977.

————. *Some Sort of Epic Grandeur: The Life of F. Scott Fitzgerald*. New York: Harcourt Brace Jovanovich, 1981.

Buttitta, Tony. *After the Good Gay Times*. New York: The Viking Press, 1974.

Coindreau, M. F. "The Faulkner I Knew." *Shenandoah* 16 (Winter 1965): 29.

Connolly, Cyril. *Previous Convictions*. London: Hamish Hamilton, 1963.

Cowley, Malcolm. *The Dream of the Golden Mountains: Remembering the 1930s*. New York: The Viking Press, 1980.

————. *The Literary Situation*. New York: The Viking Press, 1954.

————. *A Many-Windowed House*. Carbondale: Southern Illinois University Press, 1970.

Crane, Hart. *Complete Poems*. Edited by Brom Weber. Newcastle upon Tyne: Bloodaxe Press, 1984.

Dardis, Tom. *Some Time in the Sun*. New York: Charles Scribner's Sons, 1976.

Davenport-Hines, Richard. "All Sorts and Conditions." *Times Literary Supplement*, November 14, 1986: 1263.

Donaldson, Scott. *By Force of Will: The Life and Art of Ernest Hemingway*. New York: The Viking Press, 1977.

Falkner, Murry. *The Falkners of Mississippi: A Memoir*. Baton Rouge: Louisiana State University Press, 1967.

Faulkner, William. *Collected Stories*. New York: Random House, 1950.

————. *Essays, Speeches and Public Letters*. Edited by James B. Meriwether. New York: Random House, 1965.

————. *A Faulkner Miscellany*. Edited by James B. Meriwether. Jackson: University Press of Mississippi, 1974.

————. *Pylon*. New York: Harrison Smith and Robert Haas, 1935.

————. *Sanctuary*. New York: Cape and Smith, 1931.

————. *Selected Letters of William Faulkner*. Edited by Joseph Blotner. New York: Random House, 1977.

————. *The Sound and the Fury*. New York: Cape and Smith, 1929.

Fitzgerald, F. Scott. *All the Sad Young Men*. New York: Charles Scribner's Sons, 1926.

————. *As Ever, Scott Fitz —: Letters Between F. Scott Fitzgerald and His Literary Agent, Harold Ober*. Edited by Matthew J. Bruccoli and Jennifer M. Atkinson. Philadelphia: J. B. Lippincott, 1972.

————. *Correspondence of F. Scott Fitzgerald*. Edited by Matthew J. Bruccoli and Margaret M. Duggan. New York: Random House, 1980.

————. *The Crack-Up*. Edited by Edmund Wilson. New York: New Directions, 1945.

————. *Dear Scott/Dear Max: The Fitzgerald-Perkins Correspondence*. Edited by John Kuehl and Jackson R. Bryer. New York: Charles Scribner's Sons, 1971.

———. *F. Scott Fitzgerald's Ledger: A Facsimile*. Washington, D.C.: Microcard Editions, 1972.

———. *The Last Tycoon*. New York: Charles Scribner's Sons, 1941.

———. *The Letters of F. Scott Fitzgerald*. Edited by Andrew Turnbull. New York: Charles Scribner's Sons, 1963.

———. *The Price Was High: The Last Uncollected Stories of F. Scott Fitzgerald*. Edited by Matthew J. Bruccoli. New York: Harcourt Brace Jovanovich, 1979.

———. *Taps at Reveille*. New York: Charles Scribner's Sons, 1935.

Floyd, Virginia. *The Plays of Eugene O'Neill: A New Assessment*. New York: Frederick Ungar Publishing Co., 1985.

Ford, Hugh. *Four Lives in Paris*. San Francisco: North Point Press, 1987.

Friede, Donald. *The Mechanical Angel*. New York: Alfred A. Knopf, 1948.

Fuentes, Norberto O. *Hemingway in Cuba*. Secaucus: Lyle Stuart, 1984.

Gelb, Arthur and Barbara. *O'Neill* (enlarged edition with a new epilogue). New York: Harper and Row, 1973.

Gilmore, Thomas D. *Equivocal Spirits: Alcohol and Drinking in Twentieth-Century Literature*. Chapel Hill: University of North Carolina Press, 1987.

Graham, Sheilah. *The Real F. Scott Fitzgerald: Thirty-five Years Later*. New York: Grosset and Dunlap, 1976.

Griffin, Peter. *Along with Youth: Hemingway — The Early Years*. New York: Oxford University Press, 1985.

Haffenden, John. *The Life of John Berryman*. Boston: Routledge and Kegan Paul, 1982.

Hastings, Warren H., and Richard F. Weeks. "Episodes of Eugene O'Neill's Undergraduate Days at Princeton." *Princeton University Library Quarterly* 29 (1968): 208–15.

Hellman, Lillian. *An Unfinished Woman*. Boston: Little, Brown, 1969.

Hemingway, Ernest. *Across the River and into the Trees*. New York: Charles Scribner's Sons, 1950.

———. *Death in the Afternoon*. New York: Charles Scribner's Sons, 1932.

———. *For Whom the Bell Tolls*. New York: Charles Scribner's Sons, 1940.

———. *The Garden of Eden*. New York: Charles Scribner's Sons, 1986.

———. *Green Hills of Africa*. New York: Charles Scribner's Sons, 1935.

———. *Islands in the Stream*. New York: Charles Scribner's Sons, 1970.

———. *A Moveable Feast*. New York: Charles Scribner's Sons, 1964.

———. *Selected Letters, 1917–1961*. Edited by Carlos Baker. New York: Charles Scribner's Sons, 1981.

———. *The Short Stories of Ernest Hemingway*. New York: Collier Books/Macmillan, 1987.

———. *To Have and Have Not*. New York: Charles Scribner's Sons, 1937.

Hemingway, Jack. *Memoirs of a Fly Fisherman*. Dallas: Taylor Publishing, 1986.

Hemingway, Mary Welsh. *How It Was*. New York: Alfred A. Knopf, 1976.

Henderson, Philip. *Swinburne*. New York: Macmillan, 1974.

Horace. *Epistles*. Translated by Smith Palmer Bowie. Chicago: University of Chicago Press, 1959.

Hotchner, A. E. *Papa Hemingway*. New York: Random House, 1966.

Howe, Irving. *William Faulkner: A Critical Study*. Third edition. Revised and expanded. Chicago: University of Chicago Press, 1975.

Jackson, Charles. *The Lost Weekend*. New York: Farrar and Rinehart, 1944.

Johnson, Diane. "Obsession." *Vanity Fair* 48, no. 5 (May 1985): 116–19.

Kert, Bernice. *The Hemingway Women*. New York and London: W. W. Norton and Co., 1983.

London, Jack. *John Barleycorn*. New York: Macmillan, 1913.

Lorenz, Clarissa. *Lorelei Two: My Life with Conrad Aiken*. Athens: University of Georgia Press, 1983.

Lynn, Kenneth S. *Hemingway*. New York: Simon and Schuster, 1987.

Mayfield, Sara. *Exiles from Paradise*. New York: Delacorte Press, 1971.

Meade, Marion. *What Fresh Hell Is This?* New York: Villard Books, 1987.

Mellow, James R. *Invented Lives: F. Scott and Zelda Fitzgerald*. Boston: Houghton Mifflin, 1984.

Meyers, Jeffrey. *Hemingway: A Biography*. New York: Harper and Row, 1985.

Mizener, Arthur. *The Far Side of Paradise: A Biography of F. Scott Fitzgerald*. Revised edition. Boston: Houghton Mifflin, 1965.

Nathan, George Jean. *The Intimate Notebooks of George Jean Nathan*. New York: Alfred A. Knopf, 1932.

Newlove, Donald. *Those Drinking Days: Myself and Other Writers*. New York: Horizon Press, 1981.

O'Neill, Eugene. *The Iceman Cometh*. New York: Random House, 1946.

———. *Long Day's Journey into Night*. New Haven: Yale University Press, 1956.

———. *The Plays of Eugene O'Neill*. 3 volumes. New York: Random House, 1951.

———. *Selected Letters of Eugene O'Neill*. Edited by Travis Bogard and Jackson R. Bryer. New Haven: Yale University Press, 1988.

———. *A Touch of the Poet*. New Haven: Yale University Press, 1957.

Piper, Henry Dan. *F. Scott Fitzgerald: A Critical Portrait*. New York: Holt, Rinehart and Winston, 1965.

Ranald, Margaret Loftus. *The O'Neill Companion*. Westport, Conn.: Greenwood Press, 1984.

Reynolds, Michael S. *The Young Hemingway*. Boston: Basil Blackwell, 1985.

Ring, Frances Kroll. *Against the Current: As I Remember F. Scott Fitzgerald.* Berkeley: Donald S. Ellis/Creative Arts Book Company, 1985.

Rorabaugh, W. J. *The Alcoholic Republic.* New York: Oxford University Press, 1979.

Ross, Lillian. *Hemingway.* New York: Simon and Schuster, 1961.

Rudd, Hughes. *My Escape from the CIA and Other Impossible Events.* New York: E. P. Dutton, 1966.

Saint-Exupéry, Antoine de. *The Little Prince.* New York: Raynal and Hitchcock, 1943.

Sanford, John. *A More Goodly Country.* New York: Horizon, 1975.

Seabrook, William. *Asylum.* New York: Harcourt, Brace, 1935.

————. *No Hiding Place.* New York: Harcourt, Brace, 1942.

Sheaffer, Lewis. *O'Neill, Son and Artist.* Boston: Little, Brown, 1973.

————. *O'Neill, Son and Playwright.* Boston: Little, Brown, 1968.

Sinclair, Upton. *The Cup of Fury.* Great Neck, N.Y.: Channel Press, 1956.

Spratling, William. "Chapters of a Friendship: William Faulkner in New Orleans." *Texas Quarterly* 19 (Spring 1969), 27–34.

Stein, Gertrude. *The Autobiography of Alice B. Toklas.* New York: Harcourt, Brace, 1933.

Sulzberger, C. L. *Seven Continents in Forty Years.* New York: Quadrangle, 1977.

Tate, Allen. *Memoirs and Opinions.* Chicago: Swallow Press, 1975.

Thurber, James. *Credos and Curios.* New York: Harper and Row, 1962.

Turnbull, Andrew. *Scott Fitzgerald.* New York: Charles Scribner's Sons, 1962.

Waldron, Ann. *Close Connections: Caroline Gordon and the Southern Renaissance.* New York: G. P. Putnam's Sons, 1987.

Wasson, Ben. *Count No'Count: Flashbacks to Faulkner.* Jackson: University Press of Mississippi, 1983.

Wilde, Meta Carpenter, and Orin Borsten. *A Loving Gentleman: The Love Story of William Faulkner and Meta Carpenter.* New York: Simon and Schuster, 1976.

Wilson, Edmund. *The Thirties.* Edited by Leon Edel. New York: Farrar, Straus and Giroux, 1980.

————. *The Twenties.* Edited by Leon Edel. New York: Farrar, Straus and Giroux, 1975.

————. *The Wound and the Bow.* Boston: Houghton Mifflin, 1941.

Young, Stark. *Stark Young, A Life in the Arts: Letters, 1900–1962.* 2 volumes. Edited by John Pilkington. Baton Rouge: Louisiana State University Press, 1975.

Index